IT'S OK TO BE ANGRY ABOUT CAPITALISM

IT'S OK TO BE ANGRY ABOUT CAPITALISM

===

BERNIE SANDERS

with John Nichols

ALLEN LANE
an imprint of
PENGUIN BOOKS

ALLEN LANE

UK | USA | Canada | Ireland | Australia
India | New Zealand | South Africa

Penguin Books is part of the Penguin Random House group of companies
whose addresses can be found at global.penguinrandomhouse.com.

First published in the United States of America by Crown,
a division of Penguin Random House LLC 2023
First published in Great Britain by Allen Lane 2023
001

Printed and bound in Great Britain by Clays Ltd, Elcograf S.p.A.

The authorized representative in the EEA is Penguin Random House Ireland,
Morrison Chambers, 32 Nassau Street, Dublin D02 YH68

A CIP catalogue record for this book is available from the British Library

ISBN: 978–0–241–64328–0

www.greenpenguin.co.uk

This book is dedicated to Jane O'Meara Sanders, who has been at my side for more than forty years as wife, co-worker, and best buddy. I also want to thank my brother, Larry, who, when we were young, opened up new worlds to me and remains a mentor. It is also dedicated to my wonderful children, Levi, Heather, Carina, and Dave, and to my grandchildren, Sunnee, Cole, Ryleigh, Grayson, Ella, Tess, and Dylan. I am confident that they, and their generations, will help create a better world.

CONTENTS

CONTENTS

IT'S OK TO BE ANGRY ABOUT CAPITALISM

CAPITALISM IS THE PROBLEM

They say that the older you get, the more conservative you become. Well, that's not me. The older I get, the angrier I become about the uber-capitalist system under which we live, and the more I want to see transformational change in our country.

Some people think that it's "un-American" to ask hard questions about where we are as a nation, and where we're heading. I don't. To my view, there is nothing more American than questioning the systems that have failed us and demanding the changes we need in order to create the kind of society that we and future generations deserve.

Here is the simple, straightforward reality: The uber-capitalist economic system that has taken hold in the United States in recent years, propelled by uncontrollable greed and contempt for human decency, is not merely unjust. It is grossly immoral.

We need to confront that immorality. Boldly. Bluntly. Without apology. It is only then that we can begin to transform a system that is rigged against the vast majority of Americans and is destroying millions of lives.

Confronting that reality and mobilizing people to bring about the transformational change we need is not easy. That's why I've written this book. We need not only to understand the powerful forces that hold us down today but, equally important, to have a vision as to where we want to be in the future.

It is my strong belief that in the wealthiest country in the history of the world, with exploding technological progress that will greatly increase worker productivity, we can finally end austerity economics and achieve the long-sought human dream of providing a decent standard of living for all. In the twenty-first century we can end the vicious dog-eat-dog economy in which the vast majority struggle to survive, while a handful of billionaires have more wealth than they could spend in a thousand lifetimes.

The Oligarchs Own America

Let's be clear. While the middle class continues to decline, the system we have today is doing extremely well, for the people who own it. These oligarchs have enormous wealth. They have enormous power. In fact, for the 1 percent, things have never been better. They have their mansions all over the world, their private islands, their expensive art, their yachts, their private jets. Some of them have spaceships that, someday, may take them to Mars. These oligarchs like the way things are going and, with unlimited resources at their disposal, will do everything possible to defend what they have and maintain the status quo.

Yes. We live in a "democracy"—but they own that democracy. They spend tens of billions of dollars on campaign contributions to both major political parties in order to buy politicians who will do their bidding. They spend billions more on lobbying firms to influence governmental decisions at the federal, state, and local levels.

That is why, over the last fifty years, we have consistently seen public policy that benefits the very rich at the expense of everyone else.

Yes. We have freedom of speech and a "free press." But, to a significant degree, the oligarchs own that media. That is why the "personalities" they employ on TV, radio, newspapers, and social media do not ask embarrassing questions, and rarely raise issues that will undermine the privileged position of their employers. That's why, despite the many thousands of television networks, radio stations, and websites they own, there is little public discussion about the power of corporate America and how oligarchs wield that power to benefit their interests at the expense of working families.

The good news is that while the oligarchs, and the institutions they control, work frantically to maintain the status quo, we are now beginning to see cracks in the system. Millions of Americans are starting to look at the society in which they live from a new and different perspective. They are beginning to think big, not small. They are asking hard questions, and demanding answers that take them beyond the incremental politics and mainstream ideology of today. Many of them are finding answers in union organizing, as they seek a greater say in their workplaces, along with better wages, benefits, and working conditions.

Taking On the Economic and Political Establishment

I know a little bit about all of this, having run two of the most progressive grassroots campaigns for president in modern American history. In 2016 my campaign shocked the political establishment by winning twenty-two states and more than thirteen million votes in the Democratic primaries where I took on the party's anointed candidate. That's not what was supposed to happen. That's not what the Big Money interests wanted. That's not what the corporate media wanted. That's not what super-PACs and wealthy campaign contributors wanted. That's not what the super-delegates wanted. But that's what happened.

Four years later, in 2020, we won the popular vote against a huge field of candidates in the first three Democratic primary states—Iowa, New Hampshire, and Nevada. The result: a panicked political establishment came together behind Joe Biden, the one candidate they thought could beat us. The other candidates were asked to drop out.

The most important lesson of those campaigns was not just the list of states that we won as we took on the greed and recklessness of the ruling class, or the total number of votes we received. More important was *where* the votes were coming from. They were coming, in overwhelming numbers, from young people under forty—the future of our country.

In state after state, and in national polls, we won the support of young Americans by landslide proportions. These voters—Black, white, Latino, Asian American, Native American—understood from their lived experience that America's uber-capitalist system was not working for them. It was not working for them economically, as they were experiencing a lower standard of living than their parents. It was not working for them from an environmental perspective, as they faced a planet that was growing increasingly unhealthy and uninhabitable as a result of climate change. It was not working for them in terms of ending the kinds of systemic racism, sexism, homophobia, and xenophobia that they detested. During our campaigns, millions of young people in this country made it clear: They wanted change, real change.

These Americans understand that proposals that tinker around the edges are an insufficient response to the enormous crises we face. For them, there is a rapidly growing recognition that this country has deep *systemic* problems and that it is not good enough to deal only with the symptoms of the problem. We have got to get to the root causes. We have to confront the destructiveness of modern-day uber-capitalism. We have got to change the system. While polling shows that a majority of Americans still view capitalism favorably, the support level has been sliding steadily in recent years—dropping to well below 60 percent in an Axios-Momentive survey conducted in

June 2021. Among Americans aged 18–34, negative views about capitalism surged from 38 percent in 2019 to 49 percent just two years later. Among Gen-Z adults—those Americans aged 18–24 who are getting their education and looking to enter the job market—54 percent say they have a negative view.

The political reality of this moment in history, however, is not just the need to fight for a more democratic, just, and humane society. Now is the time when, with all our energy, we must also oppose the reactionary and neo-fascist forces in this country that are undermining American democracy and moving us toward authoritarianism and violence as they scapegoat minorities and attempt to divide us based on our race, our gender, our sexual orientation, or our ethnicity.

That is why, after I lost the Democratic nomination in 2020, I worked with the progressive movement to do everything we could to defeat Trump and elect Joe Biden as president. While Biden and I have very different political views, I have known him for years and consider him to be a friend and a very decent human being.

During that campaign, which took place during the COVID pandemic, I organized dozens of livestreams and rallies for Biden and Harris that were viewed by many hundreds of thousands of people. We also focused, working with a number of grassroots organizations, on voter registration and increasing voter turnout among young people, trade unionists, and nontraditional voters. And that worked. One of the reasons that Biden won and Democrats did well in 2020 was the unprecedented turnout that we saw among new and younger voters. To the surprise of the pundits and the pollsters, much the same thing happened in the 2022 midterm elections, when overwhelming support from young voters helped Democrats to defy expectations and keep control of the Senate. Unfortunately, they lost the House, and with it the ability to advance much of President Biden's agenda.

In 2020, and again in 2022, I did my best to alert the American people that Trump was not a normal political figure and that these were not normal elections. The 2020 campaign wasn't a "clash of ideas." It was a battle over whether we would remain a democracy.

Over and over again I made it clear that Trump was not only a pathological liar and despot but that, if he lost, it was unlikely he would abide by the Constitution, accept defeat, and leave office voluntarily. Tragically, the insurrection of January 6, 2021, and later disclosures made it abundantly clear that my concerns were justified, and that much of the national Republican Party has descended into right-wing, anti-democratic extremism. That was all the more evident in 2022, when Trump-backed election deniers ran in states across the country on the Republican line. And it will remain true in 2024, as Trump again bids for his party's nomination and the presidency,

Why People Vote for Trump

One of the more disturbing aspects of the 2020 election was that, while Biden won, Trump got ten million more votes than he had received in 2016. He did especially well in white, rural, economically depressed parts of the country. Why? Why did working-class people, many of them struggling economically, vote for Trump? Why was he able to hold rallies in the middle of nowhere that drew tens of thousands of enthusiastic followers?

I know that some pundits and politicians respond to those questions by suggesting that all of Trump's supporters are racists, sexists, and homophobes; that they really are "deplorable" and there is nothing to be done. Sorry. I don't agree. And I should know. I have been to almost every state in this country and, unlike corporate pundits, have actually talked with Trump supporters. Are some of them racists and sexists who vote for bigotry? Absolutely. But many are not.

I think the more accurate answer as to why Trump has won working-class support lies in the pain, desperation, and political alienation that millions of working-class Americans now experience and the degree to which the Democratic Party has abandoned them for wealthy campaign contributors and the "beautiful people."

These are Americans who, while the rich get much richer, have seen their real wages stagnate and their good union jobs go to China and Mexico. They can't afford health care, they can't afford child-care, they can't afford to send their kids to college and are scared to death about a retirement with inadequate income. Because of what doctors call "diseases of despair," their communities are even seeing a decline in life expectancy.

Many of these voters have spent their lives playing by the rules. They worked hard, very hard, and did their best for their kids and their communities. During the worst of the pandemic, they didn't have the luxury of sitting behind a computer at home doing "virtual" work. They were putting their lives on the line at jobs in hospitals, factories, warehouses, public transportation, meatpacking plants, and grocery stores. They kept the economy going, and many thousands of them died as a result.

Many of these so-called racist Americans voted for Barack Obama, our first Black president, and for "hope" and "change" and "Yes We Can." And they voted to reelect him. But their lives did not get better.

After almost fifty years of wage stagnation, Democrats were in charge—but we did not raise wages for workers. After a massive amount of illegal corporate anti-union activity, we did not make it easier for workers to join unions. We did not improve job security. We did not address corporate greed or the massive levels of income and wealth inequality. We did not provide health care for all or lower the cost of prescription drugs. We did not make childcare and higher education affordable. We did not address homelessness or the high cost of housing. We did not make it easier for working people to retire with security and dignity. We did not reform a corrupt campaign finance system.

Today, tens of millions of Americans feel deep anger toward the political, economic, and media establishment. They look at Washington and the corporate media and see rejection and contempt. They see not only a government that is ignoring their needs but politicians busy attending fundraising events with the rich, who have no clue as to what the lives of the great majority of Americans are about.

The absurdity of the current-day situation is that Trump—a phony, a pillar of the establishment, a billionaire, and an anti-worker businessman—has been able to fill that political vacuum and tap into that anger. Donald Trump, "champion of the working class." Beyond pathetic!

Failing to Build Back Better

Biden's inauguration in January 2021, with Democratic control of the House and Senate, gave Democrats an opportunity to finally stand up for working families. And not a moment too soon. In the first months of 2021, the country faced an unprecedented public health and economic crisis. Thousands of people were dying every day from COVID, millions had lost their jobs and were facing hunger and homelessness, hospitals were understaffed and in crisis, and schools were closing.

It was time to act, and to act boldly. As the newly elected chairman of the Senate Budget Committee, I was in a position to help lead that effort. On March 6, 2021, after much work by the Budget Committee, the $1.9 trillion American Rescue Plan passed the Senate by a party line vote of 50–49. The final amended bill was passed by the House on March 10 and signed by the president on March 11. This measure was one of the most comprehensive and consequential pieces of legislation in modern American history. In the midst of an unprecedented pandemic, exploding unemployment, and economic desperation, this bill provided the much-needed assistance that working families and state and local institutions desperately needed. The legislation was also extremely popular. In March 2021, President Biden's approval rating stood at 59 percent, the highest of his presidency. The people saw that, finally, they had a government that was working on their behalf.

Many of us understood that while the American Rescue Plan was an enormously important piece of *emergency* legislation, it was not enough. Now, with Democratic control of the White House, the

Senate, and the House, we had the opportunity to address the long-term structural crises that faced working people. The Budget Committee worked with the White House and members of Congress to put together a set of proposals to be called "Build Back Better," a comprehensive reconciliation bill that would have done more for working families than any piece of legislation in the last eighty years. It was truly transformative in nature and had wide public support. Tragically, that bill never made it to the floor. In a 50–50 Senate we needed every Democrat to pass it. Two conservative Democrats, West Virginia's Joe Manchin and Arizona's Kyrsten Sinema, both of them heavily financed by corporate interests, undermined our efforts at every turn. Because of their obstruction, the process dragged on for months. Momentum for change stalled. People lost hope. A year after the enactment of the American Rescue Plan, the Build Back Better bill died, and with it, much of the political support that President Biden and Democrats had won. A year after the passage of the American Rescue Plan, Biden's approval rating had dropped by 20 points.

Economic Rights Are Human Rights

One of the fundamental and ongoing debates in politics has to do with the role that government should play in our lives. And that discussion must necessarily involve the issue of human rights. Stated simply: In a democracy and a "government of the people, by the people, and for the people," what are citizens *entitled* to as human beings? And how can government deliver those rights?

In the long history of our country, the concept of human rights has gone through a radical evolution. We have lived through the barbarism of slavery. We have lived through the brutal subjugation of Native Americans. We have lived through a "democracy" where only wealthy white men had the right to vote. We have lived through hundreds of years when women were considered, legally and socially, as second-class citizens, and were literally denied control over their own bodies. We have lived through periods of intense bigotry and hatred toward immigrants. We have lived through a long history in which it was illegal for gay couples to openly express their love for each other.

We have also lived, throughout our history, with a profound separation between political rights and economic rights. Yes. Our Constitution and Bill of Rights guarantees us the right to vote, the right to express our opinions, the right to practice our religious beliefs, the right to assemble, and many other important political rights.

But they do not guarantee us the right to a decent job, health care, education, food and shelter. They do not guarantee us the right to the basic necessities that allow human beings to live decent and secure lives. In 1944, in a largely overlooked State of the Union address, President Franklin Delano Roosevelt spoke about this contradiction. "This Republic had its beginning, and grew to its present strength, under the protection of certain inalienable political rights—among them the right of free speech, free press, free worship, trial by jury, freedom from unreasonable searches and seizures. They were our rights to life and liberty," FDR explained. "As our Nation has grown in size and stature, however—as our industrial economy expanded—these political rights proved inadequate to assure us equality in the pursuit of happiness. We have come to a clear realization of the fact that true individual freedom cannot exist without economic security and independence."

Repeat: *True individual freedom cannot exist without economic security and independence.*

Roosevelt was right when he made that statement almost eighty years ago, and the principle remains true today. Economic rights are human rights, and true individual freedom cannot exist without those rights.

One of the great tragedies of modern American history is that we have not been able to implement Roosevelt's vision. Today, in our "free" country, 60 percent of our people live paycheck to paycheck—and real inflation-adjusted wages have not gone up for fifty years.

Some 85 million of us are uninsured or underinsured, and sixty thousand die each year because they don't get the medical care they need. We have the highest childhood poverty rate of almost any major country on earth, disproportionately among Black and Brown families, and our childcare system is a disaster. Higher education is increasingly unaffordable, and we lag behind many other countries in the academic achievements of our students. Millions of seniors lack the resources to heat their homes in the winter or buy the prescription drugs they need.

Meanwhile, while working families are falling further and further behind, the people on top have never had it so good. We now have more income and wealth inequality than ever before, with the richest three billionaires owning more wealth than the bottom half of our society—165 million people. Today, the top 1 percent owns more wealth than the bottom 92 percent and the CEOs of major corporations earn four hundred times what their employees make.

In our rigged economy we also have more concentration of ownership and price fixing than ever before. In one sector after another we see a handful of giant corporations controlling the market. Shockingly, there are now three Wall Street firms—BlackRock, Vanguard, and State Street—that control assets of over twenty trillion dollars and are major shareholders in almost every major corporation in the country—including the largest financial institutions in the country, media, transportation, agriculture, and manufacturing.

For a New America

This book, however, is not just a critique of modern American society and the uber-capitalism that shapes our lives. It offers a blueprint for progressive change—both economic and political. It calls for a political revolution in which working people come together to fight for a government that represents all Americans, not just the 1 percent. It embraces Roosevelt's belief that the U.S. government must guarantee economic rights to all of its people.

Yes. We can have a guaranteed jobs program that puts people to work at livable wages addressing the enormous unmet needs of our society. And we can move toward economic democracy in which workers have more and more power over the jobs they perform so that they no longer have to function as unhappy cogs in the machine.

Yes. We can create millions of jobs by leading the world in combating the existential threat posed by climate change and transforming our energy systems away from fossil fuels and toward energy efficiency and sustainable energy. We can rebuild our crumbling infrastructure—roads, bridges, rail, schools, water systems, and broadband—as we make our nation safer and more efficient.

Yes. We can put an end to our dysfunctional health care system and move toward a publicly funded Medicare for All system that guarantees health care as a human right, not a privilege.

Yes. We can guarantee lifetime learning through free public education for every American of every age as we create the best educational systems in the world, from childcare to graduate school.

Yes. We can end our grotesque level of income and wealth inequality through a progressive tax system that demands that the wealthy and large corporations finally start paying their fair share of taxes.

Yes. We can preserve reproductive rights and guarantee that women have the freedom to make the choices that are best for their lives and their livelihoods.

Yes. We can end all forms of bigotry as we move toward a society that truly embraces the wonderful words we learned as children: *America is a land with "freedom and justice for all."*

Yes. We can create a vibrant and inclusive democracy that ends our corrupt campaign finance system and makes it easier, not harder, for people of all walks of life to participate in the political process.

During the last years of his life, the Rev. Dr. Martin Luther King Jr. spoke with increasing passion about how the struggle for civil rights had evolved into "a class struggle." Speaking in 1967 to the Southern Christian Leadership Conference in Atlanta, the

Nobel Peace Prize recipient said, "Capitalism forgets that life is social. And the kingdom of brotherhood is found neither in the thesis of communism nor the antithesis of capitalism, but in a higher synthesis." To achieve that higher synthesis, Dr. King explained, "one day we must ask the question, 'Why are there forty million poor people in America?' And when you begin to ask that question, you are raising questions about the economic system, about a broader distribution of wealth. When you ask that question, you begin to question the capitalistic economy. And I'm simply saying that more and more, we've got to begin to ask questions about the whole society . . ."

That's what this book does.

NOT ME, US

*The 2020 campaign and the
fight to transform our country*

On April 8, 2020, after almost fourteen months of competing for the Democratic presidential nomination, I announced that we were suspending our campaign. The important message in the statement I made that day was "While this campaign is coming to an end, our movement is not."

Given the growing COVID-19 pandemic, and social distancing requirements that effectively ended in-person campaigning, I made the announcement through a livestream from my home. I was deeply moved that some seven million people ended up viewing it. During my remarks, I chose to focus less on the practicalities of a campaign that had fallen short in the delegate count and more on the historic nature of what we had accomplished.

"I cannot in good conscience continue to mount a campaign that cannot win and which would interfere with the important work required of all of us in this difficult hour," I explained. "But let me say this very emphatically: As you all know, we have never been just a campaign. We are a grassroots, multiracial, multigenerational move- ment which has always believed that real change never comes from the top on down but always from the bottom on up."

Our campaign was like none other in modern American history. Built upon the foundation of a 2016 bid that had proposed a political revolution, we forged a grassroots working-class movement that was national in character, and which sought to overcome the overwhelm- ing barriers to progress in the Democratic Party and the broader pol- itics of the United States.

I ran, as had been the case since my first campaign almost fifty years earlier, as a democratic socialist who was ready and willing to take on the oligarchs, the plutocrats, and the billionaire class that had turned our economic system into their plaything. But this time was different. While my ideas were still dismissed as "radical" by political elites and many in the media, I began the 2020 campaign with a base of supporters that numbered in the millions and was prepared to fight for fundamental change. By the time the campaign was done, we had taken on Wall Street and the enormously powerful economic interests that control not just the economy but the politics of our nation. We had challenged the billionaire class and the corpo- rate elite, their media and their super-PACs. We had taken on the political establishment in both major parties.

From the start, we achieved victories that shocked the pundits. We won the popular vote in the first three primary states on the way to se- curing almost ten million votes nationwide for a campaign that was sus- pended before more than two dozen primaries were held. We won California, the most populous state in the country, by more than 450,000 votes. For a time, we led the national polls, not only in the race for the Democratic nomination but in head-to-head matchups against Donald Trump. And we built a movement powered by young people who were prepared to trudge through snow to knock on doors in northern New Hampshire and to sweat through ninety-degree days in South Texas.

We had organized the most ambitious and most successful progressive presidential campaign in a century. Our ideas, which just a few years earlier had been dismissed as too extreme to be politically viable, had become part of the mainstream Democratic Party agenda. Our supporters and allies had begun to be elected to seats in Congress, and to chair state parties. We had expanded political consciousness and gotten millions of Americans to embrace a new understanding of what they had a right to expect from their government.

Most important for the long term, as a result of our campaign, young people were participating in the political process at an unprecedented rate. It turned out that our ideas and our movement were, in fact, the future of the Democratic Party. While poll after poll showed us doing more poorly than we'd hoped with older voters, those same polls showed that we were swamping the other candidates among younger voters—winning overwhelming support from Black, Latino, Asian American, Native American, and white voters under age forty. What was striking was that these young people were not only voting for us; they were the foundation of our grassroots campaign. They were the ones handing out literature, making phone calls, texting, raising small contributions, and volunteering in a hundred different ways.

A Campaign Finance Revolution

Our campaign attracted a new generation of voters because we revolutionized modern presidential politics.

At a time when virtually all campaigns were funded by super-PACs and the very rich, we broke that long-established mold and created an entirely new approach to raising sufficiently large sums of money to run a truly national presidential campaign. We did not hold one fundraiser in a billionaire's mansion. We did not seek the support of super-PACs. Our campaign was fueled by the working class—teachers, postal clerks, Amazon warehouse workers, nurses, small-business owners, farmers, and veterans—with more than two million individual donors making ten million contributions that averaged $18.50. No campaign in American history had ever received that kind of support. We had revolutionized campaign financing, developing an entirely new model that rejected Big Money and put the people in control.

The way we ran our campaign was intentional. We knew that, to reach people who had grown justifiably cynical about politics, we had to abandon the practices that had caused tens of millions of Americans to lose faith in both major parties. We didn't just talk about "rejecting the influence of big corporate money"—although I did that a lot—we actually did it. And we explained why it was absolutely necessary to reject "greed-fueled, corrupt corporate influence over elections." The simple truth, as I said in every stump speech, is that no elected official is going to represent ordinary Americans and take on the special interests if they are beholden to Big Money. You can't receive campaign contributions from the pharmaceutical industry and lower the outrageous cost of prescription drugs. You can't rely on funding from the fossil fuel industry and combat climate change. You can't take big checks from CEOs who have made their fortunes running non-union plants and then implement pro-worker labor law reforms. You can't do fundraising events with billionaires and help develop a fair and progressive tax system.

Ultimately, of course, this country needs to enact fundamental campaign finance reforms to overturn the disastrous Supreme Court ruling in *Citizens United* and establish public funding of elections. But to get to the point where we can enact those reforms, candidates have to break free from the stranglehold of Big Money. And the only way to do that, as I learned a long time ago, is by relying on contributions from working-class people. Our campaign showed it was possible to do this even at the level of presidential politics.

Initially, we were told our approach was impractical. That it could never work. I knew that was wrong. So I went on social media and wrote: "I have a wild idea: I want to challenge you to help our campaign hit a goal that will absolutely astonish the political and financial establishment." People from all across the country responded and political veterans were, indeed, astonished when our campaign raised $45 million in a single month—February 2020—with more than 2.2 million donations. *The Guardian* newspaper said we'd "established a gold standard for small-dollar fundraising."

I was enormously proud of what we accomplished. I was prouder still of the legacy of our grassroots online fundraising efforts, which can be seen in the campaigns of a new generation of candidates, especially those running for Congress, who have rejected all corporate PAC money, basing their fundraising on small donations—ensuring they will never have to bend to pressure from Big Money interests.

Seizing the Political Power of Social Media

It was not just our fundraising efforts that fundamentally changed presidential politics. It was our new approach to social media.

It was extremely important for us to get out our ideas, new and unfamiliar to many people, as far and wide as we could. Our hard-working staff developed innovative social media and livestream platforms that communicated directly to tens of millions of Americans, allowing us to reach people without having to rely on corporate media—which was unfriendly when the campaign began and grew downright hostile as it progressed. Of course, I did a zillion newspaper and radio interviews with mainstream media outlets, and appeared on every Sunday morning and late-night network television talk show. But social media provided me the opportunity to go beyond the usual twelve-second sound bites and speak in detail with Americans about the big issues in their lives.

From the start, our campaign had far more Facebook and Instagram interactions than any of the other candidates. An April 2019 *Newsweek* headline announced, "Bernie Sanders Is Most Popular 2020 Democrat on Social Media." While I still had work to do to catch up with Trump, we were clearly in the process of getting there.

By February 2020, I had more than 11.5 million Twitter followers and more than 5 million Facebook followers.

During the campaign it was not uncommon for a two-hour rally in Iowa, New Hampshire, or Nevada, which may have drawn 2,000 people to the actual venue, to be viewed by 250,000 people via livestream. This was revolutionary in the history of political communications. People were now being exposed to new political ideas and new ways of campaigning—day after day, week after week. With the large crowds that we often drew, Americans could see, with their very own eyes, that there was nothing "fringe" about our effort. They were discovering that they were not alone in seeking fundamental social and political change.

Speaking to Voters in Their Own Languages

While we developed new approaches to fundraising and social media, we did not ignore old-style politics. Our campaign knocked on millions of doors. We went to communities that had rarely if ever been visited by candidates. In particular, we went to the low-income neighborhoods that have always been neglected by politicians and strategists.

We wanted to meet people where they lived. Our belief, from the start, was that this campaign was about reconnecting with people who had given up on the political process—and about making new connections with people who had never been a part of it. For example, pundits asked why our campaign went out of its way to visit Native American reservations in 2016 and again in 2020, and to meet with representatives of the tribes. My answer was that we were going to open up conversations with people who had for too long been ignored.

In North Dakota, supporters like state representative Ruth Buffalo—an enrolled citizen of the Mandan, Hidatsa and Arikara Nation and the first Native American Democratic woman elected to that state's legislature—took the message to urban and rural communities with large Native populations. Thanks to Ruth and others like her, we won a majority of the overall vote statewide. And we secured over 75 percent of the vote in Cannon Ball, where members of the Standing Rock Sioux Tribe mounted mass protests against the Dakota Access Pipeline.

We wanted to connect with new voters in ways that worked for them. "Our goal is to talk to people where they're at, in languages that they understand," said Supreet Kaur, the National Asian American and Pacific Islanders organizer for the campaign; and to that end, we translated our campaign materials into at least eleven Asian languages, including Mandarin Chinese, Korean, Vietnamese, Tagalog, Hindi, and Punjabi. Spanish-language materials, advertisements, and campaigning at front doors and workplaces were critical to our victories in a number of states.

In the Nevada caucuses, for instance, we won 53 percent of the Latino vote. The next closest candidate, Joe Biden, got 16 percent. That did not happen by accident. Our Latino organizers developed strong outreach efforts within communities where they were known and trusted. In addition, we invested in media designed to reach young Latinos who are almost always ignored politically, especially in California, where we worked with respected members of the diverse AAPI community. In Iowa, where African immigrants had become a major presence in the meatpacking industry, we hired staffers and brought in volunteers who spoke Ethiopian and Somali dialects and could appeal directly to these workers. At a satellite caucus in Ottumwa, Ethiopian immigrant workers showed up before their shift began and voted 14–1 in favor of our campaign.

Taking the Message Directly to the People

Just as we did our best to speak in the languages of voters we were reaching out to, we sought to take our campaign to the places where they lived. Our rallies deviated from the normal route that took candidates from one big city airport tarmac to the next. We went to more cities and towns than the other candidates did, and we stayed longer. Our rallies lasted for hours because we didn't just want to mouth a few talking points; we wanted to go into depth about what was really going on in the country. We had things to say, and we knew people had things to say to us. The truth is that I love campaigning and meeting people. While doing three or four rallies and town meetings a day can be tiring, it is also inspiring. I remember, after a large rally in California, when a young man grabbed my hand and said, "Senator Sanders, the reason I like you is that you treat us like we're intelligent human beings." In order to do that, we scheduled more events than any other campaign. During one stretch, around the time of the Iowa caucuses, we were on the road for forty-five consecutive days. By some estimates, a substantial majority of the people who voted for me in the first caucus and primary states of Iowa and New Hampshire actually heard me speak. That is how democracy is supposed to work.

I know that many people showed up at these events as committed supporters, and I suppose that at least some listened to me and then decided to vote for other contenders in the crowded field. But I'm convinced that we won new supporters who got to hear a full discussion of the issues we were running on and, in many cases, had the chance to ask questions about those issues. That was especially true in rural areas, where Democrats have struggled in recent election cycles. While we certainly held plenty of rallies in the largest cities in America, before huge crowds—in many cases the largest turnouts these cities had seen in decades—we also held town hall gatherings in small towns such as Orient, Iowa, population 368. It was near there that I met with hundreds of people at the homestead where former vice president Henry Wallace was raised. I held similar events in neighboring counties, and in even smaller towns. In Iowa alone we held well over a hundred meetings in every region of the state, including towns of a few hundred people. These gatherings offered a reminder of something too many Democrats have forgotten: There are thousands of voters in rural areas ready to engage with candidates who are prepared to listen to them.

As the senator from the most rural state in the nation, I know that getting to rural areas can take a little more time. Let me tell you, it's a long car ride to the Pine Ridge Reservation in South Dakota—and to Story City, Iowa. But it's worth the ride. Once you arrive at a place where people aren't used to seeing candidates for president, you can make connections that cross lines of partisanship and ideology, and that help people reengage with a political system they have come to feel, with good cause, has abandoned them. For a candidate who is willing to devote the time and energy to going that extra fifty miles down a country road, the experience can be deeply moving, and highly instructive.

Unlike our large rallies, which had sophisticated sound systems, music, and guest speakers, and were attended by a lot of media, the rural events we did in early caucus and primary states were low-key and down-to-earth. Nothing fancy. We would rent a school gym or a church basement. I would welcome people to the event, say a few words, and be followed by a panel of local residents who spoke briefly about issues of community concern. At these meetings, we always tried to include immigrants, many of whom were employed as farmworkers or were opening businesses that revitalized neglected Main Streets. I also insisted that, wherever possible, there be at least one young person on the panel. I thought it was important to hear their perspectives, as I knew that young people in rural areas feel particularly alienated from politics. I wanted to see if we could overcome that alienation together, and often we did.

After the panelists spoke, I'd answer questions and listen to comments. An hour or two later, following a lot of discussion, we headed on to the next town. But I remained in contact with people from these communities, many of whom became enthusiastic and dedicated supporters of our campaign. Some of them even went to national conventions as Sanders delegates.

Making these connections gets to the fundamentals of campaigning. I wanted their votes. They wanted to know if I would represent their interests. We talked. And they made their decision. I must say that even at meetings where there were strong differences of opinion, and there were many of those, the interactions were always civil and respectful. It seemed to me to be a process that people enjoyed. Maybe that's because, at some deep level, we all feel that this is what America is supposed to be about.

What impressed me most about those town meetings, and moved me emotionally, was the willingness of people, often perfect strangers, to open up about their lives and share their pain, their anxiety, and the frustrations they had been experiencing. There were very few meetings where tears were not shed. Often I would start things off by saying, "Just give us your name, and tell us your story." That was all it took.

In Grundy Center, a man spoke about his anxiety over going to the hospital emergency room when he thought he was having a heart attack. He knew the tests were going to cost a fortune, and he said he kept worrying about dying and leaving his wife with a pile of medical debt. Then he sighed and said, "It's humiliating." The people around him nodded. A moment later, there was more nodding when a woman talked about having to pay thousands of dollars in premiums each month to retain an inadequate health care plan that was linked to her husband's job. They didn't have the option of finding another plan, she said. "I'm not healthy," the woman quietly explained. "We can't do other things."

In Decorah, a woman who had been paying $1,750 a month for health insurance explained how her life changed when she was finally able to enroll in Medicare. I asked if she found our proposal for a Medicare for All system, which would serve people of all ages, appealing. "Yes!" she replied. "Why don't people get it?"

The range of issues that people brought up offer a reminder of the wide variety of struggles facing working Americans:

- "I'm a family farmer, and I can't compete against corporate agriculture."

- "Will I ever reunite with my husband who has been deported back to Mexico?"
- "I have an arrest record for smoking marijuana. That's crazy."
- "I work full-time but I can't afford to take care of my kids on nine dollars an hour."
- "I didn't realize I would leave college fifty thousand dollars in debt. How am I going to pay that off on the low wages that I make?"
- "Why does the school that my child attends, which is disproportionately Black, get less state funding than white schools?"

Our rallies and town meetings, held in state after state, ended up attracting hundreds of thousands of attendees, and millions more watched via livestream. We were making connections, and it was having an impact: Against a far more crowded field than we'd faced in 2016, and with many other contenders adopting progressive stances, polls consistently showed our campaign was in the top three. In key caucus and primary states, we were at or near the top. A late September 2019 CNN poll had me tied with Joe Biden for first place in Nevada, and I was devoting as much time to that state—with its large and diverse population—as I was to the traditional "first" states of Iowa and New Hampshire.

"You're Having a Heart Attack"

On a Tuesday evening at the start of October, I was meeting in Las Vegas with members of the Muslim community. Suddenly, for the first time in all my years of speaking at public meetings, I realized I needed to sit down. I couldn't keep standing. We did the question and answer session, but I knew something was wrong. I felt I had to get out of there, and we cut the meeting short. When we got in the car, I said, "Let's get back to the hotel." But my aide, Ari Rabin-Havt, said, "No, I think we'd better go to a doctor's office."

We went to an urgent care facility, where the doctor told me,

"You're having a heart attack." I couldn't believe it. In my ignorance, I'd thought that if I was having a heart attack I would collapse—that I'd literally be on the floor. Instead I was in an ambulance, headed to a hospital. Then I was surrounded by a team of doctors and nurses. The next thing I knew, I woke up in a hospital gown. A few hours later my wife, Jane, who had been up all night and taken the first plane out of Burlington to Las Vegas, was at my side. We learned that I'd had a procedure in which stents were placed in my arteries to open them up and restore blood flow. I didn't feel any real pain when I woke up that morning; I was just very weak. In many respects, the heart attack was more a psychological blow than a physical blow. I have been blessed with great health all my life, and couldn't believe that my body had failed me.

I was very fortunate in that the care I received at the Desert Springs Hospital Medical Center was excellent. The doctors explained what had happened, and I began learning more about cardiology than I ever wanted to know. The nurses helped me get back on my feet and walked with me around the corridors—which was tough at first. I still felt weak days after the surgery. I was also not much in the mood to answer many of the phone calls that were coming in. What did cheer me up, however, was getting a visit from my friend Harry Reid, the former majority leader of the U.S. Senate who had recently retired as the senior senator from Nevada. In the midst of all I was going through, it was good to see an old friend.

My heart attack was a big news story, and media interest in my medical condition was intense. Reporters and TV camera crews crowded around the hospital entrance, peppering anyone who appeared with questions. How serious was the attack itself? What kind of damage had been incurred? Was Sanders dropping out of the race? If not, when was the seventy-eight-year-old candidate with a heart condition returning to the campaign trail, and what would that campaign look like?

Immediately after my surgery, we really didn't know the answers to the political questions. Indeed, we had our own questions: Would

I be strong enough to continue the campaign? Could I do it full-time? In my condition, could I assure the American people that I would be healthy enough to manage the incredibly stressful responsibilities that go with serving as president of the United States? Being president in your eighties is one thing. Being president in your eighties with a heart condition, that's something more. As David Axelrod, a former top adviser to President Obama, said to *The New York Times,* "Running for president is a physical and emotional trial, and the presidency itself is even more demanding. While we all wish Senator Sanders well, this has to be a big flashing light for him. And given his age, it may be for some voters as well." Axelrod was right. It was a flashing light—but not necessarily a flashing red light.

While we were uncertain about the future, one thing was clear. For me, after months of going nonstop, the campaign was at least temporarily on hold. I was heading home to Burlington to rest and recuperate, spend time with my family, and talk with close aides such as my campaign manager, Faiz Shakir. Media speculation about whether I would quit the race intensified with each passing day. Reporters were hanging out in front of the house. But that wasn't what I was thinking about. I was focused on getting stronger. Before my heart attack, walking several miles was not a problem. Now, I was running out of breath after going a few blocks. The good news was that, as the days passed, I could go farther and farther. While I was not at 100 percent, the walks around our backyard were getting easier. I was coming back. Having never experienced a health emergency like this before, I didn't know how long it would take for me to feel like my own self. But I had a growing sense that I was going to get there.

Jane and I talked a lot about whether we wanted to return to the campaign. We both agreed that we did, and when the time felt right, we called together a small group of family members and aides and began to chart our course going forward.

The first real test would come on October 15, when I was scheduled to participate in a CNN debate with the other Democratic candidates. Some debates last an hour, some an hour and a half; but, my luck, this was a long one: two hours. I was nervous about how I would do physically. The other candidates were kind, especially Kamala Harris, to whom I had not been all that close up to that point. Backstage, she was at my side asking: "Do you need to sit? Did you eat?" The expressions of concern from other candidates—including my fellow senators Elizabeth Warren, Amy Klobuchar, and Cory Booker—were genuine, and I truly appreciated them. But they also reminded me that this was a pivotal night, when voters would be watching to see whether I could stand up for two hours, and how I would perform when it came to answering questions about not just the issues but my health.

Two hours on your feet, speaking in front of millions of viewers, is never an easy thing. In this instance, it was the most demanding task I had taken on since the heart attack. If I had been forced to walk off the stage because of fatigue, it's likely the campaign would have been over right there. I don't remember if I "won" the debate or not, but I did stay up on my feet, spoke more than most of the other candidates on the stage, answered questions about everything from breaking up monopolies to protecting the Kurds in Syria, called Trump the most corrupt president in American history, and earned some generous rounds of applause. We were back.

The debate was critical to renewing the campaign. But just as important was a call I got from Representative Alexandria Ocasio-Cortez, who had not made an endorsement up to that point. Alexandria, who during her first year in Congress had become enormously popular with the progressive community and young people across the country, had been courted by several of the candidates. But she contacted me shortly before the debate to say that she had decided to endorse our campaign. Later she explained, "For me, it wasn't even about helping the senator. It was a moment of clarity for me personally in saying, 'What role do I want to play? And I want to be a part of a mass movement.'"

It turned out that she was not alone in that view. Representative

Ilhan Omar made a video in which she endorsed our campaign and announced, "Bernie Sanders isn't fighting to win just one presidential election—he's fighting for the soul of our democracy." Representative Rashida Tlaib, another member of "the Squad"—as Ocasio-Cortez had dubbed the four young, progressive congresswomen elected in 2018—called and said she wanted to make her endorsement at a rally in her hometown of Detroit. It was just remarkable. All of these young members of Congress, to whom I felt very close ideologically and personally, were calling to say they wanted the campaign to continue, and that they wanted to be a part of it.

On the Saturday following the debate, we held a rally in Queens, New York, where I was joined by many longtime supporters, including campaign co-chairs Nina Turner, a former state senator from Ohio, and Carmen Yulín Cruz, the mayor of San Juan, Puerto Rico. Tiffany Cabán, who would go on to be elected to the New York City Council, introduced Alexandria, who told the crowd, "I'm proud to say that the only reason I had any hope in launching a long-shot campaign for Congress is because Bernie Sanders proved that you can run a grassroots campaign in an America where we almost thought it wasn't possible."

The crowd of 27,000, the largest of the campaign to that point, welcomed me warmly when I took the stage. I knew that we had passed the test. And let me say this: It was an indescribable feeling to stand on a stage and look out, as far as the eye could see, at a crowd of supporters from every conceivable background who had come out on that fall day to carry forward a campaign for fundamental change. I thought about the beauty of our country, and the potential of our movement to realize *all* of its promise.

During that speech I introduced a slogan developed by Jeff Weaver—a fellow Vermonter who had been working with me on campaigns for decades—that perfectly encapsulated what our run was about: "Not Me, Us!" We were not merely making a race for the presidency. We were building a movement to transform the politics, and the future, of the United States.

This was America at its best, and it created in me an incredible sense of optimism about what could be accomplished by a campaign that in many senses was only beginning to hit its stride. I did not shy away from talking about the heart attack. "There is no question that I and my family have faced adversity over these last few weeks," I told the crowd. "The untold story is that people everywhere in this country, in the wealthiest nation in the history of the world, are facing their own adversities." That was a message that I could take back on the road.

Confronting the Status Quo

We worked harder than ever. Traveling to more states. Holding more rallies and town meetings. Issuing more position papers and going deeper in our discussions of the issues. Our poll numbers started ticking upward. After months of trailing Joe Biden, sometimes by double digits, a January national poll from CNN put me in first place. Then an NBC poll did the same. But polls are one thing. Winning actual votes is another.

In Iowa, where the process began, the caucuses were a debacle. The state party screwed up the vote count so badly that it took days to get a result. But when it finally came, I had won the most votes—thanks to overwhelming support from young people and rural communities where we had held all those town meetings. A week later we won New Hampshire, beating nineteen other candidates and carrying seven of the state's ten counties.

I was now the clear front-runner.

The momentum we were building terrified the defenders of status quo politics in the upper echelons of the Democratic Party and in the media. An Associated Press report from January 8, 2020, warned, "Fears of Sanders win are growing among the Democratic establishment." As our campaign went from strength to strength, the outcry from the establishment grew louder. A front-page story in *The New York Times* on February 13 featured the headline "Sanders on

Rise, Anxiety Deepens Among Centrists." It reported that "within the Democratic establishment, the results have deepened a mood of anxiety and frustration." The article also mentioned growing enthusiasm on the part of party leaders for Michael Bloomberg, the multibillionaire who was spending hundreds of millions on TV ads to win the nomination. While Bloomberg and his supporters were claiming that I would ruin the party's chances in November, polls consistently showed me leading Trump. Indeed, around the same time the AP report was published, a CNN poll had me seven points ahead of the incumbent.

What was the real source of that "anxiety and frustration" on the part of establishment Democrats? Was it because our campaign couldn't beat Trump? Of course not. Polls showed that we were beating him by wider margins than the other candidates. Was it that our ideas were unpopular? No. Working families across the country were reacting enthusiastically to our messages on the economy, health care, climate, and social and racial issues; and we were bringing far more people out to our events than any other candidate. Were the insiders sincerely concerned that our campaign would divide and weaken the party? Not if they were paying attention to what was happening in the caucus and primary states. Our campaign was bringing millions of people from all backgrounds—especially young people, the future of the party and the country—into the political process.

Let's be honest. What the establishment was anxious about was the fact that we were beginning to transform the Democratic Party from an election machine dominated by wealthy campaign contributors and corporate interests into a multiracial, multiethnic, urban and rural movement of the working class. What frustrated the insiders was the prospect that they and their wealthy friends, the lobbyists and the consultants, were losing control of a party they thought of as their personal possession. It became clear to me that what the struggle really came down to was a question of whether the Democratic establishment was prepared to stop coddling corporate power and begin to challenge it—as Franklin Roosevelt had done in the

New Deal era—or whether they would continue working the cocktail-party circuit for donations from billionaire investors and corporate CEOs. In other words, our campaign threatened a very cozy status quo, which answered that threat with a cry of "Anybody but Bernie."

After I won a landslide victory in the critical Nevada caucuses—with a 2–1 lead over the next closest contender, Joe Biden—and began to show strength in states from California to Maine, a *USA Today* opinion piece declared, "Moderate Democrats have a duty to consider Sanders. He has a clear path to beating Trump." Voters agreed. A national Reuters/Ipsos poll from late February found that Democratic and Independent voters felt I would be the strongest Democratic contender in a head-to-head race with the president. Unfortunately, our surging momentum rattled the establishment even more. It was clear they were preparing to throw everything they could against us.

In the final debate before the February 29 primary in South Carolina—a southern state where Biden had strong support, and where he would prevail with relative ease—I wanted to talk about taxing billionaires, ending student debt, and caring for the 87 million Americans who had no health insurance or were underinsured as the coronavirus pandemic began to take hold. My rivals had other ideas. Before the first round of questioning was done, Mike Bloomberg was claiming that Russian president Vladimir Putin wanted me as the nominee against Trump "so you will lose to him." Former South Bend mayor Pete Buttigieg warned, "If you think the last four years has been chaotic, divisive, toxic, exhausting, imagine spending the better part of 2020 with Bernie Sanders versus Donald Trump." The moderators egged them on, literally encouraging the other candidates to attack as unworkable the proposal I had made for implementing Medicare for All: a system similar to those of other Western democracies. It was an absurd and unsettling night. Issues were discarded as the other candidates kept pushing the line that nominating me would destroy Democratic chances in November. "Bernie will lose to Donald Trump," declared Bloomberg. "The House and the Senate

and some of the statehouses will all go red. And then, between gerrymandering and appointing judges, for the next twenty or thirty
years, we're going to live with this catastrophe."

When moderator Norah O'Donnell called on me to respond, I
couldn't resist observing, "Mayor Bloomberg has a solid and strong
and enthusiastic base of support. The problem is, they're all billionaires." I could have gone on, pointing out that Bloomberg had no
clue about how to build a genuine grassroots campaign and was only
trying to buy the nomination with TV ads. But I quickly got to the
point, saying, "Of the last fifty polls that have been done nationally,
Mr. Bloomberg, I beat Trump forty-seven of those fifty times."

I knew I was right. But I also knew that this wasn't an argument
about electability. This was a fight between a new vision of politics
and the status quo vision that had for decades thwarted progress in
the party and the country. As "Super Tuesday" voting on March 3 ap-
proached, the status quo made its move. This was, very probably, its
last chance to stop us. Super Tuesday was the most important election day in the race for the Democratic nomination. Fourteen states,
from Maine to California, were holding their primaries and caucuses,
and the candidate who did well on that day, with over one-third of
pledged delegates at stake, would be well positioned to win the nomination.

The good news for us was that polling showed we were winning
many of the Super Tuesday states, including the two that would
choose the largest numbers of delegates, California and Texas. The
bad news for us was that the establishment fully understood the
threat they faced, and it was prepared to do everything in its power
to prevent us from prevailing. It wasn't a secret. *Time* magazine reported on February 27 that "Big-Money Democratic Donors Are Trying to Stop Bernie Sanders," while a March 2 *New York Times*
headline announced, "Democratic Leaders Willing to Risk Party
Damage to Stop Bernie Sanders."

On the eve of Super Tuesday, the establishment struck. Despite
having raised tens of millions of dollars, and having run campaigns

that were still seen in many circles as credible, two of the leading moderate Democrats in the race, Pete Buttigieg and Minnesota senator Amy Klobuchar, abruptly canceled their candidacies and endorsed Biden. Both flew to Texas, the most hotly contested of the primary states, to appear with the former vice president. They were joined by another former candidate, Texan Beto O'Rourke, in a highly choreographed show of support. The establishment had succeeded in uniting, in support of Biden, the candidates who had been dividing up the moderate vote. Meanwhile, the liberal and progressive vote continued to be divided between Massachusetts senator Elizabeth Warren and myself. Despite poor showings in Iowa, New Hampshire, Nevada, and South Carolina, Warren chose to stay in the race. I was closer to her on the issues than any other candidate. But, at a point where her endorsement could have been significant in a number of Super Tuesday states, she chose not to give it.

Even as the centrist vote coalesced around Biden, and the progressive and liberal vote was divided, our campaign still won California, Colorado, Utah, and Vermont on Super Tuesday. But Biden beat us in Texas by around sixty thousand votes. That narrow win, along with solid victories in Virginia, Massachusetts, and Minnesota, gave the former vice president a huge boost. Our campaign, which days earlier had been expected to win the most delegates on Super Tuesday, was suddenly trailing. Biden had the lead, and the momentum. Warren left the race a few days later, and with the exit of Bloomberg, what had been a twenty-three-candidate contest was down to a two-man race between Biden and me.

We soldiered on through the next rounds of primaries, and won in places such as North Dakota. But Biden was taking the big states, and the onset of COVID-19 made it impossible for us to hold the rallies and mount the door-to-door campaigns that were needed to have a chance in states I had won in 2016, such as Michigan, Washington, and Wisconsin. After a loss in the Wisconsin primary on April 7, we reached the decision that it was time to suspend our campaign.

Needless to say, it is difficult to end a campaign that has been sustained by thousands of active volunteers and attracted the support of millions of voters. It is even more difficult when that campaign has become a movement that has aroused a sense of possibility about finally addressing the most challenging issues facing the nation. I would be less than honest if I failed to acknowledge that many of my staffers wanted to carry on, arguing that even if we could not win we should take the message forward. But, to my mind, as painful as the decision was, there did not appear to be any other option. As I said to our supporters when we suspended our effort, "If I believed we had a feasible path to the nomination, I would certainly continue the campaign. But it's just not there."

Ending a Campaign; Carrying a Movement Forward

My decision to suspend our campaign was about something greater than the primary fight in which I had been involved. I could not justify making a futile effort that might have undermined the united front we needed to build in order to defeat Trump. I had started my 2020 campaign with a determination to defeat the most dangerous president in the modern history of the country, and I intended to do everything I could to boot Donald Trump from office. I concluded that we might as well get started on that effort as soon as possible.

So it was that, on the morning of April 8, 2020, I began the livestream broadcast from my home.

It was not a typical concession speech, because ours had not been a typical campaign. I, of course, congratulated Joe Biden as "a very decent man who I will work with to move our progressive ideas forward." I spoke of how I would work with him to forge a progressive platform and how, together, standing united, we would defeat Donald Trump.

But my main message had to do with what we had accomplished with a campaign that really meant it when we said: "Not Me, Us!"

I reminded the millions of Americans who watched the livestream that we had built "an unprecedented grassroots political campaign that has had a profound impact in changing our nation."

"Together we have transformed American consciousness as to what kind of nation we can become, and have taken this country a major step forward in the never-ending struggle for economic justice, social justice, racial justice, and environmental justice," I said, before recalling a quote from Nelson Mandela: "It always seems impossible until it is done."

What Mandela meant, and what I strongly believe, is that "the greatest obstacle to reach social change has everything to do with the power of the corporate and political establishment to limit our vision as to what is possible and what we are entitled to as human beings. If we don't believe that we are entitled to health care as a human right, we will never achieve universal health care. If we don't believe that we are entitled to decent wages and working conditions, millions of us will continue to live in poverty. If we don't believe that we are entitled to all of the education we require to fulfill our dreams, many of us will leave schools saddled with huge debt, or never get the education we need. If we don't believe that we are entitled to live in a world that has a clean environment and is not ravaged by climate change, we will continue to see more drought, floods, rising sea levels, an increasingly uninhabitable planet."

While we did not win the nomination, I said, we changed public consciousness. "It was not long ago that people considered [our] ideas radical and fringe," I explained. "Today they are mainstream ideas, and many of them are already being implemented in cities and states across the country. That is what we have accomplished together."

If that does not sound quite like the language of defeat, it's because I believed the setback we suffered in 2020 was only temporary. Why was I so confident? Because, I said, "not only are we winning the struggle ideologically, we are also winning it generationally. The future of our country rests with young people. And in state after state, whether we won or whether we lost the Democratic primaries or caucuses, we received a significant majority of the votes, sometimes an overwhelming majority, from people not only thirty years of age or under, but fifty years of age or younger. In other words, the future of this country is with *our* ideas."

2

TAKING ON TRUMP

Our progressive movement's struggle to defeat the most dangerous president in American history

Almost all presidential candidates, when they lose an election, simply close shop, pack up, and go home. That was never something we were going to do. That was not what "Not Me, Us!" was about. We were building a grassroots movement that was about transforming the country. So, while the "Bernie Sanders for President" campaign was finished, the struggle for economic, racial, social, and environmental justice would carry forward. Through the fall of 2020, it would be focused on preventing Donald Trump from winning a second term. Not only were Trump's policies reactionary and anti-worker, there was real uncertainty about whether democracy would survive if he remained in power.

With a campaign staff reduced to about fifteen employees, headed up by Misty Rebik, who had formerly been my Iowa state director, we began our efforts to do everything possible to defeat

Trump. Further, I wanted to make sure that our campaign organization, with its millions of supporters, could help progressive candidates around the country who were running for federal, state, and
local office. We also wanted to support the great grassroots organizations that we had worked with during the campaign.

What I Liked About Joe Biden

I met Joe Biden when I was elected to the Senate in 2006. He was a
senior Democratic senator, with more than thirty years of experience
in the chamber. I was a freshman senator who arrived not as a Democrat, but as an Independent who would caucus with Democrats
under the leadership of the late Harry Reid. We were not on the
same committees, and we did not travel in the same circles. Joe was
the ultimate insider. I, to say the least, was not. Yet, while Joe was a
good deal more conservative than I was on foreign and domestic policy issues, I liked him personally. He was a decent man, down-to-
earth, family-oriented, warm, and good-humored. He talked a lot
about his working-class roots, which I appreciated, as I did his enthusiasm for organized labor.

When Joe served as President Barack Obama's vice president, he
invited me several times to the Naval Observatory, the vice presidential residence in Washington. He took an interest in my 2016 presidential campaign and, while he remained neutral in the competition
between Hillary Clinton and myself, he was not shy about offering
insights and advice. That drew us closer, as did the fact that my wife,
Jane, and Joe's wife, Jill, developed a friendship as Senate spouses
and, eventually, on the campaign trail.

Joe and I got to know each other better during the 2020 campaign.
We debated each other almost a dozen times, usually amid a crowd of
other contenders but, finally, in a one-on-one event that was broadcast
from a CNN studio in Washington, D.C., during the initial COVID-19
surge. We also participated in dozens of forums that put us in the same
place at the same time. I was always impressed by his decency when,

during breaks in these multi-candidate events, he would go out of his way to comfort a candidate who had just been attacked or who had stumbled in answering a question. Even though we took different positions on the issues, and even though we were trying to outmaneuver each other in pursuit of the nomination, we developed a sort of camaraderie. There's a behind-the-scenes relationship that opens up among candidates who are on the same long campaign trail—especially for those of us who have known each other for years. We share reactions to news stories, compare notes on hotels, complain about early wake-up calls, and commiserate with each other about the challenge of finding a good meal on the road.

After our campaign was suspended in early April of 2020, Joe and I began talking on the phone quite a bit about how we could best work together to defeat Trump. Our staffs, led by Ron Klain from his team and Analilia Mejia from ours, began to communicate on a regular basis. During our initial calls, we agreed to do two things. First, we would participate in a livestream broadcast together, where I would formally endorse his candidacy. Second, we would establish a set of task forces to see what kind of consensus the two campaigns could reach on the major issues facing our country.

During the half-hour livestream—which, due to COVID, we joined from our respective homes on April 13—I wanted to send the clearest message I could. "I'm asking every Democrat, I'm asking every Independent, I'm asking a lot of Republicans to come together in this campaign to support your candidacy, which I endorse," I said, telling Joe "we need you in the White House."

Joe accepted the endorsement warmly, saying, "You don't get enough credit, Bernie, for being the voice that forces us to take a hard look in the mirror and ask ourselves if we've done enough. And we haven't . . . I am going to need you, not just to win the campaign, but to govern." Joe was signaling his understanding of the need to form a political alliance against Trump. The issue task forces would solidify that alliance. "It's no great secret, Joe, that you and I have our differences, and we are not going to paper them over. That's real," I said. "But I hope that these task forces will come together, utilizing the best minds and people in your campaign and in my campaign, to work out real solutions to these very, very important problems."

How Task Forces Gave the Biden Campaign a Progressive Agenda

In establishing the task forces, there was excellent cooperation between the campaigns. We agreed to address six of the major crises facing the country: the economy, health care, education, climate change, immigration, and criminal justice. The Biden campaign would have five members on each task force; we would have three.

Biden's positions on most issues were of course more conservative than mine. We appealed to different groups of voters. It was obvious that, if Biden was going to win, he needed to attract our supporters. The task forces, therefore, served both of our interests. We wanted to move him in a more progressive direction. He wanted to adopt policies that could create some degree of excitement within the progressive community. As part of the protocol for the task forces, we agreed that we would keep their ongoing discussions private, and do our best to prevent leaks to the media.

The work began immediately. Our shared understanding of the importance of building genuine unity for the fall campaign against Trump made the process of establishing the task forces far smoother than is usually the case in politics.

When it came to the actual makeup of the task forces, my team didn't want Biden's to name right-wing Democrats who were viscerally opposed to the progressive agenda. They agreed. For their part, they didn't want us to include progressives who had, in a personal way, attacked Biden. We agreed. The Biden camp selected some of the most prominent Democrats in the country, including former presidential candidate and secretary of state John Kerry and former U.S. attorney general Eric Holder, as well as a number of members of Congress. Our campaign came up with eighteen strong progressives to represent us on the task forces.

The task forces provided a rare opportunity for the moderate and progressive wings of the Democratic Party to debate, collaborate, and look for areas of agreement. The discussions were serious, and often animated. Our campaign's task force members pushed aggressively for an agenda that would represent working families, protect the environment, and take on powerful corporate interests. Sometimes our ideas prevailed. Sometimes they failed. Most times, the two teams found middle ground on which progress could be achieved.

The process proved to be an honest, difficult, sometimes frustrating and sometimes encouraging give-and-take:

> *Should we raise the federal minimum wage to $15 an hour?*
>   Agreement.
> *Should we move forward toward a Medicare for All single-payer program?* Disagreement.
> *Should we have Medicare negotiate prescription drug costs?*
>   Agreement.
> *Should we legalize marijuana?* Disagreement.
> *Should we be aggressive in combating climate change and create a Civilian Climate Corps?* Agreement.
> *Should we forgive all student debt?* Disagreement.
> *Should we lower the age of Medicare eligibility to sixty?*
>   Agreement.
> *Should we make public colleges and universities tuition-free?*
>   Disagreement.
> *Should we end private prisons and detention centers?* Agreement.
> *Should we impose a wealth tax on billionaires?* Disagreement.

Would I have liked to see the Biden camp agree with us on all these issues? Of course. But there was no question that we had succeeded in pushing Biden in a more progressive direction. Even *The New York Times,* which was often hostile to our campaign and its agenda, recognized that we had achieved significant progress on the issues, and on the work of uniting the party to take on Trump: "The new policy recommendations for Joseph R. Biden Jr., crafted jointly by allies of Mr. Biden and Senator Bernie Sanders of Vermont, are the clearest sign yet that the moderate and progressive wings of the Democratic Party are trying to unite far more than they did in 2016," reported the paper of record. "But the ideas put forth on Wednesday are also indications that progressives succeeded in pushing some proposals leftward, influencing Mr. Biden's policy platform as he prepares to accept his party's nomination for president next month."

The Most Progressive Platform in the History of the Democratic Party

The task forces provided an outline for the party platform, which would be written in the weeks leading up to the August 17–20 Democratic National Convention. Several of the representatives who served on the task forces joined in the drafting process, and they continued to push for even more progressive positions, arguing that the coronavirus pandemic and the economic hardship that extended from it demanded that the party adopt a bolder agenda. That was especially true on the question of whether to expand Medicare to cover all Americans. "We have an opportunity to go bigger because this moment demands it," argued Dr. Abdul El-Sayed, as he advocated on behalf of Medicare for All. The amendments proposed by our campaign were rejected by the platform committee, which was dominated by Biden delegates. But the final document did nod to our advocacy, embracing calls to add a public option to the Affordable Care Act.

On a number of other issues, there was measurable progress. *Scientific American* announced, "Democrats released their strongest climate platform in history." The platform also featured robust support for labor unions, acknowledging that "the global trading system has failed to keep its promises to American workers"; and embraced anti-trust and antimonopoly initiatives that had been popularized by our supporters, such as Fordham professor Zephyr Teachout. The document echoed our campaign's populist message with a declaration: "We will make sure the wealthy pay their fair share in taxes. We will make sure investors pay the same tax rates as workers and bring an end to expensive and unproductive tax loopholes, including the carried interest loophole. Corporate tax rates, which were cut sharply by the 2017 Republican tax cut, must be raised, and 'trickle-down' tax cuts must be rejected." The planks on abortion rights and LGBTQ rights were strong, reflecting well-founded concerns that an increasingly conservative U.S. Supreme Court would begin to reject its own precedents. And, following the outcry over the murders of George Floyd and Breonna Taylor, the party took a dramatically stronger stand in favor of criminal justice reform.

The platform was not as bold as the one I would have run on. But there was no doubt in my mind that it outlined a program that would, if adopted into policy, make Biden the most progressive president since Franklin Delano Roosevelt. That was a case I made in a prime-time speech on the opening night of the Democratic National Convention (which was held virtually, because of COVID). The other keynote of the evening was given by former first lady Michelle Obama.

Addressing the Democratic National Convention

Given that the address was going to be carried live by every major television network in the country, it would be one of the most important speeches I would ever deliver, and my staff and I put a good deal of time into preparing the text. What made it especially challenging to prepare was that I had only eight minutes to deliver it. Much to say. Little time to say it. Further, I would be looking into a camera, rather than feeling the energy of a crowd. That's a tough way to deliver any major speech.

Speaking from the Hotel Vermont in downtown Burlington, I used my eight minutes to discuss the existential threats facing the nation, the enormous differences between Biden and Trump, and the catastrophic prospect of continuing Donald Trump's presidency.

"We are facing the worst public health crisis in a hundred years and the worst economic collapse since the Great Depression," I said. "We are confronting systemic racism, and the existential threat to our planet of climate change. And, in the midst of all this, we have a president who is not only incapable of addressing these crises but is leading us down the path towards authoritarianism. This election is the most important in the modern history of this country. In response to the unprecedented set of crises we face, we need an unprecedented response—a movement, like never before, of people who are prepared to stand up and fight for democracy and decency—and against greed, oligarchy, and bigotry."

The vast majority of the Americans who were listening to me understood the pandemic as an immediate threat and a personal challenge. I used my address to put it in perspective politically. By rejecting science, Trump had "put our lives and health in jeopardy," I said. "Trump has attacked doctors and scientists trying to protect us from the pandemic, while refusing to take strong action to produce the masks, gowns, and gloves our health care workers desperately need. Nero fiddled while Rome burned; Trump golfs. His actions fanned this pandemic, resulting in over 170,000 deaths and a nation still unprepared to protect its people."

While the pandemic was the most pressing issue of the moment, I felt it was possible—and necessary—to make a connection in the minds of voters between Trump's reckless disregard for the health and safety of Americans during this particular crisis and his broader disregard for the welfare of the people he was supposed to serve.

"The American people have caught on that this president and his administration are, to put it bluntly, frauds. In 2016, Trump promised he would stand with working families," I explained. "He said that he would 'drain the swamp,' take on Wall Street and powerful special interests. He would protect Social Security, Medicare, and Medicaid and, by the way, he would provide health care to 'everybody.' Well. None of that was true. Instead, he gave trillions to the top one percent and large corporations, and filled his administration with billionaires. He tried to throw thirty-two million people off of their health insurance, eliminate protections for preexisting conditions, and submitted budgets that proposed slashing Medicaid, Medicare, and Social Security."

Drawing a stark contrast with Trump, I made the case for Joe Biden as an honorable man who was running—thanks to the work of the task forces—on a progressive platform.

While all of the issues mattered, what weighed on me most as I prepared to deliver the speech was the mounting evidence that Donald Trump would do anything to maintain his grip on power. "Under this administration authoritarianism has taken root in our country. I, and my family, and many of yours, know the insidious way authoritarianism destroys democracy, decency, and humanity."

The reference to my family in those remarks was deliberate. I'm Jewish, and my family came from Poland. My father's family was almost entirely wiped out by Hitler and his violent white nationalism. I am profoundly conscious of the threat that white nationalism and other forms of racism pose. It was with this in mind that I pledged in my convention address: "As long as I am here, I will work with other progressives, with moderates, and, yes, with conservatives to preserve this nation from a threat that so many of our heroes fought and died to defeat."

That was an appeal to unity in support of Joe Biden's candidacy, which I was more than happy to make. But there was more to it than that. I was appealing to the conscience of Americans who I hoped would recognize that "the future of our democracy is at stake."

"My friends," I concluded, "the price of failure is just too great to imagine."

That was the core message I wanted to deliver, and I was pleased on the second night of the convention when my supporters echoed it. As the traditional roll call of the states was conducted virtually that evening, the more than one thousand delegates who were pledged to support my candidacy got a chance to honor the will of primary voters. They did that, but many of them also made a point of talking about how they were uniting behind the Biden-Harris ticket to build a movement strong enough to defeat Trump and Trumpism. Former United Auto Workers president Bob King formally nominated me for the presidency, while Alexandria Ocasio-Cortez seconded the nomination and celebrated our "mass people's movement working to establish twenty-first-century social, economic, and human rights, including guaranteed health care, higher education, living wages, and labor rights for all people in the United States."

Building the Anti-Trump Movement

Defeating Trump was never going to be easy. The man is a demagogue and a pathological liar. Many people called him crazy, and I did not necessarily disagree with them. But Trump was not stupid. He was a master at identifying the vulnerabilities of his opponents and then ruthlessly exploiting them. Given the Democratic Party's failure to address the needs of a struggling working class over many years, on issues ranging from trade policy to deindustrialization to wages, Trump seized every opportunity to claim he was the man to fill the void. There was a risk in 2020 that, despite the miserable job he had done, Trump would continue to attract support from working women and men who were growing increasingly desperate as the pandemic raged.

With millions of Americans falling further and further behind economically, losing faith in government, and feeling ignored by the political establishment, Trump played on their anger and resentment through sometimes subtle but often overt appeals to racism, sexism, homophobia, and xenophobia. He employed the classic calculus of the authoritarian. People needed enemies—and Trump gave them plenty. It is no small feat that in four short years Trump annihilated the long-standing leadership of the Republican Party and converted a center-right political organization into a vehicle for right-wing extremism that drew comparisons with European neo-fascist parties.

What was even more alarming was the fact that millions of Americans, following Trump's lead, now told pollsters they had lost faith in democracy. A growing number of them agreed with the statement that "true American patriots may have to resort to violence in order to save our country." Trump's most fervent supporters were agitated, and they were activated. They would turn out. The question was whether Democrats could mobilize the tens of millions of voters who believed in democracy but who were not necessarily excited by Joe Biden and Kamala Harris.

As the Democratic nominee, Biden would set the tone for the campaign. His team, with its long experience and hundreds of millions in campaign funds, would frame the messaging against Trump. Our team wrestled with an essential question: How could we effectively support a candidate who was far more conservative than I was without compromising our progressive principles or disappointing our supporters?

Biden hoped to reach out to Republicans and moderates by contrasting his basic decency and honesty with an authoritarian president who frequently expressed racist and xenophobic views, presided over the most corrupt administration in modern history, and lied all the time. While this was a different strategy from the one I would have pursued as the Democratic nominee, it certainly wasn't illogical and, if carried forward skillfully, had the potential to lead to victory. The problem with it, though, was that it left a whole lot of potential voters out of the campaign.

By pursuing a predictably cautious approach, what was Biden saying to the tens of millions of Americans who were demanding bold and transformative change? How was he going to connect with young people who were not only struggling economically but were deeply concerned about the crises of climate change, systemic racism, and student debt? What was he saying to working-class people who were unable to make it on $10 an hour, who had no health insurance, and, as a result of the pandemic, had lost their jobs or their homes? What was he saying to the millions of people in Black, Latino, Asian American, and Indigenous communities who were fighting economic and social injustice every single day? The answer: Not enough.

We had a lot to say to disenchanted and disenfranchised Americans, and it quickly became clear that the best way for us to help Biden was to reach out to people who had not voted for him in the primaries, who were not particularly excited about his candidacy, and with whom he was not effectively communicating. The political danger for Biden was not that these people would vote for Trump. The danger was they might not vote at all. We believed that we could get them to the polls.

If it had been a normal time and a normal campaign, I would have been on a plane flying from state to state, doing rallies and town meetings, speaking to tens of thousands of people. Unfortunately, 2020 was not a normal year, and most of our campaigning had to take place through livestreams and social media. Not optimal, and not something that I liked, but it was what we had to do.

Our Mostly Virtual Campaign for Joe Biden and Kamala Harris

We made it work by teaming up with grassroots organizations and doing as many livestream events as we could. We held nineteen virtual rallies in the battleground states. We also held eleven with particular constituencies that we wanted to reach out to, including young voters, trade unionists, the Latino community, rural Americans, climate change activists, criminal justice reform advocates, and campaigners for a just immigration system. Our major goal in these livestreams was not only to get people registered, but to make sure they voted.

We also wanted to reach potential voters in states that were not priorities for the Biden campaign and the Democratic Party. Fall presidential campaigning in recent decades has been focused almost exclusively on so-called battleground states, where both parties are competitive and polls tend to be tight. I understand the logic of this approach in a closely contested race where securing the needed 270 electoral votes is a priority. But it has always frustrated me, because a narrow focus diminishes prospects for ultimately changing the direction of our politics. That was particularly true in 2020. There were people in reliably "red" Republican states and reliably "blue" Democratic states who needed to be mobilized in order to win local, state, and congressional contests—and also to build out the base for the presidential ticket. With this in mind, we organized livestream rallies in red, blue, and purple states. We also encouraged the Biden campaign and the Democratic Party to consider some basic logic that is too frequently ignored by politicians: You can't change people's political views if you don't talk to them and treat them with respect.

Our first two livestreams were in Kentucky and West Virginia on August 15. We then proceeded to Iowa and Wisconsin, then to Colorado and Texas, and on and on. It's a big country. Most often the meetings consisted of panel discussions in which we heard from local people who were struggling with unemployment, low wages, and a lack of health care. I talked about what the election could mean for their lives. We also heard from national leaders, including U.S. senators, progressive members of Congress, governors, and folks who headed up major progressive national organizations. At one rally, held on the Thursday before the election, Democratic vice presidential nominee Kamala Harris joined Service Employees International Union president Mary Kay Henry and Ai-jen Poo, one of the nation's leading advocates for home care workers, to discuss the fight for living wages. On the Saturday afternoon before the election, I joined one of my most ardent supporters in the primaries, Congressional Progressive Caucus co-chair Mark Pocan, for a rally with students on the University of Wisconsin–Madison campus, where the mascot is a badger. I told the virtual crowd, "I know sometimes it's uncomfortable badgering your friends to come out and vote. Well, you're going to feel a little bit more uncomfortable if Trump wins Wisconsin by a handful of votes." Students gave a vital boost to Biden, who won Wisconsin by 20,682 votes, for a 0.63 percent margin over Trump.

Given the constraints that we were operating under, the "turn-outs" for these virtual rallies were impressive. The national livestreams often drew more than 200,000 viewers, while events that were targeted toward individual states drew as many as 10,000 people. By Election Day, the overall viewership numbered in the millions.

While the virtual rallies were successful, I kept getting encouragement to leave the television studio and hit the road. Despite a good deal of nervousness on my wife's part, I agreed to hold in-person rallies for Biden in three battleground states: New Hampshire, Michigan, and Pennsylvania. The Biden team went out of its way to assure that these trips were as COVID-safe as possible. We had our own plane, everyone around me was tested and wore masks, the security was strong, and the physical spaces we occupied were wiped clean. The primary goal of these trips was not to bring out large crowds of people, which would have been inappropriate and impractical during the pandemic. What we hoped to do was attract local media. And that we did, in no small measure because of the novelty of the events we organized.

They were certainly the weirdest public events I have ever done.

In Lebanon, New Hampshire, the Biden campaign rented a beautiful field at a ski resort outside of town. The weather was wonderful. Under normal circumstances, the event would've drawn thousands of people from a state that neighbored Vermont and where I'd twice won as a presidential primary contender. But, because we limited attendance and kept people far apart, we had only a few hundred. I'll admit that it was a disconcerting experience to address so few voters and so much grass.

An event we did in Macomb County, Michigan, was even stranger. We did a "car rally." For the first time in my life, I had the opportunity to address a parking lot full of cars and trucks—hundreds of them. Instead of being interrupted by cheers and applause, I was greeted with honking horns. The character of the event—an auto-focused rally in the nation's preeminent auto-making state— apparently unsettled the Republicans. A number of Trump supporters attempted to disrupt my remarks, but the police—and the honking horns of our supporters—made it a good day for the Biden campaign.

We organized another car rally, outside of Pittsburgh. There were terrific warm-up speeches from Lieutenant Governor John Fetterman and a pair of rising stars in the Pennsylvania legislature, state representatives Summer Lee and Sara Innamorato. I had supported all three of them in their election bids and it was great to see them out on the campaign trail. Two years later, John would be elected to the U.S. Senate, while Summer would be elected to the U.S. House. When we spoke together on that fall day in 2020, hundreds of enthusiastic young workers showed up for the event, which gave me a sense of optimism for what might happen in Pennsylvania on Election Day.

As it happened, Biden won both Michigan and Pennsylvania with relative ease, and he narrowly carried Wisconsin. Those were three of the five states that backed Trump in 2016 but flipped to the Democrats in 2020, thanks to a historic mobilization of new voters that saw Biden win nationally with a seven-million popular vote margin.

Reelecting the Squad and Electing Some Allies

Electing Joe Biden wasn't our only political mission in 2020. We knew that, if we were going to build a strong grassroots political movement, progressives had to win down-ballot races for seats in state legislatures and on city councils, county commissions and school boards. They had to be elected as district attorneys and state attorneys general. We ended up endorsing more than two hundred candidates for a wide variety of positions in 2020. They were extraordinary candidates, often young and energetic, many of them people of color. Even though our resources were limited, and even though we backed contenders in a lot of tough races, more than 150 of our endorsed candidates ended up winning.

From the beginning, we recognized that it was absolutely imperative to maintain the dramatic gains progressives had made in the congressional elections of 2018. We were determined to protect progressive incumbents, including the members of the Squad—Representatives Alexandria Ocasio-Cortez of New York, Ilhan Omar of Minnesota, Ayanna Pressley of Massachusetts, and Rashida Tlaib of Michigan—who had come under fierce attack from not just Republicans but many establishment Democrats, and much of the media, during their initial terms in office.

All four members of the Squad had played outsized roles in shaping congressional debates in 2019 and 2020, giving voice to often neglected ideas, issues, and communities. They represented a breath of fresh air in Washington, in no small measure because they were not afraid to speak boldly and bluntly. Their new style of politics was successful in energizing young people, not only in their own districts, but from coast to coast.

I knew I had a lot in common with these women. Yes. I was at least forty years older than they were. Yes, I was a man and they were women. Yes, I was white and they were people of color. Yet several of us were immigrants or children of immigrants. We all came from working-class families that had struggled economically. And we all had to elbow our way into politics by taking on and defeating establishment candidates with campaigns that relied on grassroots support rather than the money power of the billionaire class.

Given the bigotry and xenophobia that had come to define Trump's Republican Party, it was no surprise that AOC, Omar, and Tlaib were under fierce and constant attack by the president and his right-wing allies. Alexandria's family came from Puerto Rico, Rashida's from Palestine, and Ilhan's from Somalia. Rashida and Ilhan were Muslims. Because of their backgrounds, their strong progressive views, and their willingness to speak up on hot-button domestic and foreign policy issues when so many other Democrats were shamefully silent, the three of them were subjected to incredibly vitriolic assaults. Trump's suggestion that they should "go back and help fix the totally broken and crime-infested places from which they came" was one of the most racist and divisive statements of his presidency. What was especially unsettling, if not entirely surprising to me, was the extent to which these members of the Squad were vilified not just by Trump and the Republican right, but by corporate Democrats. Yet, despite the enormous pressure they faced, they displayed dignity and resolve in the face of dishonest and disgusting smears.

Alexandria, Ilhan, and Rashida all faced well-funded opponents in the 2020 Democratic primaries. Our team decided early on that we would make it our mission to provide them with the strongest possible political and financial support in those races. Given their popularity in the progressive community, and especially among backers of my campaign who appreciated the support they had given me, we were able to raise hundreds of thousands of dollars for each of them and to help generate volunteer support for phone banks and door-to-door campaigning.

On June 23, Alexandria won her primary with 74 percent of the vote; on August 4, Rashida won with 66 percent; and on August 11, Ilhan, who faced the most determined and expensive challenge, won with 57 percent. Those decisive wins sent a loud and clear message to the world that the initial victories of Squad members in 2018 were not "flukes." Their progressive views spoke to the needs of their constituents, and proved to be enormously popular.

The original Squad members had new allies among the 2020 winners in Democratic primaries across the country. Just as AOC had upset an entrenched incumbent in her 2018 Democratic primary, so Jamaal Bowman of New York City and Cori Bush of St. Louis defeated powerful veteran incumbents in their 2020 Democratic primaries. Mondaire Jones, another strong progressive we backed, won an open seat in New York's Westchester and Rockland counties. In 2022, more candidates who identified with the Squad were elected, including Greg Casar in Texas and Summer Lee in Pennsylvania.

Each of these wins sent a powerful message that the political revolution was advancing. Progressives were on a roll, at the federal level and in communities across the country. In addition to major victories in congressional primaries, each week brought news of wins for candidates we backed for state legislature, district attorney, and local posts. These wins, by candidates such as José Garza, who was elected district attorney in Travis County, Texas, and George Gascón, who was elected to serve as district attorney for Los Angeles County, were essential not just for the progressive movement but for America in a moment of racial reckoning.

Campaigning Against Systemic Racism

The murder of George Floyd in late May of 2020 horrified the nation and the world, and inspired an extraordinary mobilization on behalf of long-delayed criminal justice reforms and a meaningful response to systemic racism. As many as 26 million Americans, in cities and towns across the country, joined in what survey researchers described as the largest protest mobilization in American history. Young people of all races and backgrounds took to the streets to demand an end to police brutality and greater civilian control over public-safety departments. Floyd's murder came after the deaths of Eric Garner, Michael Brown, Tamir Rice, Walter Scott, Alton Sterling, Breonna Taylor, and dozens of others in police custody. The Black community was sick and tired of the brutal and illegal behavior of too many police officers, and they were joined by people of all races in demanding accountability and a redefinition of what policing meant.

Minnesota attorney general Keith Ellison, my friend and long-time supporter, organized the successful prosecution of Derek Chauvin, the police officer who murdered George Floyd. Keith put things in perspective when he said, "In our society, there is a social norm that killing certain kinds of people is more tolerable than other kinds of people." That, said Keith, is systemic racism, and I agree with him. And it does not show itself only in policing. Keith explains that systemic racism can be identified "through housing patterns, through employment, through wealth, through a whole range of other things," and he is right when he argues that we all must begin the hard work of addressing it by reforming policing—so that unarmed Black men are no longer murdered by police officers who too frequently operate with impunity.

Police brutality is just one manifestation of the broad economic, social, and racial injustice that continues to warp our society. And we saw that injustice on stark display in 2020. The pandemic shined a light on inequality in ways that could no longer be denied, or ignored. Millions of people lost their jobs and income, and were suffering in a way that had not been seen in almost a century. "Essential" workers in hospitals, drugstores, grocery stores, mass transit, and warehouses were forced to go to work to feed their families. They were quite literally putting their lives on the line to provide the basic services Americans needed. Many of these workers were not provided with safe working conditions or adequate protective equipment. As a result, tens of thousands contracted the virus and died. They were disproportionately people of color. In response to the incredible distress within minority communities, grassroots organizations across the country sprang into action. They marched for justice. They provided support for the unemployed, the sick, and the poor. And we did our best to help. During the month of June 2020, our campaign raised over $6 million for these groups and causes, and got many thousands of our supporters involved. It's important to remember that electoral politics is not the only venue for achieving transformational change.

Raising Political Consciousness

The tumultuous events of the summer and fall of 2020 reminded us that it was imperative to continue doing what the corporate media does not do: educate working-class people about the realities of the economic and political system in which they live and struggle. Our presidential campaign was over. But we still had 15.4 million Twitter followers, 5.6 million Facebook followers, and 6.6 million followers on Instagram, as well as an email list that numbered in the millions. That's a lot of people, and those totals do not even include the almost 20 million more who follow our non-political U.S. Senate social media accounts.

As part of our campaign organization we maintained a full communications and video staff. This enabled us to post statements and messages every day on multiple platforms, and to produce high-quality videos that would receive millions of views. NPR even did a feature headlined "Bernie TV: How the Sanders Campaign's Live Videos Help It Build Community," noting how, during the primary campaign, our once modest livestreaming project had become an epic endeavor: "The numbers are really big: more than 85 million views over the course of the campaign, spread across traditional social media platforms like Facebook and YouTube, and newer, more niche platforms like the gaming network Twitch." We were not CNN, MSNBC, or Fox, let alone CBS, NBC, or ABC. But, with our relatively small operation, we were doing important work in providing people with information they might not otherwise receive about progressive perspective on issues that shaped their lives.

If we had just shut down the campaign in April, we would have lost all that capacity to spread the word not just about candidates, but about issues. That wasn't a mistake we were going to make.

Battling Against COVID-19, and Pandemic Profiteering

Battling with Trump and the Republicans on issues related to the pandemic that raged throughout 2020 was immensely frustrating. While my campaign was done, the president's was ongoing—and he was playing politics with matters of life and death.

The fundamental reality of that miserable year was that the Trump administration failed horribly in providing national leadership to combat the pandemic. My state of Vermont, like every other state in the country, had been seriously impacted by the pandemic and the

economic meltdown associated with it. I was saddened and stunned
to see, just a few blocks from my home, hundreds of Vermonters
lined up in their cars for emergency food boxes. Hunger, desperation, and fear were rampant all over the country.

As a member of the Senate Democratic leadership, I fought for
the strongest possible legislation to protect working people during
this unprecedented crisis. Tens of thousands of people died unnecessarily because Trump rejected the advice of doctors and scientists.
The United States had far higher hospitalization levels and death
rates than other major countries because our response to the pandemic was weak, unfocused, and often dishonest. Trump literally
bragged to *Washington Post* journalist Bob Woodward that he down-
played the pandemic at a time when millions of lives were at stake,
and when thousands of lives were being lost.

As the pandemic spread, misleading information from the
Trump administration made things worse. For instance, the president and his aides sent conflicting and often disingenuous signals
about the importance of wearing masks—one of the most vital ways
to stop the spread of the virus. Along with a number of other senators, I introduced legislation that would send three reusable N-95
masks to every person in this country. I also fought to make certain
that all doctors and nurses had an adequate supply of the highest-
quality personal protective equipment. It was clear to me that we
had to utilize the Defense Production Act to break our dependency
on other countries for the supply of masks and equipment that was
desperately needed. Yet, while the Trump administration initially
made some moves in the right direction, it generally relied on ineffectual "market solutions" at a time when government intervention
was vital.

At the same time, the billionaire class that Trump had served so
faithfully was cashing in on the crisis. According to Americans for
Tax Fairness and the Institute for Policy Studies, $731 billion in
wealth was accumulated by 467 billionaires—the richest 0.001 percent of all America—from March 18, 2020, when COVID-19 case

numbers and deaths began to spike, until August 5, 2020. During roughly the same period, 5.4 million Americans lost their health insurance and 50 million applied for unemployment insurance.

On August 6, 2020, I introduced legislation that sought to address the growth of income and wealth inequality during the pandemic, as well as the inadequacies of our health care system, which the pandemic had made so apparently clear. My Make Billionaires Pay Act proposed a 60 percent tax on the new wealth accumulated by billionaires during the pandemic. The $422 billion raised by this bill would be used to expand Medicare to cover all Americans during the crisis. It was beyond absurd that in the midst of a major health care crisis, many millions of Americans had no health insurance or were trying to get by with inadequate coverage. It was equally absurd that the nation's wealth was being redistributed upward at a time when everyone was supposed to be engaged in "shared sacrifice." When I introduced the bill, I explained, "In my view, it is time for the Senate to act on behalf of the working class who are hurting like they have never hurt before, not the billionaire class who are doing phenomenally well and have never had it so good."

The legislation, which was cosponsored by Senators Ed Markey of Massachusetts and Kirsten Gillibrand of New York, was well received. Polls consistently showed that the vast majority of Americans favored taxing the rich. In fact, a Reuters/Ipsos poll released shortly before I introduced the Make Billionaires Pay Act legislation found that nearly two-thirds of respondents agreed that the very rich should pay more. Yet my proposal never got a hearing in a Senate that was then controlled by Republicans under the leadership of Kentucky senator Mitch McConnell, one of the chief benefactors of the billionaire class's campaign largesse. Nor did it have a chance with a president, Donald Trump, who proudly declared himself to be a member of that class.

This was just another example of how the will of the people was being thwarted during Trump's democracy-crushing presidency.

The Fight for Democracy

Throughout Trump's time in office, and especially during the period leading up to Election Day 2020, I became increasingly concerned that, if the president lost the election, he would not abide by the results. Unlike all previous presidents, he so obviously did not respect democracy or the rule of law. I feared that, for the first time in American history, our country would not see a peaceful transfer of power.

I thought that it was enormously important for the American people to have a clear understanding of the threat that Trump's rejection of democracy posed. The more advanced warning Americans got, the better chance there would be to prepare ourselves to thwart an assault on the foundations of our country's elections and governance. Over a period of weeks following the Democratic National Convention in August, I attended a number of meetings with lawyers and scholars who had studied the possible strategies that a defeated Donald Trump might utilize to try to overturn the election result. On September 24, 2020, at George Washington University, I delivered a major address in which I reflected on what turned out to be the most serious—and ultimately terrifying—issue of 2020.

CBS News described my address as "an impassioned speech" that raised the prospect of "President Trump's refusal to commit to a peaceful transfer of power." I don't know how "impassioned" it was, but I do know that it was one of the most important speeches I ever gave. In an exclusive interview with CBS News's Cara Korte after I delivered the address, I made it clear that I was deeply concerned about the threat of violence and chaos in this country following the election.

"Too many people fought and died to defend democracy to allow him to destroy it," I said of Trump. "If he wins, he wins. But if he loses, he is going to leave office because we are going to defend American democracy." I was laying down the gauntlet in a fight that, just five months later, would see me voting at the close of a Senate impeachment trial to convict Trump for inciting a deadly insurrection that sought to overturn the results of a free and fair election.

If we take one thing away from the tumultuous election of 2020 and its even more tumultuous aftermath, it is that we must be far more serious about maintaining the basic infrastructure of democracy. That infrastructure is as strong as we make it, and we must be ever cognizant of the fact that there are totalitarians among us who would destroy it.

"What I am going to talk about is something that, in my wildest dreams, I never thought I would be discussing," I said at George Washington. "And that is the need to make certain that the president of the United States, if he loses this election, will abide by the will of the voters and leave office peacefully." Americans, I argued, needed to wake up to the reality that Trump was, in fact, "prepared to undermine American democracy in order to stay in power."

I understood that there would be those who thought I was the one who was going to extremes, that I was "crying wolf" in order to stir fears among my supporters and potential Democratic voters. The media in this country tends to see everything in terms of one side versus the other, without recognizing there are existential issues that transcend the narrow boundaries of partisanship and ideology. In my speech, I sought to promote that recognition.

"This is not just an election between Donald Trump and Joe Biden. This is an election between Donald Trump and democracy— and democracy must win," I argued. "But today, under Donald Trump, we have a president who has little respect for our Constitution or the rule of law. Today, that peaceful transition of power, the bedrock of American democracy, is being threatened like never before. And in that regard I think it is terribly important that we actually listen to, and take seriously, what Donald Trump is saying."

I quoted from Trump's speech to the Republican National Convention in August, when he said, "The only way they can take this election away from us is if this is a rigged election." Trump was addressing his party's convention at a point when almost every national poll had him behind, and when he was trailing in polls in most battleground states. "Think about what that statement means," I said.

"What he is saying is that if he wins the election, that's great. But if he loses, it's rigged, because the only way, the only way, he can lose is if it's rigged. And if it's rigged, then he is not leaving office. Heads I win. Tails you lose. In other words, in Trump's mind, there is no conceivable way that he should leave office."

Trump's anti-democratic raving continued into the fall. On the night before I delivered my speech at George Washington, Trump went further down the path of authoritarianism, making himself the first president in the history of this country to refuse to commit to a peaceful transition of power if he lost the election. During a briefing at the White House, a reporter asked point-blank: "Win, lose or draw in this election, will you commit here today for a peaceful transferal of power after the election?" Trump responded: "We're going to have to see what happens. You know that I've been complaining very strongly about the ballots, and the ballots are a disaster. We want to get rid of the ballots and you'll have a very peaceful—there won't be a transfer, frankly. There will be a continuation."

I updated my speech to reflect on those remarks, and to provide a blunt retort to his views regarding the transfer of power: "That's not his choice. That's for the American people to determine. Let us be very clear: There is nothing in our Constitution or in our laws that give Donald Trump the privilege of deciding whether or not he will step aside if he loses. In the United States the president does not determine who can or cannot vote, and what ballots will be counted. That may be what his friend Putin does in Russia. It may be what is done in other authoritarian countries. But it is not and will not be done in America. This is a democracy."

To defend democracy, I argued, Democratic, Republican, and Independent officials needed to vigorously oppose voter suppression and voter intimidation, to make sure that every vote was counted, and to take necessary steps to ensure that no one was declared the winner until those votes were counted. "To my Republican colleagues in the Congress," I said, "please do not continue to tell the American people how much you love America if, at this critical moment, you are not prepared to stand up to defend American democracy and our way of life. Stop the hypocrisy."

Fearing that hypocrisy might prevail, I offered a plan for averting disaster:

- "First, it is absolutely imperative that we have, by far, the largest voter turnout in American history and that people vote as early as possible. As someone who is strongly supporting Joe Biden, let's be clear: A landslide victory for Biden will make it virtually impossible for Trump to deny the results, and is our best means for defending democracy."
- "Second, with the pandemic and a massive increase in mail-in voting, state legislatures must take immediate action now to allow mail-in votes to be counted before Election Day—as they come in."
- "Third, the news media needs to prepare the American people to understand there is no longer a single election day and that it is very possible that we may not know the results on November third."
- "Fourth, social media companies must finally get their act together and stop people from using their tools to spread disinformation and to threaten and harass election officials."
- "Fifth, in the Congress and in state legislatures, hearings must be held as soon as possible to explain to the public how the Election Day process and the days that follow will be handled. As we count every vote, and prevent voter intimidation, everything possible must be done to prevent chaos, disinformation, and even violence."

Unfortunately, barely three months later, the violence came, in the form of an unprecedented and deadly assault on the U.S. Capitol.

Many of my worst fears had been realized. Yet, on the night of January 6, after the rioters were driven from the building and order was restored, I returned to the Capitol and voted with my fellow Democrats and the majority of Senate Republicans to certify Biden's 306–232 Electoral College victory over Trump. After one of the longest and most challenging campaigns in American history, Joe Biden would become the forty-sixth president of the United States.

The events of January 6, 2021, scarred America. Democracy won out that day, but the struggle over its future continues—as Trump and his supporters still refuse to accept the results of the 2020 election, and plot new strategies for voter suppression that threaten to warp the election of 2024.

I knew in the fall of 2020, and I know now, that our duty is to make it clear to Americans, no matter what their political persuasion, that our democracy will not be destroyed. This country, from its inception and through the sacrifices of millions, has been a model to the world with regard to representative government. In 1863, in the midst of the terrible Civil War, Abraham Lincoln at Gettysburg stated that this government "of the people, by the people, for the people, shall not perish from the earth." The struggle Lincoln identified more than a century and a half ago is not finished. In our time, we must ensure the forces of liberty and justice will prevail.

3

THE FIGHT TO BUILD BACK BETTER

*Why do Democrats have such a hard time
delivering on the promise of transformational change?*

Joe Biden won the 2020 election by seven million votes nationally, flipped five states that had backed Donald Trump in 2016,
and carried the Electoral College 306–232. The focus we had
placed on reaching out to young and working-class voters in the battleground states of Wisconsin, Michigan, and Pennsylvania had paid
off. Those three historic manufacturing states, all of which had been
in Trump's column in 2016, shifted to Biden in 2020. But Biden's
personal mandate did not translate into the sort of House and Senate
majorities that would make it easy for him to govern. In fact, Democratic control of the Senate was not achieved until two months after
the November election—on January 5, 2021—when Democrats Jon
Ossoff and Raphael Warnock won a pair of runoff contests for U.S.
Senate seats representing Georgia.

Their wins gave Democrats the two seats that were needed to

displace Republican Mitch McConnell as majority leader of the Senate, and to replace him with Democrat Chuck Schumer. With the Georgia wins, everything became possible for the new administration. Not easy, mind you, but with a 50–50 split in the Senate, and with Vice President Kamala Harris ready to break ties, there was an opening for Joe Biden and for those of us who knew that transformational change was needed.

How Economic Populism Flipped the Senate

My role in the Georgia campaigns began shortly after the November election, when the Senate was wrestling with the question of how to respond to the devastating economic instability associated with the pandemic. In December, I led the fight to provide a $2,000 direct payment for every working-class adult in the country and their children. I made the case that, with so many Americans suffering hardship, it was imperative that we immediately put cash into their hands so that they could pay the bills and put food on the table.

My strategy involved doing something I had never done before. I used my power as a United States senator to object to several "unanimous consent" requests to hold a quick vote on the "must-pass" defense bill until Senate leaders agreed to a separate vote on the plan for the $2,000 direct payments.

Things got tense. On December 28, 2020, three days after Christmas and three days before New Year's Eve, I announced: "This week on the Senate floor Mitch McConnell wants to vote to override Trump's veto of the $740 billion defense funding bill and then head home for the New Year. I'm going to object until we get a vote on legislation to provide a $2,000 direct payment to the working class. Let me be clear: If Senator McConnell doesn't agree to an up-or-down vote to provide the working people of our country a $2,000 direct payment, Congress will not be going home for New Year's Eve. Let's do our job."

My maneuver was not enthusiastically received by members of

the Republican Caucus. The Democratic response was equally cool—at least initially. The last thing most of my colleagues wanted to do was spend New Year's Eve and New Year's Day in Washington. Leadership on both sides of the aisle wanted to hold a quick vote on the defense bill on Wednesday, December 30, and get out of town for the remainder of the year. I was not going to let them do that.

My message to the Democrats, with whom I caucused, was that we had an opportunity to finally show the American people that Democrats were on the side of working families. We also had a chance to force McConnell to make a choice: Support the $2,000 direct payments and help people who were hurting, or confirm that a Republican-controlled Senate was never going to deliver for tens of millions of Americans who were experiencing hard times.

We had to seize this moment!

Eventually, Chuck Schumer warmed up to the idea and joined me on the floor of the Senate to demand a vote on the $2,000 direct payments. To his credit, Schumer pressed the issue, and in short order we had the entire Democratic Caucus on our side. McConnell was furious. He didn't just object to the procedural move. He made the ridiculous claim that $2,000 direct payments for working-class families was somehow "socialism for the rich."

You can't make this stuff up. The same Republican leader who had led the charge to hand over a trillion dollars in tax breaks to the rich and to multinational corporations, in the uber-capitalist orgy of Trump's first two years in office, was suddenly claiming that $2,000 direct payments to working-class Americans was "socialism." McConnell's argument was absurd, and it put him in opposition to the 78 percent of Americans who supported the idea.

For me, the fight for those $2,000 payments became an opportunity to highlight how far McConnell and his allies were willing to go in order to redistribute wealth upward. I seized on the opportunity, making note of the fact that—after Trump's tax bill was signed into law—McConnell had been more than happy to see energy tycoon Charles Koch pocket a $1.4 billion tax break. He had no problem with Amazon, one of the most profitable corporations in America, receiving a $129 million tax rebate check from the IRS after paying nothing in federal income taxes. But, suddenly, in a harsh winter for millions of Americans, he was "very concerned" that someone making $75,000 a year might receive a $2,000 check to help pay their bills. The hypocrisy was off the charts.

My staff director, Warren Gunnels, blew up a few of the tax rebate checks into giant posters that I brought with me to the Senate floor to show the American people who were watching on C-SPAN and social media. How was it acceptable to provide enormous tax rebate checks to profitable companies such as IBM, Delta Airlines, Chevron, and Netflix—and, of course, Amazon, an online retailer that was reporting record profits in the year of the pandemic? How were such payouts appropriate when these mega-corporations didn't pay a penny in federal income taxes? In what cruel calculation was it acceptable to provide billions in bailouts to corporations that did not need them, and then to deny a $2,000 check to struggling working moms during a global pandemic? The only people any of this made "sense" to were Mitch McConnell's millionaire campaign contributors.

It made no sense economically. And it made no sense politically, as the Georgia runoff race would make clear.

The debate over the $2,000 direct payments became a huge issue for the Democrats in Georgia. Warnock and Ossoff supported my proposal while their Republican opponents—both sitting senators who were members of McConnell's caucus—were either unable or unwilling to get the majority leader to schedule a vote. On the day before the Georgia election, President-elect Biden traveled to Georgia to deliver a blunt message: The only way working Americans would see those $2,000 payments was if Warnock and Ossoff were elected and Democrats gained a majority in the Senate. The issue electrified turnout and, as liberal and conservative pundits would agree, contributed to the close yet definitional victories for the two Georgians who would give Democrats control on Capitol Hill.

The Georgia results showed us the best of democracy, as working-class voters rose up to demand that government take their side.

Unfortunately, within hours of the victory celebrations, we saw the worst of those who rejected democracy.

In the Middle of a Violent Assault on Democracy

I had predicted in my September speech at George Washington University that Donald Trump would try to overturn the election results in every way possible, including the incitement of violence. But even I didn't imagine how far the defeated president would go on January 6, 2021. Even in my wildest imagination, I had never contemplated that a violent group of extremists, many of them white nationalists inspired by a vile doctrine of racist and anti-Semitic hatred, would storm the Capitol, overwhelm the Capitol Police, physically take over the U.S. Senate chamber, and threaten the lives of the vice president and Speaker of the House. Being trapped in a room with other senators, guarded by police officers and FBI agents with machine guns, was a scene I never could have predicted—and that I never want to see again. But I knew then, as I know now, that the deep divisions Trump and his allies had opened up in America, and which they continue to inflame, make the possibility of more anti-democratic violence real. That was one of the many reasons why I later voted to convict Trump for inciting an insurrection, and why I would do so again.

For weeks before and after Biden's inauguration on January 20, 2021, thousands of well-armed National Guard units from states across the country, including Vermont, established checkpoints around the Capitol and secured the perimeter. This was a far cry from the usual peaceful transfer of power from one administration to another that our nation was accustomed to. Instead of what we read about in eighth-grade civics class, Washington on those winter days felt like a city beset by civil war. When I spoke with guardsmen and -women, I was struck by the fact that they knew exactly why they were there. They were defending the Constitution and preserving our fragile democracy.

A Pair of Mittens

Not everything that happened in that epic moment was so consequential, as I learned on Biden's Inaugural Day. I have been involved in public life for over fifty years. I have run for mayor, governor, the U.S. House and the U.S. Senate. I ran for president of the United States twice. But I have never received so much attention as I did when, on a bitter cold winter day, I took my place in the stands that had been erected for the inauguration of Joe Biden and Kamala Harris. As a sensible Vermonter, I was wearing a heavy coat and a pair of homemade mittens.

Vermont, it's fair to say, is not a "flashy" state in terms of attire. There's a reason for that: Vermonters know that it can get very cold in the winter, and they know how to stay warm. We are a practical and functional people, and when we are outside in the winter—which lasts a lot longer in our part of the country than in most—we wear boots, sweaters, warm coats, and funny-looking hats. Style is not our focus. Staying warm is.

Like every other member of Congress, I had received an invitation to attend the ceremony on that January 20. In normal times we would have been packed together on the west front of the U.S. Capitol, facing the National Mall. These, however, were not normal times. We were in the midst of the worst pandemic in one hundred years and our seats were spaced far apart from one another. We were wearing face masks. And the proximity to the January 6 insurrection made security a top priority. Everything about Inaugural Day was unusual—including the fact that Donald Trump, facing an impeachment trial and still in the sway of his "Big Lie" delusion over his election loss—did not intend to show up for the actual transfer of power.

Frankly, it never occurred to me to wear anything to the inauguration other than my warm Vermont coat, the coat I always wore and the only coat I had in Washington. We were going to be outside for several hours. It was a blustery day with the possibility of snow. What else would I wear? And to keep my hands warm I had, as I always did, a pair of mittens in my pockets that were knitted by Jen Ellis, a schoolteacher from Essex Junction, Vermont. She had kindly sent them to me, and I gladly wore them on Inaugural Day. That was the whole story.

Except.

When I got back to my office after the ceremony I was informed by Mike Casca, my communications director, that a photo of me sitting alone in mask and mittens had gone viral on the internet. That was weird. But it got weirder. Within a few days, we were seeing memes from all across the globe. There I was with my mittens on the moon, at the Last Supper, on the *Titanic,* alongside Forrest Gump, next to Spider-Man, on top of skyscrapers. It turned out that this photo, shot by Agence France-Presse photographer Brendan Smialowski, generated more memes than almost any other taken in 2021. Who would have thought?

Not only did the photo, and the many permutations it inspired, create a lot of smiles, it also enabled us to raise much-needed money for organizations that serve low-income Vermonters. Our campaign organization sold T-shirts and sweatshirts with the photo that raised some $2 million, which went to Meals on Wheels and other excellent agencies around the state.

But after Biden was inaugurated, I had more on my mind than mittens and memes. Thousands of Americans were dying every day from COVID, and we were in the midst of the worst economic downturn since the Great Depression. Shops and restaurants had shut down. Unemployment was skyrocketing. People were going hungry and facing eviction. Hospitals were still overwhelmed with COVID patients. Children were not attending school.

Chairman of the Senate Budget Committee

Congress had to act boldly. With Biden as president, we had an opportunity to put Trump's malignant neglect behind us. And as chairman of the Budget Committee, I was in a position to make things happen.

I was well aware of the arcane rules of a dysfunctional U.S. Senate, including the requirement that sixty votes be obtained to open up a debate on legislation that only takes fifty-one votes to pass. I knew about the cumbersome "Byrd rule" regarding budgetary matters, and I understood the incredibly powerful role that the unelected parliamentarian plays in determining what the Senate can include in certain bills. And I certainly knew that, in January 2021, the Senate was evenly, and bitterly, divided between the two parties, and that the Democratic majority in the House was slim.

Yet, despite all of those impediments, I felt a sense of urgency in Congress and the White House that I had never experienced before. The country faced enormous challenges, and it was clear to me—and to a lot of other members of the House and Senate—that people wanted Congress to think big, not small. Our campaigns for president, the growth of the progressive movement, and the work of the Biden-Sanders task forces had, I believed, created an understanding that the Democratic Party needed to do more than just manage the crises. Americans were hurting and uncertain about the future and they wanted action. They had voted for a new president. They had given that president a Congress where, though the margins were small, his party was in charge. It was time to start getting things done.

President Biden understood this. In our conversations, he made it clear that he wanted to deliver more than the incremental fixes that people had come to associate with previous Democratic administrations. He shared with me, and with the American people, a willingness to do what politicians rarely do. He was ready to develop policy from the ground on up, to take a hard look at the problems facing the country, both immediate and long-term, and to actually address them.

Thus, work began on a reconciliation bill that we called the American Rescue Plan. It turned out to be the most significant and

successful piece of legislation passed by Congress in the modern history of the country.

What? You have no clue about what a "reconciliation bill" is?
Don't worry. Most people don't—not even, I learned, a few of my
colleagues. Here's all you need to know: When the majority party
wants to pass something important and doesn't have the sixty votes it
needs to schedule the vote, it uses the reconciliation process to get
around the filibuster rule—which allows a minority of senators to
deny the majority the power to act. Under reconciliation, it is possible to pass legislation with fifty-one votes. Theoretically, the reconciliation process is only supposed to be used for "budgetary" measures,
not policy. But that's not the reality. In recent years, it has been used
by Republicans to allow drilling for oil in the Arctic National Wildlife
Refuge and to push through Trump's tax breaks for billionaires and
corporations. Republicans also used it to try to repeal the Affordable
Care Act.

As the incoming chairman of the Budget Committee, I was determined to use the reconciliation process not to benefit the wealthy
and the powerful, but to respond to the unprecedented needs of
working families, children, the elderly, the sick, and the poor.

So were President Biden and the Democratic leaders in Congress. Of course, we had our disagreements. But in those early days
of the Biden administration, we all understood that we would need
to pass at least two reconciliation bills during the president's first two
years in office. The initial bill was the American Rescue Plan, which
would deal with the public health and economic emergency of the
moment. The second bill, which came to be known as the Build
Back Better Act, was supposed to address the long-term structural
problems working-class families had been struggling with for more
than forty years. It also had to combat the existential threat of climate change.

Taking these urgent steps was important not just from an economic and moral perspective. It was vital to restoring faith in our
democracy. From one end of the country to the other, working fami-

lies had become disillusioned and disgusted with a corrupt political system. They were susceptible to bogus conspiracy theories that offered "explanations" for why their lives had grown increasingly difficult. We needed to make clear to the American people that they now had a government that would respond to their needs.

Tragically, those needs kept growing and growing. January 2021 marked the deadliest month of the pandemic, with over ninety thousand Americans dying of COVID. Millions were infected with the disease. Yet. Ninety million Americans were uninsured or underinsured and could not afford to go to a doctor when they got sick.

More than twenty-four million Americans were unemployed, underemployed, or had given up looking for work. Hunger in our country was at its highest level in decades as millions of Americans, many for the first time in their lives, waited in lines sometimes stretching for miles just to collect emergency packages of food. Almost fifteen million Americans owed an average of $5,800 in back rent and were terrified that they would soon be evicted from their homes.

It was time to get to work.

Crafting the American Rescue Plan

In January, I presented a legislative outline for the first reconciliation bill to Senator Schumer and the White House.

My message was "Go big!"

I argued that the American Rescue Plan had to provide that $2,000 direct payment for every working-class American adult, and for their children. We'd made a promise that if our candidates won in Georgia, these checks would be on the way. Now it was time to keep that promise.

The $2,000 payments represented an emergency response that addressed immediate pain. But they were not sufficient to meet the crisis. Not by a long shot.

On some issues, there was broad agreement. For instance, everyone knew we had to provide urgent assistance to state and local governments in order to prevent mass layoffs of teachers, firefighters, and other workers in the public sector. As a former mayor, I knew how desperately the federal money was needed by communities that had spent down their budgets dealing with the pandemic.

All of us agreed that the bill needed to include robust funding to make it possible for public schools to reopen safely, to feed the hungry, to prevent evictions and foreclosures, to provide accommodations for people who had lost their homes, to keep public transportation services running, and to expand high-speed internet for regions where remote learning and work had made the digital divide an even more urgent equity issue.

One of my top priorities was a massive expansion of summer school and after-school programs to benefit working-class kids whose education had been set back by the pandemic. Senator Schumer agreed to include this essential investment in the bill.

But not every issue was so easily resolved.

All of us wanted to extend supplemental emergency unemployment benefits for the eighteen million workers who lost their jobs during the pandemic. The question was, how much to provide and for how long? A year earlier, in the first stages of the pandemic, Congress had passed the CARES Act, a major relief bill that included $600 a week in supplemental unemployment benefits. Republicans initially backed that commitment, but soon began to attack it with the false argument that this relatively modest benefit was keeping people from going back to work. The reality was that corporate donors wanted to force people to go back to work at low wages, but unfortunately the Republican argument gained traction in the media—and even with some Democrats. Trump eventually cut the program in half.

When we began talking about the reconciliation bill, I advocated for restoring the $600 a week commitment as part of the measure. But we ended up with just $300 a week, and extended funding only through the end of September.

We also needed, in my view, to end the international embarrassment of the United States having the highest child poverty rate of virtually every major country on the planet. Senators Michael Bennet, Sherrod Brown, and Cory Booker had a proposal to provide every working family in America with a $300 monthly payment per child by expanding the Child Tax Credit. This provision alone could lift nearly ten million children out of poverty and allow working families the opportunity to raise their kids with dignity and security.

My progressive colleagues and I wanted to make the expanded Child Tax Credit a permanent feature of the tax code, as part of the reconciliation bill. But, because this first bill was being framed as a response to the economic emergency, an agreement was reached to allow the credit to expire in December 2021. I didn't like the compromise, but I respected assurances that it would be extended before the expiration date. Shamefully, that never happened.

There was general agreement that we needed to respond to the public health emergency that was still overwhelming the country. But here again, differences emerged on the question of how bold we should be in meeting the challenge.

In my view, the best way to get more people vaccinated and give more people access to health care was by expanding Medicare, the most popular and comprehensive care program in America. During the economic crisis, millions of Americans, when they lost their jobs, also lost the health insurance tied to those jobs. Suddenly, it was dawning on Americans that health care should not be an employee benefit. It should be understood as a human right.

While I recognized that we did not have the votes to include the response I really wanted—a Medicare for All plan—in the bill, we needed to empower Medicare to pay all of the health care bills of the uninsured and the underinsured for the duration of the pandemic. Unfortunately, that turned out to be a bridge too far for a number of Democratic senators who still depend on the private health insurance industry and huge pharmaceutical companies to fund their campaigns.

Speaker Pelosi, Majority Leader Schumer, and President Biden wanted to lower the cost of health care for low- and middle-income Americans who receive coverage on the Affordable Care Act exchanges. I also wanted to reduce the costs for working families, but I was not a fan of their proposal for how to achieve the goal. Providing massive subsidies to private health insurance companies, I argued, would continue to prop up a dysfunctional health care system that puts profits ahead of the well-being of the American people.

The Democratic leadership refused to bend. But at least I was able to get them to agree to include my proposal to substantially expand funding for community health centers so that more Americans could get the primary care, dental care, and mental health care they desperately needed—as well as low-cost prescription drugs. These health centers have been enormously successful in Vermont, providing high-quality health care to roughly one out of every three people in my state.

Another issue I've long been involved with came into play as the debate continued. There was growing support for a move to prevent millions of truck drivers, miners, bakery workers, plumbers, and pipefitters from seeing their pensions cut by as much as 65 percent. The final reconciliation bill included a provision my pro-labor colleagues and I had pushed for years—to shore up troubled pension plans that had been decimated by the mismanagement and greed of Wall Street money managers.

The legislation outline I proposed as Budget Committee chair would also have substantially lowered prescription drug prices by requiring Medicare to negotiate with the pharmaceutical industry. It would have made preschool and childcare free for working families. It would have guaranteed paid family and medical leave for every worker in our country. It would have made it easier for young Americans to go to college, and it would have canceled student debt.

This proposal was a progressive, unprecedented, and transformational plan. No Republican would come close to supporting it, and a number of conservative Democrats also had objections. Senator Schumer wanted to postpone a debate over these issues. He said we needed to address the emergency first. While I understood that argument, I was fearful that this could be our one opportunity to achieve the long-neglected changes our country needed. I worried that whatever was left out of the first reconciliation bill might not make it into future legislation that could be sent to President Biden's desk by an evenly divided Senate.

Sadly, my fears turned out to be justified.

The Fight for $15

The one structural change that I thought absolutely needed to be included in the first reconciliation bill was an increase in the minimum wage to at least $15 an hour—with a mechanism for increasing wages to keep up with inflation. The federal minimum wage had not been raised since 2009. Even worse, the $2.13 an hour tipped minimum wage for waiters, waitresses, bartenders, barbers, and hairstylists had not been raised since 1991—my first year in Congress. That was outrageous. I was convinced that the only way we could raise the minimum wage in this Congress was through reconciliation. President Biden, Senator Schumer, and Speaker Pelosi said they agreed. But there were two problems. First, we would either have to convince the Senate parliamentarian that increasing the minimum wage was not in violation of the so-called Byrd rule—which prohibits policy provisions that are supposedly "extraneous" to the budget from being included in a reconciliation bill—or we would have to disregard her opinion if she tried to block us. Second, we would have to convince all fifty Democrats in the Senate to support our position.

With respect to the first challenge, my view was that the parliamentarian's opinion was irrelevant. The Senate parliamentarian is an unelected staffer who serves at the pleasure of the Senate majority leader. Under the Constitution and the Senate's rules, it is the vice president who determines what is and what is not permissible under reconciliation. If the parliamentarian disagreed with us, Senator Schumer could simply replace her with someone else who agreed with our position—as the Republicans did twice when they were in the majority. Or the vice president, in her capacity as the president of the Senate, could ignore the parliamentarian's advice—which was a common practice in the 1960s, when many of President Lyndon Johnson's Great Society proposals were enacted by the Senate.

Frustratingly, my opinion did not prevail. In a one-sentence opinion, the parliamentarian said that increasing the minimum wage was a violation of the Byrd rule and could not be included in the reconciliation bill. Supposedly, that was the end of the line.

But I was unwilling to give up. This issue was too important. It was shameful that, in the richest country on earth, breadwinners who worked forty hours a week would live in poverty. Every top-tier Democratic candidate for president in 2020 had supported a $15 minimum wage. The 2020 Democratic Party platform included a $15 minimum wage plank. The Democratic House of Representatives passed legislation twice to increase the minimum wage to $15 an hour. I wasn't going to let this issue go.

At the very least, we had to show the American people that the overwhelming majority of the Democratic Caucus in the Senate supported the increase. We had to create a situation in which those who voted against this legislation would have to explain their thinking to angry constituents in their home states.

I made the decision to offer an amendment to the reconciliation bill that would increase the federal minimum wage to $15 an hour, knowing that it would take sixty votes to pass. My plan was to put every senator on the record: Were they on the side of workers who clearly needed a raise, or were they on the side of corporate lobbyists and CEOs who did everything they could to keep wages low?

Only forty-two senators voted for my amendment. No one was shocked when all fifty Senate Republicans voted "no." Disappointingly, Democratic Senators Joe Manchin, Kyrsten Sinema, Tom Carper, Chris Coons, Maggie Hassan, Jeanne Shaheen, and Jon Tester, along with Angus King, an Independent who caucuses with the Democrats, joined the Republicans in voting "no."

What was so galling was the fact that polls showed there was overwhelming support for increasing the minimum wage to at least $15 an hour. If you were worried about voter sentiments, there was nothing difficult about casting this vote. Yet fifty-eight senators, including eight Democrats, refused to do so.

A Single Vote Lifted Millions of Americans Out of Desperation

Obviously, I did not get everything I wanted in the American Rescue Plan. But we got a lot of what America needed. After more than twenty-five hours of debate and votes on thirty-nine amendments, the United States Senate finally passed the American Rescue Plan largely intact at 12:30 P.M. on Saturday, March 6, 2021. The vote was 50–49. Every Democrat voted for it. Every Republican present voted against it.

By a single vote, we had lifted millions of men, women, and children out of desperation.

In the midst of a pandemic that had caused an unprecedented health care crisis, and an unprecedented economic crisis, Congress had done exactly what a democratic government in a civilized society is supposed to do. It responded to the needs of people who were in despair.

This legislation provided much-needed direct payments to struggling families, protected the unemployed, fed the hungry, prevented evictions, and allowed small businesses to survive. It jump-started the economy, helping to create four million new jobs and to cut the unemployment rate by nearly 50 percent. Even more important, it provided funding for the government to expand the vaccine program that would save an untold number of lives.

The American Rescue Plan was enormously successful. And enormously popular. According to a Morning Consult survey conducted as Congress was settling the issue, 76 percent of the American people supported the $1.9 trillion plan. One week after President Biden signed this historical legislation into law, his approval rating shot up to 59 percent—the highest it has been during his time in the White House.

The American people appreciated that their government was finally standing up for working families.

The Slow Road to Building Back Better

I wanted to build on the momentum we had achieved with the American Rescue Plan by immediately passing a second reconciliation bill to create millions of good-paying jobs, substantially improve the lives of working families, and combat the existential threat of climate change. Unlike the Rescue Plan—which was an emergency measure—we would fund it by making the wealthiest Americans and the most profitable corporations pay their fair share of taxes and lower the outrageous price of prescription drugs.

We needed to act, and act quickly. Unfortunately, the thousands of corporate lobbyists who roam the halls of Congress, and the billionaires who finance the campaigns of politicians on both sides of the aisle, disagreed. They had, for the most part, gotten nothing out of the American Rescue Plan and were not about to let that happen again. It was time for their revenge.

The first major bill that was put on the Senate floor after the American Rescue Plan was a sweeping corporate giveaway masquerading as legislation to increase American competitiveness with China. The centerpiece of the Endless Frontier Act proposal was a plan to provide a $53 billion blank check to the highly profitable microchip industry, with no protections for taxpayers. Oh, and by the way, it also included a provision to provide a $10 billion bailout to Jeff Bezos so that his space company, Blue Origin, could receive a contract from NASA to rocket off to the moon.

Needless to say, I strongly opposed this legislation. Americans were sick and tired of corporate greed. They wanted us to make sure that corporations finally paid their fair share of taxes, not hand out corporate welfare to some of the most profitable and powerful com-

panies in America—companies that were responsible for outsourcing hundreds of thousands of good-paying jobs to low-wage countries
overseas.

Unfortunately, I was the lone voice inside the Democratic Caucus opposing this bill.

The Endless Frontier Act passed the Senate 68–32 on June 8,
2021.

Three months had come and gone since the American Rescue
Plan was signed into law, and we had done nothing to pass a second
reconciliation bill.

Next up was infrastructure. There was a vigorous debate inside
the caucus about whether to include a major infrastructure package
in the second reconciliation bill, or try to work with Republicans and
pass a more modest bill with sixty votes.

As someone who had run for president with a bold proposal to
repair our crumbling infrastructure, I fully appreciated that the nation's bridges, roads, railways, airports, sewers, and dams needed
massive improvements. In 2015, I was the first senator to introduce
a $1 trillion bill for a five-year infrastructure plan.

My view was that we should include infrastructure in the reconciliation bill and that, if we could not get any Republican support, we
should pass it with fifty votes. I was also very concerned that if a bipartisan infrastructure bill passed, it would reduce our leverage and
jeopardize chances of getting the rest of President Biden's agenda to
improve the lives of the American people signed into law.

Unfortunately, my view, and the views of many other progressive
members of Congress, did not prevail.

In early June 2021, while conservative Democrats were working
behind closed doors with Republicans to come up with an agreement on an infrastructure bill, Senator Schumer gave me an assign-
ment. He asked me, as chairman of the Budget Committee, to write
a framework for the second reconciliation bill that could gain the
support of all eleven Democrats on the Budget Committee. Of
course, I agreed. Finally, after months of doing little but catering to

the needs of corporate America, we were beginning to get back to addressing the long-neglected needs of working families and saving the planet from a climate catastrophe.

Senator Schumer gave me and my staff some $5.6 trillion in funding requests to consider, with roughly half of them paid for by taxing large corporations and the wealthy and lowering the cost of prescription drugs. I asked Senator Schumer if we could increase the package to $6 trillion. He agreed.

The $6 trillion reconciliation framework I presented to the Senate Budget Committee on June 16, 2021, addressed both the human and physical infrastructure needs that we have ignored for decades.

It would have ended the absurdity of the United States having the highest levels of childhood poverty of almost any major nation by extending the $300 a month Child Tax Credit through 2025.

It included $500 billion to radically improve our dysfunctional childcare system so that no working family would have to spend more than 7 percent of its income on childcare, and it would have made pre-kindergarten universal and free to every three- and four-year-old in America.

It would have expanded higher education and job-training opportunities for students, not only by making community colleges tuition-free but by making two years of public university tuition-free.

It would have guaranteed twelve weeks of paid family and medical leave to every worker in America.

It would have expanded Medicare to include dental, vision, and hearing benefits while lowering the program's eligibility age to sixty. It would have also extended comprehensive dental care to millions of veterans for the first time in our nation's history.

It included $560 billion to address the housing crisis in America by building millions of affordable rental units, providing rental assistance, repairing public housing, and expanding homeownership.

It included $400 billion to provide over 800,000 seniors and people with disabilities the long-term home health care they urgently need, while substantially increasing pay for home care workers.

Further, it would have provided undocumented people living in the shadows of American society with a pathway to citizenship, including Dreamers and the essential workers who courageously kept our economy running in the middle of a deadly pandemic.

Perhaps most important, it provided over $1.1 trillion to begin the process of shifting our energy system away from fossil fuels and toward sustainable energy to combat the existential threat of climate change. It included a nationwide clean-energy standard that would have moved our transportation system, electrical generation, buildings, and agriculture toward clean energy. It also included $60 billion to create a Civilian Climate Corps to hire hundreds of thousands of young people to protect our natural resources and fight against climate change—a proposal I worked on with Rep. Alexandria Ocasio-Cortez and Senator Ed Markey.

My proposal would have taken on the greed of the pharmaceutical industry by requiring it to negotiate prescription drug prices with Medicare—saving at least $500 billion over the next decade.

Finally, the plan would have ended the travesty of billionaires and large corporations making billions of dollars in profits and paying nothing in federal taxes. At the same time, it would have cracked down on offshore tax scams and tax evasion.

Yes, $6 trillion was a large and unprecedented number. But we were living then, and continue to live in, an unprecedented moment. We had reached the point in our history where we had the opportunity and the power to address the long-term structural crises in a country where the rich got much richer while working people experienced a steady decline in their standard of living. This was the time to make government work for all Americans, not just the powerful few.

Getting Democrats on Board for Build Back Better

The response I received from my Democratic colleagues on the Senate Budget Committee was overwhelmingly positive. Nine out of the eleven members were in agreement that we needed a $6 trillion reconciliation bill. One member, Virginia senator Tim Kaine, was mostly supportive, but wanted to push the number down to $4 trillion or perhaps $4.5 trillion. That left Virginia senator Mark Warner.

I like Senator Warner and consider him a friend. He is, however, a fiscal conservative. At the time, he was in the middle of negotiating the bipartisan infrastructure bill. For weeks, we waited for a signal from him.

Finally, about a month after I released my proposal, Senator Warner gave us his bottom line for reconciliation: $3.5 trillion. I wasn't happy; $3.5 trillion was not nearly enough to fulfill President Biden's campaign promises. It wasn't enough to meet our commitments to deal with climate change. It would not be enough to reduce the Medicare eligibility age and provide health care to millions of Americans. And it was a totally arbitrary number. But I could not convince him to go any higher.

My own view was that before agreeing to go down to $3.5 trillion, we needed to get a firm commitment from Senator Manchin of West Virginia and Senator Sinema of Arizona—the two Democrats who were most dependent on corporate campaign contributions—that they would not try to cut this bill down any further. Unfortunately, that was not a commitment we could get. Senator Schumer thought it was vital for us to show progress on moving the reconciliation bill forward, and so did every single Democrat on the Budget Committee. I reluctantly agreed.

At roughly the same time, centrist Democrats and Republicans put infrastructure back on the table, with an agreement for a $550 billion spending plan.

On August 10, 2021, the Senate passed the infrastructure bill by a vote of 69–30. I voted for it. It was a reasonably good piece of legislation. But I voted for it with the absolute belief that Democratic leadership in the House and the Senate would not send the infrastructure bill to the president's desk without passing the Build Back Better Reconciliation Act.

That's what Speaker Pelosi said. That's what Majority Leader

Schumer said. That's what President Biden said. Unfortunately, that was not the position of two corporate Democrats in the Senate and a handful of conservative House Democrats who were taking campaign contributions from at least twenty-five Republican billionaires.

I knew this was going to be a fight. We needed to get something on paper.

On August 11, 2021, the Senate passed the budget resolution legislation I helped write. This measure allowed the Senate to pass a $3.5 trillion reconciliation bill with fifty votes instead of sixty. Every single Democrat voted for it, including Manchin and Sinema. We were on our way to a historic victory for the working class of America.

Or so it seemed.

So Close and Yet So Far

The next year would prove to be one of the most difficult, demanding, and demoralizing years of my three decades in Congress.

Yes. We were the closest we had ever been to finally making the transformational changes to our society that would fundamentally improve the lives of working families with children, the elderly, the sick, and the poor, and reduce soaring income and wealth inequality. And yet we were so far away.

Only over time did it become clear that, while they had voted for the American Rescue Act and the infrastructure plan, Manchin and Sinema were never going to support legislation that took on corporate interests as aggressively as did the Build Back Better Act.

It didn't matter that, in poll after poll, the overwhelming majority of Americans supported the entirety of the $3.5 trillion reconciliation plan that was backed by the president and the Budget Committee, or that the majority of Manchin's and Sinema's constituents in West Virginia and Arizona supported Build Back Better.

No. What mattered was that billionaire campaign contributors and lobbyists were determined to do everything they could to defeat our agenda.

The reality was that they held the upper hand.

In order for Build Back Better to be approved, we needed 100 percent of the Democratic Caucus in the Senate behind us. Meanwhile, all that the billionaire class and the special interests needed to defeat this legislation was a single member of that same caucus. It wasn't a fair contest. In fact, for the wealthy and the powerful, who have unlimited resources at their disposal, defeating the bill was as easy as shooting fish in a barrel.

We had forty-eight out of the fifty Democratic senators to support the $3.5 trillion plan. The moneyed interests had two Democratic senators to oppose it, along with every single Republican.

Our only hope had been an agreement that the House would not approve the infrastructure bill—which both Manchin and Sinema wanted—without also approving Build Back Better. But on November 2, 2021, Democrats suffered a significant setback in off-year elections that saw Virginia—a state that had voted overwhelmingly for Biden—elect a conservative Republican governor, as the GOP made gains in other states across the country. Democratic leaders in Congress panicked. They recognized—correctly—that Americans were frustrated with the lack of action on Capitol Hill. But, instead of going big, they went small.

On November 5, 2021, the modest bipartisan infrastructure bill passed the House. But the chamber failed to take up the Build Back Better Act. We had lost our leverage.

Two weeks later, in a futile attempt to secure the votes of Senators Manchin and Sinema, the House cut the Build Back Better bill in half and passed a scaled-back version of what had been proposed.

What was left out of the House bill was heartbreaking.

Gone was an extension of the $300-a-month Child Tax Credit. The next month, after this program expired, the child poverty rate skyrocketed by 41 percent.

Gone was free community college.

Gone was the expansion of Medicare to provide eyeglasses, hearing aids, and dental care to seniors and people with disabilities, which had been the most popular provision in the bill.

Gone was the repeal of Trump's tax breaks for the wealthy that virtually every Democrat, including Senator Sinema, had campaigned to eliminate.

While the paid family and medical leave provision survived, it was trimmed down from twelve weeks to four.

And yet, when all was said and done, even the modest measure that the House proposed would go nowhere.

Early in 2022, Senator Manchin finally acknowledged on Fox News what many of us had long believed to be the case: that he would never support a meaningful investment in the country's future. Build Back Better, Manchin announced, was dead.

But that wasn't quite the case. Build Back Better was in legislative purgatory. While month after month passed as Congress did nothing, President Biden's approval ratings were beginning to tank.

There were never-ending negotiations with Senator Manchin behind closed doors. We kept hearing that Build Back Better would return in some form. But almost a year passed. As the legislation gathered more and more dust, the American people became increasingly demoralized. By the summer of 2022, President Biden's approval rating was at 36 percent, the lowest level of his presidency. In generic polling, Democrats trailed Republicans in matchups for the 2022 midterm elections. Senate inaction was becoming a crisis for the Democrats.

Why Do Democrats Fail to Hold Republicans to Account?

I wanted to break the logjam.

As circumstances grew increasingly desperate for the Democrats, I proposed a "radical idea." I wanted "the world's greatest deliberative body" to actually start deliberating. I wanted Senate Democrats to bring to the floor legislation that addressed the needs of working families, and force Republicans to vote for or against these very important and very popular initiatives.

The GOP is the party that gives tax breaks to billionaires while maneuvering to cut Social Security, Medicare, Medicaid. It is a party that ignores climate change. It represents the interests of the wealthy and the powerful while turning its back on struggling working-class families. Perhaps because they take such unpopular positions, they feel a need to spend an inordinate amount of time conspiring to make it harder to vote.

Yet, despite the outrageous behavior of Donald Trump and his allies, and their unpopular agenda, Republicans had been able to escape responsibility for their reactionary positions because the Senate rarely held clear yes-or-no votes on the issues that the American people cared about the most. That wasn't only wrong from a policy perspective, it was extremely stupid politics.

The American people were sick and tired of endless "negotiations." They were sick and tired of politicians hiding behind closed doors. They wanted the Senate to vote on legislation to improve their lives. At the very least, they had a right to know where their senators stood on the issues.

But Senate leaders preferred to do nothing rather than "divide" their caucus by exposing the pro-corporate stances of a handful of their Democratic colleagues.

Building Back a Little Better

Finally, after nearly a year of delay, Senator Manchin and Senator Schumer announced that a deal had been reached. We were going to vote on a very modest reconciliation bill. It fell far short of the bold agenda that my progressive colleagues and I had been fighting to advance. The legislation included just about $434 billion in new spending over a ten-year period—$64 billion to subsidize private health insurance plans under the Affordable Care Act and $370 billion for the fight against climate change. Frustratingly, at a time of accelerating climate devastation, the agreement included massive giveaways to the fossil fuel companies. Manchin, the largest recipient of fossil fuel money, got what he wanted, but the broader Build Back Better agenda was decimated.

Enacting free and universal pre-K for three- and four-year-olds? Gone.

Making sure that no family in America pays more than 7 percent of their limited income on childcare? Gone.

Providing dental care, eyeglasses, and hearing aids for senior citizens under Medicare? Gone.

Making sure that seniors and persons with disabilities can receive the high-quality health care they need from well-paid workers in their own homes, instead of being forced into understaffed and inhospitable nursing homes? Gone.

Building millions of units of affordable housing, combating homelessness, repairing public housing, and providing rental assistance to millions of Americans who desperately need it? Gone.

Creating hundreds of thousands of jobs and providing education assistance to young Americans in order to combat climate change through a Civilian Climate Corps? Gone.

The slimmed-down reconciliation bill that was put up for a vote in August 2022 contained modest advances, to be sure. But hidden in its language were a lot of bad ideas.

Yes, for the first time in history, Medicare administrators would be allowed to negotiate with the pharmaceutical industry to lower drug prices. Unfortunately, that provision would not kick in until 2026—and it started with only ten drugs. The reconciliation bill would do nothing to lower prescription drug prices for anyone who was not on Medicare. The pharmaceutical industry would still be allowed to charge the American people the highest prices in the world—by far—for prescription drugs.

Yes, out-of-pocket prescription drug costs for seniors would be capped at $2,000 a year. This was a good provision that would benefit up to two million seniors who currently pay more than that amount for prescriptions. Unfortunately, this provision would not go into effect until 2025. Worse yet, the $25 billion cost of this provision was not going to be paid for by the pharmaceutical companies that were making record-breaking profits. The plan would be paid for by increasing Medicare premiums on virtually every senior citizen in the United States.

Yes, the price of insulin for Medicare recipients would be capped at $35 a month. But the Senate parliamentarian advised that sixty votes would be needed to extend that $35-a-month price cap on insulin to those who were not on Medicare. So most diabetics would get no protection against pharmaceutical profiteering. Because of the parliamentarian's ruling, and the failure of Democratic leadership to reject it, our effort to aid all diabetics fell short. While all fifty Democratic senators backed the proposal for a universal cap, only seven Republicans did so. The amendment lost, despite the fact that there were fifty-seven "yes" votes to forty-three "no's."

Yes, in terms of health care, this legislation would for three years extend subsidies for some thirteen million Americans who have private health insurance plans as a result of the Affordable Care Act. Without this provision, millions of Americans would have seen their premiums skyrocket, and some three million Americans would lose their health insurance altogether. This was a good provision. However, the $64 billion expenditure to pay for it went directly into the pockets of private health insurance companies, which made more than $60 billion in profits in 2021, and provided their executives with exorbitant compensation packages.

The slimmed-down reconciliation bill—dubbed the Inflation Reduction Act—proposed no action to help the more than seventy million Americans who are uninsured or underinsured, and it did nothing to reform a dysfunctional health care system that is designed not to make people well, but to make the stockholders of private health insurance companies extremely rich.

Yes, the bill did begin to make the wealthy and large corporations pay their fair share in taxes by imposing a 15 percent minimum tax on corporations. No longer would companies like AT&T, Federal Express, and Nike be allowed to make billions of dollars in profits and pay nothing in federal income tax. Further, the bill would provide the resources the IRS needs not only to audit wealthy tax cheats who have been avoiding up to $1 trillion in taxes that they legally owe, but also to help average Americans get their income tax refunds faster. But the bad news remained that this bill did nothing to repeal the Trump tax breaks that went to the very wealthy and large corporations. Trump's 2017 tax bill provided over a trillion dollars in tax breaks to the top 1 percent and large corporations. In fact, 83 percent of the benefits of the Trump tax law are going to the top 1 percent. This bill repealed none of those benefits.

Yes, by any measure, the most significant part of this bill was an unprecedented $300 billion investment in clean energy and energy efficiency, including a $7 billion solar rooftop proposal that I introduced. This bill could help increase U.S. solar energy by 500 percent and more than double wind energy by 2035. That was no small thing. But it also included that huge giveaway to the fossil fuel industry—both in the reconciliation bill itself and in a side deal, a summary of which was made public just days before the Senate voted on the bill.

In my view, it was absolutely absurd and counterproductive to be providing tens of billions of dollars in new tax breaks and subsidies to the fossil fuel industry, and opening up millions of new acres of public lands to oil and gas companies that are destroying the planet, in a bill that was touted as a historic climate bill.

I found it particularly galling that some of the worst fossil fuel polluters on the planet, including BP and Shell, endorsed this reconciliation bill, while the CEO of ExxonMobil claimed the bill was "a step in the right direction" and pronounced himself "pleased" with the "comprehensive set of solutions" it included.

A Last Chance to Get It Right

In the end, I reluctantly voted for this bill. It fell far short of what the American people needed—and begged—us to do. Overall, as I studied this more than 700-page piece of legislation, I recognized the pluses outweighed the negatives.

However, given that this was the last reconciliation bill that the Senate would be considering before the midterm elections—and, therefore, the last opportunity we had to do something significant for the American people with just fifty votes—I didn't believe the Democratic Caucus should squander that moment.

I wanted at least forty-seven other senators to join with me in supporting multiple amendments, in order to show the American people that we were on their side. We might, or might not, have the fifty votes to pass these amendments, but we could make it clear to the voters who stood with the working class and who did not. In so doing, we could draw a sharp contrast with what the vast majority of Americans stood for and what the Republicans stood against.

Unfortunately, the Democratic leadership refused to embrace this strategy. They were more interested in showing that their caucus was "unified" in favor of a modest proposal than in showing that most Democrats favored a bigger and bolder agenda.

But I wasn't giving up.

I had my staff draft five amendments, and during a marathon legislative session that started in the evening on Saturday, August 8, and concluded at about 3:00 P.M. on Sunday, August 9, I offered them one by one.

At 11:31 P.M., I proposed an amendment to prohibit Medicare from paying higher prices for prescription drugs than the Veterans Administration. If that amendment had passed, we could have cut the price of prescription drugs under Medicare in half and saved $800 billion over the next decade. It lost by a vote of 1–99.

At 1:15 A.M., I proposed an amendment to expand Medicare to cover dental, vision, and hearing benefits for seniors and persons with disabilities. It lost 3–97, with only Georgia senators Warnock and Ossoff voting with me.

A few hours later, Senator Warnock offered an amendment to expand Medicaid for over three million Americans who had been denied health care by Republican governors and state legislatures opposed to Obamacare. The amendment lost 5–94, with Senator Baldwin and Senator Susan Collins—a Republican—joining the Georgia senators and myself in its favor.

At 4:01 A.M., I proposed an amendment to establish a Civilian Climate Corps to create some 400,000 jobs and educational benefits for young Americans to combat climate change, improve the environment, and transition our economy to renewable energy and energy efficiency. It failed 1–98.

At 7:38 A.M., I proposed an amendment to extend the monthly $300-per-child tax credit for an additional four years—paid for by repealing the Trump tax breaks for the wealthy and large corporations. It failed 1–97.

Finally, at 9:38 A.M., I proposed my last amendment: to strike all of the benefits to fossil fuel companies that were included in the reconciliation bill. Shock of shocks: It failed 1–99.

It's important to note that not every amendment to the reconciliation bill was defeated. But this is not a happy end to the story.

On Sunday, just before final passage of the bill, Senator Sinema voted with the Republicans to provide a $35 billion carve-out for Wall Street private equity vultures from the corporate minimum tax. No, we couldn't expand Medicare. We couldn't take on the greed of the pharmaceutical industry or big oil companies. We couldn't provide $300 a month for low-income families to take care of their toddlers and escape poverty. But we *could* provide a last-minute $35 billion tax break to extremely profitable Wall Street firms and their executives who had contributed millions of dollars in campaign contributions to the Republicans and Senator Sinema. If you want to know why the American people are giving up on American politics, put this down as Exhibit A.

At about 10:30 A.M., I took a short walk outside of the Senate chamber with my staff director, Warren Gunnels, who had been by my side on the floor. We needed to get some fresh air. We had been wearing masks for about thirteen hours straight and we were tired. I sat down and leaned back on the Capitol steps, Warren standing a few feet from me, when we noticed a lone photographer who had started taking pictures. It was a ninety-degree day and I certainly wasn't wearing mittens, but Warren said: "This could be the start of another meme."

Sure enough, Warren was right. The *Los Angeles Times* ran a picture of me sitting on the Capitol steps.

As NPR reported: "Senator Bernie Sanders has been memed again—no mittens this time. During the marathon debate for the Inflation Reduction Act, a photo emerged of a seemingly dejected Sanders sitting on the Capitol steps resembling a 1970s cartoon character, the iconic bill from 'Schoolhouse Rock!' on the same Capitol steps. Sanders' amendments were defeated. But life imitating art, the bill passed."

That was correct. After fifteen hours of debate and votes on twenty-eight amendments, the reconciliation bill was passed by a vote of 51–50, with the vice president casting the tie-breaking vote.

It's Time to Stop Settling for Less

At a time of enormous need, pain, and discontent, at a point when too many Americans were giving up on democracy, the Senate put a Band-Aid on a gaping wound. Most people would not notice, let alone remember, what we had done. The tragedy was that, with a majority in the Senate, we could have done more than simply address specific issues. We could have given hope to millions who had lost faith, and, in the process, shown them that their government could work for *them,* as opposed to the wealthy and powerful.

Most senators tried to put the best spin on things. But I did not. I'm not interested in making excuses. I don't tell people to be satisfied with what they get—or to accept that some things will never be gotten. I tell people to demand more. And so, with this history told, it is time to talk about what more we should be demanding. It is time to look forward—to present an agenda for upending uber-capitalism and point toward that North Star future where economic and social and racial justice are not just a promise but a reality.

4

BILLIONAIRES SHOULD NOT EXIST

*Only by ending American oligarchy
can we begin to realize America's promise*

W hen I launched a plan to tax extreme wealth in the fall
of 2019, a *New York Times* reporter wondered whether I
was trying to eliminate billionaires. Actually, I replied, "I
don't think that billionaires should exist."

That sentence launched hundreds of headlines and broadcast
conversations—especially on Fox News and right-wing talk radio.
Facebook CEO Mark Zuckerberg admitted that "at some level no
one deserves to have that much money." Elon Musk tweeted a couple of snarky comments. But what struck me was that a lot of people
thought I must be kidding. I wasn't.

In case anyone missed the point, my campaign issued a BILLION-
AIRES SHOULD NOT EXIST bumper sticker. Tens of thousands of Americans displayed them because they understood what most pundits

did not: that the United States cannot afford to support a billionaire class that takes far more from this country than it gives back.

The very existence of a rapidly expanding billionaire class in the United States is a manifestation of an unjust system that promotes massive income and wealth inequality. In this system, the people on top enjoy lives of extraordinary privilege. They possess more of the planet's largesse than they could burn through in a thousand lifetimes. No luxury is beyond their reach. They are so phenomenally rich that they can spend their fortunes buying "experiences"—like a rocket trip beyond Earth's atmosphere. While an exceptionally wealthy few wallow in affluence and become exponentially richer with each passing day, the majority of Americans live lives of quiet desperation. They're not scheming to pay for trips to outer space. They're struggling to pay for the necessities of life here on Earth.

The very existence of billionaires is not just about who has the money and who doesn't. It is also a manifestation of a corrupt political system, in which immense power over the lives of the great mass of Americans is concentrated in the hands of a small number of people who—through campaign finance arrangements that can only be described as legalized bribery—buy control of our elections and the policies that extend from them.

These are the Wall Street investors and corporate CEOs who determine whether jobs will stay in this country or go abroad, what kind of incomes working people will earn, and what the price of gas, prescription drugs, and food will be. And while these oligarchs exert enormous influence over our lives, ordinary people have virtually no power, or even the concept of power, in shaping the future of the country. They lack the institutions to exert influence, and they're too busy just trying to survive.

In this unprecedented moment in American history, there is no more time for tinkering around the edges. It is time to reject "conventional wisdom" and "incrementalism." It is time to fundamentally rethink our adherence to the system of unfettered capitalism, and to address the unspeakable harm that system is doing to us all.

In a country where there is little honest debate about our economic system, and only marginally more debate about the political system that sustains it, the idea of rejecting unfettered capitalism—and of doing away with the billionaire class—may sound radical.

It's not.

The goal of any democratic, moral, and rational nation must be to create a society where people are healthy, happy, and able to live long and productive lives. Not just the rich and the powerful, but *all* people. Our greatness should be determined not by the number of billionaires who live in our country, the size of our GDP, the number of nuclear weapons we have, or how many channels we receive on cable TV. We should judge our success as a nation by looking at the quality of life for the average American. How healthy is he? How satisfied is she in her work? How happy are their children? We must move away from the economic mentality of scarcity and austerity to a mindset that seeks prosperity for all. To those who say that, in the wealthiest country in the history of the world, there is not enough to care for all the people, our answer must be: "That's absurd. Of course there's enough!" With the explosion of new technology and productivity that we are experiencing, we now have the capability to provide a good life for every American.

Our economic debates should not revolve around questions of resources. They should revolve around questions of intent, and will.

If we truly intend to make America great, we will strive to be a nation that has eliminated poverty, homelessness, and diseases of despair, where hard work is rewarded with a living wage, and where those who are too old or too infirm to work are protected by a safety net that guarantees no American will be destitute. That's not a utopian vision or some foreign construct. This country should have the best educational system in the world from childcare to graduate school—accessible to all, regardless of income. We should have a top-quality health care system allowing all people to walk into a doctor's office and get the care they need without worrying about the cost, because the system is publicly funded. Instead of spending more money on the military than the next ten nations combined, we should lead the world in diplomacy and international collaboration, especially when it comes to preventing wars and combating climate change.

Greed Is Not Good

My conservative friends often talk about the *moral* values that should be guiding the United States. Fair enough. There are moral values that should be guiding Americans into the future, and about which we should be very clear:

> Greed is not good.
> Massive income and wealth inequality is not good.
> Buying elections is not good.
> Profiting from human illness is not good.
> Charging people the highest prices in the world for prescription drugs is not good.
> Exploiting workers is not good.
> Monopolization of the economy by a handful of corporations is not good.
> Ignoring the needs of the most vulnerable among us—children, the elderly, and people with disabilities—is not good.
> Racism, sexism, homophobia, and xenophobia are not good.
> For-profit prisons that make money by locking up poor people are not good.
> Wars and excessive military budgets are not good.
> Carbon emissions that destroy our planet are not good.

The simple truth is that unfettered capitalism is not just creating economic misery for the majority of Americans, it is destroying our health, our well-being, our democracy, and our planet. If we hope to save ourselves, we must identify the people and the policies that engineer this destruction. Once we do so, it becomes clear that the time is long overdue for us to do away with billionaires, end a "winner take all" system based on greed, corruption, and rampant self-interest, and move toward a system motivated by compassion, cooperation, and common interest. We have to determine whether we are going to use our intelligence and energy to create a nation and world in which all people thrive, or whether we maintain a rigged system in which the few benefit at the expense of the many. This isn't about creating a rigid system that discourages creativity and innovation. There's nothing wrong with a business or an entrepreneur making a profit. There is something profoundly wrong, however, when massive corporations, controlled by the wealthiest people on earth, lie, cheat, bribe, and steal in order to make profits that are funded by the destruction of our lives, our environment, and our democracy.

Recently, there has been much political and media discussion about the oligarchy surrounding Vladimir Putin, the veteran KGB operative who has emerged as Russia's authoritarian leader. We have learned about the extraordinary wealth of those favored by Putin, of their illicit power and their determination to take advantage of a system that has literally allowed them to strip a nation of its assets. But oligarchy is not a uniquely Russian phenomenon. It's a global reality that our corporate media chooses to examine in only the narrowest of terms. What about the oligarchs of America? What about the perverse and destructive role that they play in shaping our society? Why is there no acknowledgment, by our political and media elites, that there is an American oligarchy every bit as dangerous as the oligarchies we decry in other countries?

If we accept that the truth will set us free, then we need to face some hard truths about American oligarchs. This country has reached a point in its history where it must determine whether we truly embrace the inspiring words in our Declaration of Independence, "that all men are created equal" and "endowed by their Creator with certain unalienable Rights." Or do we simply accept that we will continue to be ruled by a small number of extremely wealthy and powerful people who are motivated by greed and could care less for the general welfare?

We have to decide whether we take seriously what the great religions of the world—Christianity, Judaism, Islam, Buddhism, Hinduism, and others—have preached for thousands of years. Do we believe in the brotherhood of man and human solidarity? Do we believe in the Golden Rule that says each and every one of us should "do unto others as you would have them do unto you"? Or do we accept, as the prevailing ethic of our culture, that whoever has the gold rules—and that lying, cheating, and stealing are OK if you're powerful enough to be able to get away with it?

If we fail to make the right choice, it will be made for us by the powerful few who already control too much of our destiny.

Living Under Oligarchy

The establishment, through our political system, our media, and our schools, perpetuates the mythology that we are a democratic society in which "the people" are supreme and control the destiny of the nation.

Really?

The U.S. Census Bureau estimated at the start of 2022 that there were 332,403,650 people living in the United States. Yet, roughly 90 percent of the wealth of the nation is owned by one-tenth of 1 percent of that total. So 332,403 Americans own more than the other 332,071,247. But that does not begin to tell the story of wealth inequality in America.

Let's make things more concrete. Before the pandemic, just three ultra-billionaires—Jeff Bezos, Bill Gates, and Warren Buffett—controlled as much wealth as the bottom half of the U.S. population combined. During the pandemic, the fortunes of those who were already enormously wealthy boomed as we saw one of the most rapid redistributions of wealth upward in global history. According to the

Institute for Policy Studies, while most Americans were engaged in the "shared sacrifice" imposed by a global health crisis, the combined wealth of roughly 725 American billionaires increased by $2.071 trillion (70.3 percent) between March 18, 2020, and October 15, 2021, from approximately $2.947 trillion to $5.019 trillion.

The rich are not merely consolidating their wealth, they are consolidating their influence over American government and political life; billionaire contributions to election campaigns spiked from $31 million in 2010—when the Supreme Court's *Citizens United* ruling struck down many barriers to elite influence—to $1.2 billion in 2020. That 2020 figure more than doubles, to $2.6 billion, when we include billionaires who "self-fund" their own campaigns for high office, according to a study by Americans for Tax Fairness. And those numbers do not include the billions of underreported dollars flowing into the "dark money" campaigns that decide who will occupy positions of power. Once the favored candidates of the billionaire class arrive in Washington, they are greeted by thousands of lobbyists whose paychecks are funded by the same billionaires and their allies.

The oligarchy controls our economy. Three firms—BlackRock, Vanguard, and State Street—now control assets of over $20 trillion, equivalent to the GDP of the United States of America. They are the largest stockholders in the major banks in our country. They are major shareholders in more than 96 percent of S&P 500 companies. In other words, they have significant influence over many hundreds of companies that employ millions of American workers; influence, in fact, over the entire economy.

Let's talk about banking. After the Wall Street crash of 2008, there was a lot of discussion about the wealth and power of the major banks and how they were "too big to fail." Well, these three Wall Street investment firms are the largest shareholders of some of the biggest banks in America—JPMorgan Chase, Wells Fargo, and Citibank.

Let's talk about transportation. BlackRock, Vanguard, and State are among the top owners of all four major airlines—American, Southwest, Delta, and United.

What about health care? Together, they own an average of 20 percent of the major drug companies.

What about media? They are among the largest stockholders in Comcast, Disney, and Warner Bros.

With their control of so much of our politics and media, billionaires are freed to expand their wealth and power at exponential rates. Bill Gates is now recognized as the largest private owner of farmland in the United States, with some 269,000 acres across dozens of states, according to the Associated Press. Billionaire-guided investment firms such as BlackRock grabbed up 15 percent of U.S. homes that were for sale in the first quarter of 2021, driving up prices—and their profits—in markets across the country. They control huge swathes of the health care industry, the pharmaceutical industry, the energy sector, Big Tech, agriculture, and transportation. They are coming to dominate every aspect of our lives.

That is the power and influence of 0.0001 of 1 percent of our population. That is not democracy. That is oligarchy.

The Oligarchs Are Different

In the 1920s, F. Scott Fitzgerald wrote about the very rich: "They are different from you and me." That was true then, in the years just prior to the Great Depression. It is even truer now. The oligarchs of today live in a world so separate from the experience of ordinary mortals that their lifestyle is beyond the imagination of most Americans.

These people don't live in houses. They own palaces—huge mansions surrounded by manicured lawns and tall gates—which are scattered around the world. They don't go to the local emergency room when they get sick. They have the best doctors and specialists in the world on call and, when necessary, can jet off in a private "medical jet" to get the best treatment in the world. The prescription drugs they need to stay alive are readily accessible, no matter what the cost. They don't go places in compact cars or sedans. They travel in chauffeur-driven limousines and private planes. They have teams of pilots on call to whisk them off to ski in the Alps and to go snorkeling in the Caribbean. The wealthiest few are building spaceships so that they can vacation in the stratosphere.

The oligarchs don't settle into the Courtyard by Marriott or camp in a national park when they go on holiday. They "summer" in coastal enclaves and get away from the winter cold on their own private islands. They don't row boats on lakes, or kayak on rivers. They cruise the oceans on yachts that cost hundreds of millions of dollars and are so large that bridges must be removed so that they can pass through. They don't go to museums to see fine art. They buy up the great paintings and sculptures of the world for their own private enjoyment.

They do not share their wealth. They pass it on to their heirs. "The three wealthiest U.S. families are the Waltons of Walmart, the Mars candy family, and the Koch brothers, heirs to the country's second largest private company, the energy conglomerate Koch Industries. These are all enterprises built by the grandparents and parents of today's wealthy heirs and heiresses," noted the 2021 "Billionaire Bonanza" study by the Institute for Policy Studies. "These three families own a combined fortune of $348.7 billion, which is four million times the median wealth of a U.S. family."

Oligarchs don't send their babies to a local childcare center with low-paid, overworked teachers. They fly-in professional nannies and tutors to care for the kids at home. Their children don't go to overcrowded neighborhood public schools; they jet off to the finest private schools in the world and enjoy the support of teams of specialized instructors. The children of oligarchs don't go to community colleges, or struggle to figure out how to afford public universities in their states while taking on overwhelming loads of student debt. They waltz into Ivy League universities, thanks to the "legacies" of their grandparents and generous donations from their parents.

After graduation, the children of oligarchs don't send out résumés, ink the spaces on job applications, or sit through rounds of interviews in hopes of launching a career. With an assist from their grandparents and parents, they are given positions for which their qualifications may be slim but their connections are substantial. And if they run afoul of the law, they aren't dependent upon overworked and underpaid public defenders to keep them out of jail. The best lawyers that money can buy make the calls that are necessary to cause the "little problem" to go away.

Don't Hate Elon Musk, Hate the System That Made Musk Possible

The point is not to demonize oligarchs. Nor is it to envy them. People like Musk, Bezos, Zuckerberg, Gates, Buffett, the Waltons, the Kochs, and their ilk are usually smart. They tend to work hard and take risks; they're often innovative.

We harm the discourse when we get bogged down with personalities, and we create the false impression that a couple of bad eggs are the problem.

The fight against American oligarchy—and the plutocratic arrangements that foster it—has nothing to do with personalities. Inequality isn't about individuals; this is a systemic crisis.

It's time to end a culture that not only accepts but actually creates the obscene degree of inequality, injustice, and uncontrollable greed that is so damaging to our nation and world. We have to get comfortable acknowledging this fact, as citizens and as political activists and leaders. We have to start saying:

Yes. It is immoral and absurd that our country has more income and wealth inequality today than at any time since the 1920s, that 45 percent of all new income goes to the top 1 percent, that CEOs now make 350 times more than their average employees earn.

Yes. It is unconscionable that, thanks to the uber-capitalist policies of the past thirty years, we have seen a massive transfer of wealth from those who have too little to those who have too much. It is not acceptable that, during this short period in human history, the top 1 percent have seen a $21 trillion increase in their wealth, while the bottom half of the American people have actually seen a $900 billion decline in their wealth.

Yes. It is disgraceful that, despite an explosion in technology and huge increases in productivity, the average American worker today makes no more than he or she did fifty years ago in real, inflation-adjusted dollars. It is frightening to know that most of the new jobs now being created are low-skill, low-wage, and often part-time and that, everything being equal, the next generation will have a lower standard of living than their parents.

Upending a System That Attacks Our Values and Mangles Priorities

No fight makes sense until we know what we are fighting against. So let me spell it out.

Our struggle is to end a system that evaluates "worth" as a measure of market profitability, a system in which we are asked to believe—based on salaries paid—that the star athlete who helps a billionaire team owner increase his bottom line is "worth" more than a thousand teachers who help children escape poverty.

Our struggle is against a system where the top twenty-five hedge fund managers in the United States pocket more money than 350,000 kindergarten teachers combined. When did we the people make that determination? When did we decide that a drug company executive at Moderna can collect a "golden parachute" valued at $926 million for *not* working, while EMT workers who work around the clock to save lives make as little as $40,000 a year?

The answer, of course, is that the American people never approved these brutal trade-offs that insult our values. The vast majority of Americans recognize that Eugene Victor Debs was right when he said, a century ago, that "I am opposing a social order in which it is possible for one man who does absolutely nothing that is useful to amass a fortune of hundreds of millions of dollars, while millions of men and women who work all the days of their lives secure barely enough for a wretched existence."

Debs spoke in a different time. But the struggle is the same today.

It is a struggle against the dog-eat-dog, every-person-for-himself culture in which wealth and money are worshipped. We need to recognize, once and for all, that for the people on top, enough is never enough. How much do they need? The answer is always "More!" One billion dollars in wealth is not enough. Five billion is not enough. A hundred billion is not enough. Like heroin addicts, oligarchs are never satisfied with what they have. They need a new fix. More, more, and more, no matter what the consequences of their greed. The only real difference is that, while heroin addicts end up dead or in jail, destroying their lives and the lives of those around them, greed addicts never end up in jail. Instead of destroying themselves, they destroy our communities, our institutions, our society.

Our struggle is about guaranteeing the respect that is deserved for the tens of millions of working-class Americans who, day after day, do the hard work that saves and improves lives and keeps our economy and nation going. As we saw more clearly than ever during the pandemic, it is not the oligarchs who are essential. It is the doctors, nurses, teachers, childcare workers, firefighters, cops, postal workers, grocery store clerks, factory workers, packinghouse and warehouse employees, farmers and farm laborers, pilots and bus drivers and truckers who do the truly important work. Yet most of these workers earn a tiny fraction of what the Wall Street speculators grab up in a single day of trading.

Our struggle is to end the injustices of an economic system where more than half our people are working paycheck to paycheck, and millions are falling further and further behind as they try to survive on starvation wages. We should not have 500,000 people who are homeless and eighteen million who spend half their limited incomes on housing. We should not have hundreds of thousands of bright young people unable to afford a higher education, and forty-five million people who are struggling with student debt. We should not have almost a hundred million Americans who are uninsured or underinsured, sixty thousand dying each year because they don't get to a doctor on time. We should not have a circumstance where one out of four patients is unable to afford the prescription drugs their doctors prescribe. We should not have 40 percent of our older workers entering retirement with no savings at all, and 10 percent of our senior citizens living in poverty. We should not have one of the highest rates of childhood poverty among major countries. We should not have declining life expectancy when people in comparable countries are living longer, healthier lives.

We Need a New Sense of Morality

When a criminal walks into a store and shoots the clerk behind the counter, we make the moral judgment that this behavior is socially unacceptable, and that the gunman should be punished. When a public official misuses and steals taxpayer money, we make the moral judgment that the embezzler should lose his job and, perhaps, be incarcerated.

Yet, when the wealthy and powerful make calculated decisions that are destructive and life-threatening to millions of people—or to the planet—we are told that "it's just business," and that it's somehow inappropriate to make moral judgments based on their actions. No matter how heinous those actions may be. Not only do individual executives go unpunished when they harm their workers and their communities; in our uber-capitalist system, their crimes are not even acknowledged. We are told that whatever the "invisible hand of the marketplace" allows is acceptable, no matter how much pain is caused. Under uber-capitalism, where the rich and the powerful make the laws and shape the culture, their behavior is rarely if ever considered to be illegal—let alone punishable.

A few examples:

As far back as the late 1950s, physicist Edward Teller and other scientists were warning executives in the fossil fuel industry that carbon emissions were "contaminating the atmosphere" and causing a "greenhouse effect" that could eventually lead to temperature increases "sufficient to melt the icecap and submerge New York." More than sixty years ago, these executives knew they were causing global warming and therefore threatening the very existence of the planet. Yet, in pursuit of profit, the executives not only refused to publicly acknowledge what they had learned but, year after year, lied about the existential threat that climate change posed for our planet.

Today, all over the world sea levels are rising, causing increased flooding. Oceans are becoming more acidified, as fish die off. Heat waves are killing people by the thousands and droughts are making it impossible for farmers to grow the food we need. Extreme weather disturbances with massive property destruction and wildfires that destroy millions of acres are becoming such common occurrences that we literally see "100-year events" occurring year after year. In the coming thirty years, as the planet continues to warm, the World Bank estimates that more than 200 million people will be forced to migrate because of extreme weather events and steady environmental decline.

We face a future in which desperate people will search for clean drinking water and new land in which to grow their crops. This mass migration of people will lay the groundwork for future international tension and more war. Yet all of this was avoidable. Fossil fuel executives made a calculated decision to deceive the world about global warming. They determined that their short-term profits were more important than the well-being of the planet and the lives of billions of people. They sinned against humanity and against the future in the foulest of ways imaginable.

So what happened to the CEOs who betrayed the American people and the global community? Were they fired from their jobs? Were they condemned by pundits on cable television and the editorial boards of major newspapers? Were they prosecuted? Did they go to jail for their crimes? Nope. Not at all. Not a one of them. These CEOs got rich. They enjoyed their status as prominent and respected members of their communities. When oil billionaires and fossil fuel industry

CEOs die in comfortable old age, obituary writers identify them as "financial geniuses," "captains of industry," and "philanthropists."

There is zero accountability.

The same goes for other industries.

The classic example of the impunity of CEOs comes from the tobacco industry. Decade after decade, industry insiders lied about what they knew of the dangers of smoking. Even when they got caught, they kept lying, perpetuating business practices that led to the deaths of hundreds of thousands of people each year in our country, and millions around the world. In 2018, 480,000 Americans died as a result of smoking. Four hundred and eighty thousand people— almost as many as we lost in the first year of the coronavirus pandemic. Those deaths resulted from a deliberate refusal to respect science. Like the fossil fuel industry, tobacco industry insiders knew exactly what they were doing. It's no longer any great medical secret that their products are designed to addict people to nicotine and other chemicals that cause cancer, emphysema, heart disease, and many other life-threatening illnesses. It's also no secret that tobacco companies spend billions in the United States and around the world to ensnare young people, through e-cigarettes and other products, into habits that lead to a shortened life of addiction and suffering.

In other words, we have a major American (and global) industry whose business model is designed to attract young people to their products, chemically addict them, cause them terrible suffering and death, and then pass the hundreds of billions a year in medical costs on to the taxpayers.

Then there is the pharmaceutical industry. We should be horrified by the price-fixing and collusion in the industry, which results in Americans paying the highest prices in the world for prescription drugs—in some cases ten times more than other countries. We should also be horrified that almost one in four Americans cannot afford the outrageous cost of the medications their doctors prescribe, even as the drug companies make tens of billions in profits. But what should make us most furious are the ways in which the major drug companies and pharmacy benefit managers (PBMs) have *knowingly* pushed hundreds of millions of highly addictive opiate pills into communities around the country. Their actions have spawned an epidemic, which has killed at least 600,000 Americans—including more than a thousand of my fellow Vermonters. Purdue Pharma, the manufacturer of OxyContin, one of the largest-selling opiates, recognized decades ago that their product was extremely addictive and was causing a massive number of overdoses. What was the response of the billionaires who owned the company? Did they pull the product off the market and work with doctors and scientists to determine the best way to treat the addictions that they caused? Not quite. According to a *New York Times* report from May 29, 2018, "a copy of a confidential Justice Department report shows that federal prosecutors investigating the company found that Purdue Pharma knew about 'significant' abuse of OxyContin in the first years after the drug's introduction in 1996 and concealed that information."

But they did more than conceal the information. Recognizing that addiction equated with profit, they hired more salespeople, sold more product, and made even larger profits. They got caught eventually, and Purdue Pharma was required to pay billions to state governments. But those fines will not bring back the lives of those who died from Purdue Pharma drugs, or heal the pain of families that have been devastated. They will not come close to compensating taxpayers for the medical bills this epidemic has generated. Nor will they bring genuine accountability, since not one of the billionaire oligarchs in the Sackler family, which owns Purdue Pharma, or any other executive of the company, has been jailed.

The biggest producer of oligarchy in the United States is funded by American taxpayers. We're speaking, of course, of the investment banking industry.

In 2008, after major Wall Street banks knowingly peddled investment portfolios based on near-worthless subprime mortgages, they crashed the global economy, creating a Great Recession that would eventually be understood as the worst financial downturn since the

Great Depression. This was the largest act of criminal fraud in American history. They caused the bankruptcy of huge firms, the collapse of the stock market, and an agonizing economic downturn that robbed millions of Americans of their jobs, their homes, and their life savings.

What happened to the "masters of the universe" who perpetrated this brutal crime against the American people and the global economy? The Bush administration and bipartisan majorities in a Capitol controlled by the Democrats bailed out these "too big to fail" banks to the tune of hundreds of billions of dollars. Under the Obama administration, not one senior Wall Street executive faced arrest or prosecution. In fact, in 2014, after JPMorgan Chase settled out of court with the Justice Department, the bank's board of directors awarded CEO Jamie Dimon a 74 percent increase in his salary.

Are we shocked by this? Of course not. Most Americans understand that the basic function of the current criminal justice system is to lock up the poor, racial and ethnic minorities, and people who suffer from addiction and mental illness. Rich white executives, with their armies of lawyers and records of campaign donations to people in high places, don't go to jail.

Uber-capitalism has a very clear message to the American people. For the billionaire class and the corporate CEOs who are associated with it, the message is: "Heads I win. Tails you lose." Uber-capitalists operate with impunity. There is no action, no matter how blatant or reprehensible, that is punishable. Under our current value system these corporations are not doing anything "wrong." In fact, they are doing exactly what they are supposed to be doing. This is how the system works. They are making massive profits, paying out huge dividends to their stockholders, and rewarding their CEOs with extravagant compensation packages. They are succeeding. And if they step over some line and get "caught" and have to pay a fine, it is literally "just the cost of doing business."

But the truth is that they don't have to worry much about getting "caught," because most of what they do is perfectly legal. It is legal because their politician pawns write the laws.

Billionaires Cannot Be Allowed to Buy Our Democracy

Donald Trump has at least two major distinctions. He was the first billionaire to occupy the Oval Office. And he was the most anti-democratic president in American history. That ought to be a lesson to us.

Trump is the ugliest expression of a growing phenomenon in which billionaires in the United States and around the world are not only delivering massive amounts of campaign cash to the candidates and parties they support; these billionaires are actually running for office—and winning.

The influence of money in American politics is not new. It has always existed. But since the Supreme Court's *Citizens United* ruling in 2010, that influence has become much more insidious. In that decision, the court reversed long-standing campaign finance law and argued that restrictions on campaign spending were a violation of the First Amendment guarantees to free speech. That ill-thought conclusion led to the creation of super-PACs, which corporations and billionaires now use to "express their freedom" by spending unlimited amounts of money to influence the results of election campaigns.

Most Americans express their political views by casting ballots. Some of them make modest contributions to the candidate of their choice, and I am extremely proud that in my two campaigns for president millions of Americans made donations of less than $50.

But a handful of Americans—billionaires—participate in elections differently. They attempt to buy them through the expenditures of huge amounts of money, which they are allowed to spend on races for every office, from the city council to the presidency. Billionaires have bought their ways into both major parties. In 2019 and 2020, Republican mega-donor Sheldon Adelson and his wife, Miriam, contributed $218 million. Early in 2020, ABC News noted in a report on the presidential candidacy of former New York City mayor Michael Bloomberg, a Republican who became a Democratic mega-donor, that "over the past two decades, Bloomberg has funneled more than $160 million to various candidates and groups across the political spectrum." That's outrageous. But there are now multibillionaires who claim that they are prepared to spend up to one billion dollars on campaigns.

In the 2020 presidential election, billionaires played a major role in both the primaries and the general election. According to *Forbes,* 230 billionaires contributed to the Biden campaign, while 133 billionaires contributed to the Trump campaign and 61 billionaires contributed to the campaign of former South Bend mayor Pete Buttigieg. More recently, Florida newspapers reported that 42 billionaires had contributed to Florida governor Ron DeSantis's 2022 campaign. And *Forbes* reported that 25 billionaires had contributed to West Virginia senator Joe Manchin, while 21 had contributed to another corporate-aligned Democrat, Arizona senator Kyrsten Sinema. These contributions are, of course, in addition to the massive infusions of undisclosed "dark money" that flow into super-PACs and so-called independent expenditure groups.

The Big Money campaign contributions are not even ideological. Some of the biggest donors give to Democrats *and* Republicans. Major corporations and interest groups on Wall Street, the pharmaceutical industry, insurance companies, defense contractors, and fossil fuel companies contribute to both major political parties at the same time. Whether you're a Democrat or Republican, the billionaires and the Big Money interests want you on their side. They understand that a few million dollars in campaign contributions are peanuts compared to a provision in a piece of legislation—or the removal of provisions, as we saw in the Build Back Better fight—that could clear the way for them to reap billions in corporate welfare or tax deductions.

Does all this money matter? Do big donations really influence the direction of campaigns, and of the governing that extends from those campaigns? Silly questions. Of course they do. Let me give you a few personal examples.

When I ran for president in 2020, one of my major opponents was Michael Bloomberg. During that campaign there was nothing particularly exceptional about the views that Bloomberg espoused. He was a moderate Democrat, as were a number of other candidates. What was exceptional about him was his wealth, and the amount of his own money that he was prepared to spend to win the Democratic nomination. Bloomberg was the eighth-wealthiest person in the world at the time he announced his candidacy, according to *Forbes*. (Trump ranked a pathetic 275th.)

Bloomberg entered the campaign late, months after the other contenders. But in the relatively short period of time that he was in the running, he spent some $900 million—more than four times as much as my campaign spent over a far longer period, and far more than any other contender. In the primary states that he contested, Bloomberg spent millions to fill the airwaves with wall-to-wall advertising. The result: While he did not win the nomination, Bloomberg went, in a very short time span, from being a relatively unknown candidate to one of the major contenders. There was only one reason why his campaign got as far as it did. Bloomberg was a multibillionaire who could open his checkbook and spend a hundred million dollars, and then another hundred million, and then another hundred million, until he got almost to a billion—and until the debates revealed him to be woefully unprepared.

I'll give Bloomberg credit, however. At least in 2020, he spent his money openly and honestly on himself.

A far uglier manifestation of the plutocratic politics that has overtaken America comes when billionaires and millionaires spend their money surreptitiously in order to achieve results that the ads they buy don't even mention.

During the 2022 Democratic primary season, I became involved in a number of congressional races in support of progressive candidates for Congress, such as Summer Lee in Pennsylvania and Jessica Cisneros in Texas. In her primary for an open seat, Summer, a brilliant young state legislator, beat a lawyer with lots of ties to the party establishment, while Jessica lost her challenge to a conservative Democratic incumbent. But in a sense, both of them faced the same opponent: an outside super-PAC funded by wealthy donors who wanted to beat progressives standing with the working class of this country.

On the Republican side of the ballot, PayPal co-founder Peter Thiel was buying Senate nominations for his friends—and the friends of Donald Trump. After the Ohio Republican U.S. Senate primary in May 2022, CNN reported that Thiel, who has an estimated net worth that exceeds $7 billion, gave $15 million to a group called "Protect Ohio Values," a super-PAC that supported one candidate: his former employee and longtime associate J. D. Vance. Running against a former state treasurer and a former chair of the Ohio Republican Party, Vance, who had never held public office and had spent much of his adult life outside Ohio, won the nomination with ease. He then won in November, and will sit for the next six years in the U.S. Senate. Do you think Senator Vance will ever say no to Peter Thiel? I don't.

The current American campaign finance system is a disaster and an embarrassment to anyone who seriously believes in democracy. If someone tomorrow were to offer a senator $100 to vote for or against a piece of legislation, it would, by any court of law, be considered a "bribe." Taking that bribe could land that person offering it—and the senator taking it—in jail. If that same person were to put $100 million into a super-PAC for that senator, their spending would be considered perfectly legal. It would also, if successful, win the donor a very close and grateful relationship with a very powerful elected official.

The role of Big Money in politics is so absurd that it is increasingly common for super-PACs to spend more money on campaigns than the candidates themselves. In fact, there are House and Senate races where the real competition comes down to the TV ads run by competing super-PACs. The candidates are bystanders to their own campaigns.

So, too, quite frequently, are the issues that matter. High on the list of those issues is the one that the oligarchs are most excited about keeping off the table: taxation of the rich and of the corporations they control.

Tax the Rich!

Taxing the rich has always been a good idea. Now, in a moment of rapidly expanding economic inequality, it is one of the most necessary ideas of our time. This is why I have repeatedly proposed strategies for taxing the billionaire class down to size. The most ambitious of these were a pair of 2021 proposals: the For the 99.5 Percent Act and the Corporate Tax Dodging Prevention Act.

The For the 99.5 Percent Act proposed a new progressive estate-tax rate structure on the top 0.5 percent of Americans—the tiny portion of our population who because of accidents of birth or marriage have inherited over $3.5 million in wealth. Under the plan, 99.5 percent of Americans would not pay a penny more in taxes. But the families of billionaires in America—who have a combined net worth of over $5 trillion—would owe up to $3 trillion in estate taxes. Specifically, this legislation would impose a 45 percent tax rate on estates worth $3.5 million, and a 65 percent tax rate on the value of estates worth over $1 billion. The measure also outlined plans to end tax breaks for dynasty trusts and close loopholes in the estate and gift tax, with an eye toward ensuring that the wealthiest Americans could no longer use legal gimmicks to avoid paying their fair share.

What kind of money are we talking about? When I proposed the bill, with support from a number of my Senate colleagues, we estimated that it would produce $430 billion in revenues in a decade. Specifically:

- The Walton family, the owners of Walmart, would pay up to $85.8 billion more in taxes on their $221.5 billion fortune.

- The family of Jeff Bezos, the founder of Amazon, would pay up to $44.4 billion more in taxes on his $178 billion fortune.
- The family of Elon Musk would pay up to $40.4 billion more in taxes on his $162 billion fortune.
- Facebook CEO Mark Zuckerberg's family would pay up to $25.3 billion more in taxes on his $101.7 billion fortune.

The Corporate Tax Dodging Prevention Act was even more ambitious. It set out to raise over $2.3 trillion in revenue by preventing corporations from shifting their profits offshore to avoid paying U.S. taxes. It also proposed to restore the top corporate tax rate to 35 percent—which was hardly a radical idea, as that's what it was before Donald Trump and his allies restructured tax policy to make it easier for corporations to avoid paying any taxes at all.

Reversing what Trump and Republicans like former House Speaker Paul Ryan did to benefit corporations is really just a first step. But it is an essential one, as it undoes a circumstance that—in the first year after Trump signed the 2017 Republican tax bill into law—allows more than ninety Fortune 500 companies to not only avoid paying federal income taxes, but to actually receive massive tax rebate checks from the IRS. Remarkably, in 2018:

- Amazon received a $129 million check from the IRS after making $10.8 billion in profits
- Delta received a $187 million check from the IRS after making $5.1 billion in profits
- Chevron received a $181 million check from the IRS after making $4.5 billion in profits

With language barring corporations from sheltering profits in tax havens like Bermuda and the Cayman Islands, the Corporate Tax Dodging Prevention Act was designed to stop giving tax breaks to corporations—and their owners—for shipping jobs overseas. It also outlined plans to:

- End the rule allowing American corporations to pay a lower or zero-percent tax rate on offshore earnings compared to domestic income
- Close loopholes allowing American corporations to shift income between foreign countries to avoid U.S. taxes
- Repeal "check the box" loopholes for offshoring money
- Prevent multinational corporations from stripping earnings out of the United States by manipulating debt expenses
- Prevent American corporations from claiming to be foreign by using a tax-haven post office box as their address

I was proud of these detailed proposals—not just because they made sense but because they opened up a discussion about using tax policy to address inequality.

Legislative initiatives to tax the rich are often framed as efforts to raise funds for noble and necessary purposes, such as providing health care for all Americans or making college free. That's a good argument, to my mind. I agree with Gabriel Zucman, a professor of economics at the University of California–Berkeley, when he says, "What makes nations prosperous is not the sanctification of a tiny number of ultra-wealthy individuals; it is investment in health care and education for all." But the benefits that extend from taxing the wealthiest Americans go beyond budgetary considerations. Fair and progressive taxation, which has as its goal the redistribution of the nation's largesse from a handful of billionaires to the great mass of Americans, is one of the best ways to tackle wealth inequality, address the long-term damage done by systemic racism, and free up working Americans to create, innovate, and strengthen the United States.

History and common sense tell us that the market will not get it right. More than a century ago, former president Theodore Roosevelt, a Republican who possessed considerable wealth of his own, recognized that taxing extreme wealth was necessary not merely to collect revenues but to preserve and extend democracy. "The ab-

sence of effective state, and, especially, national, restraint upon un-
fair money-getting has tended to create a small class of enormously
wealthy and economically powerful men, whose chief object is to
hold and increase their power," he warned in the 1910 "New Nationalism" speech, where he outlined a plan to "change the conditions
which enable these men to accumulate power which it is not for the
general welfare." At the heart of Teddy Roosevelt's plan was an ambitious wealth tax that targeted both the income and the estates of the
robber barons of his time.

Today, taxing the rich is one of the most popular ideas in American politics. A Reuters/Ipsos poll from 2020 found that 64 percent of
voters agreed that "the very rich should contribute an extra share of
their total wealth each year to support public programs." Yet Democrats remain cautious about using tax policy to right the course of the
nation. That caution is wrongheaded. They should be inspired by
President Franklin Delano Roosevelt, who explained in 1935, "People know that vast personal incomes come not only through the effort or ability or luck of those who receive them, but also because of
the opportunities for advantage which Government itself contributes. Therefore, the duty rests upon the Government to restrict such
incomes by very high taxes."

How high?

Earlier in this book, I described the Make Billionaires Pay Act,
which I proposed at the height of the pandemic. The measure would
have imposed a 60 percent tax on the wealth gains made by 467 billionaires between March 18, 2020, and January 1, 2021.

But why stop at one year? And why see progressive, necessary
taxation as only an emergency response?

This isn't a radical new idea. President Franklin Roosevelt's administration used a tax on the windfalls of the wealthy to prevent
profiteering during World War II. It was far more aggressive than
anything proposed by contemporary lawmakers: Top tax rates could
go as high as 90 percent on the excess profits of corporations, and
95 percent for wealthy individuals. These taxes worked so well dur-

ing the war that they were continued in its aftermath. Under Republican president Dwight Eisenhower, who served during the economic boom times of the 1950s, the top tax rate for the wealthiest Americans was around 92 percent. America thrived. Unions were strong. Working-class Americans could afford to support themselves and buy homes on a single income. Inequality existed, but not like today. In the early 1950s, the richest 20 percent of Americans controlled 42.8 percent of wealth. That was too much. But as we know, today, concentration of wealth is accelerating at such a rapid rate that there is a lively discussion in the financial press about which of these ultra-billionaires will be America's first trillionaire. We shouldn't have trillionaires. And we shouldn't have billionaires.

5

ENDING GREED IN THE HEALTH CARE SYSTEM

Health care is a human right, not a privilege

W e all want to live long, happy, and productive lives. We want the health and strength we need to have a meaningful work life. We want to avoid chronic and debilitating illness. We want to remain mobile. We want to have good sight and hearing. We want our cognitive faculties to remain strong. We want to be around long enough to welcome our great-grandchildren into the world.

The quality of health care that a nation provides is not only a major factor in determining whether we achieve those goals; it gets to the heart of what a country stands for and what its values are. In a sense, there is nothing more important. Do we really ascribe to the lofty words in our Declaration of Independence that "all men are created equal, that they are endowed by their Creator with certain unalienable Rights, that among these are Life, Liberty and the pursuit of Happiness"? Or is our quality of life, our health, and our longevity determined by how much money we have and by the greed of very powerful special interests?

A System That Works for Investors, Not Patients

The current American health care system is working exactly the way it is designed to operate—for the people who own it. In 2021, the health care industry made over $100 billion in profits, stock prices soared, and the CEOs of insurance companies and drug companies received extremely generous compensation packages. As a result of billions spent on lobbyists and campaign contributions, the industry is one of the dominant political players in Congress and state legislatures, has enormous influence within both major political parties, and significantly influences national health care policy. What more can be said? Our health care system is a true American success story.

But, you might ask, *how is the health care system doing for ordinary Americans, the people who utilize the system as opposed to the people who own the system?*

Well, that's a very different story. For the average American our current health care system is a disaster—extremely expensive, inaccessible, and bureaucratic. In fact, it is a broken system that must be completely transformed.

One of the great political challenges we now face is whether to maintain a system designed to create enormous profits and wealth for the insurance companies, the drug companies, and the billionaires who own them; or do we create a new system based on the principle that health care is a human right and that every man, woman, and child in this country should, in a cost-effective way, be guaranteed quality and equitable health care regardless of their economic status. Do we continue the national embarrassment of remaining the only major country on earth not to provide health care to all? Further, should our system prioritize wellness and disease prevention and the creation of a healthy society, rather than just the treatment of illness?

With regard to the current health care system, here's where we are today. According to a West Health–Gallup poll published in March 2022, "An estimated 112 million (44 percent) American adults are struggling to pay for health care, and more than double that number (93 percent) feel that what they do pay is not worth the cost." The report tells us: "Americans are finding it increasingly harder to pay for health care. Over the past year, the percentage of Americans who report skipping needed care due to cost has increased to 30 percent. Meanwhile, nearly the same percentage of Americans, 29 percent, report that they could not access affordable care if they needed it today. But a lack of affordability is not the only issue affecting Americans' experiences with the health care system— they are also dissatisfied with its value. More than half of the country (52 percent) reports that the care provided is simply not worth the cost. And in an open-ended question, 38 percent of respondents, representing an estimated 97 million adults, used the word 'expensive' to characterize the health care system, while another 13 percent used the word 'broken,' the second-most-used word."

In America, we spend almost twice as much per capita on health care as the people of any other country, over $12,530 each year for every man, woman, and child—a total of $4 trillion, or about 20 percent of our GDP. This is an astronomical expenditure, and it continues to rapidly increase and devour the resources of individuals, families, businesses, and government at an unsustainable rate.

In comparison, the United Kingdom spends just $5,268 per capita on health care, Canada spends $5,370, France spends $5,564, and Germany spends $6,731. At a fraction of the amount that we spend, all these countries guarantee health care to all their people.

One might think that with this huge outlay of money, the quality of health care in the United States would be the very best in the world. Wrong. Very wrong.

The sad truth is that, despite the enormous amount of money we spend, the American health care system ranks close to the bottom of major industrialized nations in outcomes: longevity, accessibility, coverage, equity, and efficiency. In other words, we are getting a terrible return on our huge expenditure on health care.

The essential problem of our "system" is that it is not really a system. It is a disjointed, complicated, non-transparent collection of thousands of entities dominated by powerful forces who have made health care a commodity, and who seek to gain huge profits from it. The goal of this "system" is not to cure disease or keep people healthy. It is to make as much money as possible for the people who own it.

In a rapidly changing world, with new challenges and technologies, no country has a "perfect" system—and never will. The question that must be asked, however, is: What is the *goal* of the system? Should an entire layer of corporate bureaucracy called "insurance companies"—which employ hundreds of thousands of people who have absolutely nothing to do with the actual *provision* of health care—be allowed to continue determining policies and priorities with the sole purpose of maximizing profits?

The CEOs of top insurance companies, each of whom makes tens of millions a year in compensation, do not perform heart surgery or brain surgery. They don't treat people who are suffering with cancer, diabetes, Alzheimer's disease, COVID, or mental illness. They don't keep our children healthy and provide annual checkups. They don't do the research we need to discover the causes of terrible illnesses that afflict millions. They don't build hospitals or clinics or educate medical and nursing students.

That doesn't make them "evil" or "terrible" people. They aren't supposed to do those things. That's not their job. They are businesspeople, and their sole purpose in the "industry" (funny name for health care) is to make as much money as possible for their stockholders and for themselves—and they do that very well.

If the goal of insurance company CEOs and their employees is NOT to provide quality care for all, if their goal is NOT to implement a cost-effective system, if their goal is NOT to prevent disease and create a healthy society, if their goal is NOT to accomplish anything that will lower their profit margins, then what has been the result of their efforts?

60,000 Unnecessary Deaths and $60 Billion in Profits

Today, because of the profiteering, dysfunctionality, and misplaced priorities of the current system, over 85 million Americans are uninsured or underinsured. From 2016 through 2020, in the richest country on earth, there were over 437,000 GoFundMe medical campaigns for Americans who had no other way to pay their doctor or hospital bills. They had to beg for money in order to get medical treatment.

In fact, while it is rarely discussed, our health care system is so flawed, so feckless, that over sixty thousand Americans die each year because they do not get the care they need when they need it. These are people who get sick and wait and hope that their condition will improve. Sometimes that doesn't happen—and they die. Sometimes they suffer for years. What an unspeakable outrage! Sixty thousand people die from preventable deaths every year in the United States while insurance companies make huge profits.

Meanwhile, the six largest health insurance companies in America made over $60 billion in profits in 2021, led by the UnitedHealth Group, which made $24 billion. And, not surprisingly, the CEOs in the industry receive huge compensation packages. In 2021, the CEO of Centene, Michael Neidorff, made $20.6 million; the CEO of CVS Health, Karen Lynch, made $20.3 million; the CEO of Cigna, David Cordani, took home just under $20 million; and the CEO of Anthem, Gail Boudreaux, received more than $19 million in total compensation.

And then there is the pharmaceutical industry.

Prescription drug therapy is an integral part of modern-day medicine. Wonderful and effective drugs, newly developed and old, save lives and ease suffering. But, in America today, almost one out of four people are unable to afford the outrageously high cost of prescription drugs their doctors prescribe. Millions go to a doctor, get a diagnosis of their medical condition, but can't purchase the medicine they need in order to treat it. Many of them get sicker, and end up in the emergency room or the hospital—costing the system far more money than the prescription drugs would have cost, not to mention the personal suffering involved. How crazy is that?

At the same time, as we continue to pay by far the highest prices in the world for prescription drugs, the pharmaceutical industry, year after year, remains one of the most profitable industries in the country. In 2021, Pfizer, Johnson & Johnson, and AbbVie—three giant pharmaceutical companies—increased their profits by over 90 percent to $54 billion; and in 2020, the CEOs of just eight prescription drug companies made $350 million in total compensation.

A Failure of Morality

If a nation is morally judged by how we treat the weakest and most vulnerable among us, our health care system fails miserably. Our infant and maternal death rates are extremely high—and for minority communities are equivalent to those of impoverished third world countries.

Further, our current health care system fails to fully recognize that health care is more than just walking into a doctor's office or entering a hospital. It's about every aspect of our lives. It must be comprehensive.

Yes. Dental care is health care. Yet tens of millions of our people, including many seniors, cannot afford to see a dentist. Many of them end up with no teeth in their mouth, unable to chew food properly, or they have chronic pain that takes them into the emergency room for temporary relief. Others are unable to smile, embarrassed by missing front teeth—a true badge of poverty.

Yes. The treatment of mental illness is health care. Yet, as a result of the pandemic, our long-standing mental health crisis is worse than ever. In 2021 we lost over 100,000 people to drug overdoses, while suicide, alcoholism, depression, and anxiety are rising. The pandemic has been especially hard on young people whose school lives and relationships with friends have been radically disrupted. It has also severely impacted elderly people who have been unable to have regular contact with friends and family. In virtually every state in the country, distraught Americans are in desperate need of affordable mental health treatment and are unable to find it.

Yes. Providing services to millions of elderly and disabled Americans in their homes is health care. Yet our home health care system, with the extremely low wages it pays its workers, is currently under enormous pressure, unable to attract the staffing levels it needs. The result: Many seniors and people with disabilities are forced into nursing homes, at greater expense to the system, when they would prefer to remain at home with family and friends.

Meanwhile, there is little debate that many of our nursing homes, as reflected by the very high death rates they experienced because of COVID, are understaffed, in disarray, and endanger the well-being of their inhabitants.

Unbelievably, despite our huge expenditure in health care, our ill-thought and ineffectual system cannot even perform one of its most basic functions—providing an adequate number of doctors, nurses, dentists, and other health care personnel. The current shortage, exacerbated by the burnout experienced by many health care providers during the pandemic, will dramatically increase, if not immediately addressed, because of the aging and coming retirement of many health care professionals.

In recent years, I have worked to substantially increase funding for the National Health Service Corps. This federal program provides debt forgiveness and scholarships for doctors and nurses who practice in medically underserved areas. In fact, in the American

Rescue Plan, we tripled funding for this vitally important program. We are making some progress, but it's not enough.

Too Few Doctors in Too Few Places

Today, as just another manifestation of our broken system, many of our young health care practitioners leave school deeply in debt. I will never forget chatting with a young woman in Iowa who informed me that she had just graduated dental school with over $400,000 in student debt—which, unfortunately, is not uncommon for young dentists, doctors, and nurses.

Unlike many other countries, which provide free or inexpensive education for mental health, dental, and nursing students, our current system negatively impacts not only individual practitioners but the overall delivery of health care. Young medical and nursing school graduates, burdened with hundreds of thousands in student loans, gravitate toward the specialties and the geographical locations that will provide them the high incomes they need to pay off their debts as quickly as possible. Deeply in debt, they are not likely to flock to rural, medically underserved areas, where they are paid far less than their urban counterparts.

This contributes to another major crisis facing our dysfunctional health care system, which is that in many parts of the country, often communities that are rural and struggling economically, residents are seeing their local hospitals shut down, and are unable to find a doctor. In fact, there are now entire counties in America where there are no doctors, and where primary care is effectively unavailable. Patients in these medical deserts are forced to travel long distances to deliver a baby, get treatment for cancer, or respond to a heart attack.

Hospital emergency rooms are structured and staffed to deal with emergencies—accidents, shootings, and strokes. Their purpose is not to treat a case of the flu or an earache. Yet across the country, emergency rooms—which provide the most extensive primary care—are overflowing with patients seeking non-emergency treatment because they are unable to find a primary care doctor of their own. Primary care in an emergency room costs ten times more than in a community health center. Not a wise expenditure of health care dollars.

In terms of the long-term financial implications for our broken health care system, approximately half of all personal bankruptcies in this country, some 500,000 per year, are connected to unpaid medical bills. People with inadequate or no insurance leave a hospital with a huge bill. After being hounded by bill collectors, under great emotional duress, they conclude they'll never be able to pay it off. They go bankrupt. Then, after declaring bankruptcy, their credit-worthiness is destroyed and they face higher interest rates on anything they purchase, which exacerbates their spiral into poverty and economic instability. Our health care system is part of a vicious circle that destroys lives when it should be saving them.

Why Does the United States Make Getting Sick So Complicated?

Not only is the current system extremely expensive, it is so complex that millions of Americans simply cannot get the care they need—even when it is available, even when they are entitled to coverage, even when it is a matter of life and death.

The enormous amount of time and energy that Americans spend trying to navigate this unbelievably complicated insurance system drives many—including those who are already anxious because of the medical condition they are seeking treatment for—into despair. There is the filling-out of forms to determine eligibility. There are the arguments with the insurance company to determine whether a procedure is or is not covered. There are the endless discussions with some bureaucrat as to why a bill has not been paid. And if by chance you get sick or have an accident away from home and outside your "network," there is the question of how much additional cost you will incur.

The system's complexity is not only a problem for patients. One of the things that most demoralizes doctors, nurses, and their staffs are the hours spent arguing with insurance companies about how they can treat their patients.

At the heart of the crisis is the reality that we really do not have a health care *system*—like most modern industrialized countries do. What we have is a *non-system* that is enormously complex, bureaucratic, and fragmented. It leaves parents bewildered and caregivers frustrated.

Let's start with Medicaid. If you are below a certain income, which of course can change year to year, you may be eligible for this federal-state program. Because each state chooses to spend more or less money on the program, the benefits and coverage you are entitled to vary significantly depending upon where you live. Also, there is no guarantee that a doctor or a dentist will accept you, because Medicaid reimbursement rates are often too low and, in some communities, busy doctors and dentists simply don't want to treat lower-income people.

In our rapidly aging society, Medicaid is the major source of funding for nursing homes. Unfortunately, to be eligible to get that care, the patient must first deplete the life savings that he/she may have accumulated and had hoped to leave to their children. Many elderly people are forced to make anguishing decisions as to whether they provide for their children and grandchildren, or take care of themselves.

If you are over sixty-five you are entitled to Medicare, a federal program funded by the FICA tax that workers and their employers pay. Medicare, with a co-payment, does provide strong and comprehensive medical and hospital coverage. But if you want dental care, glasses, or a hearing aid, you will have to select and pay for one of dozens of private Medicare Advantage plans. Good luck in making the right choice.

Then there is the Affordable Care Act (Obamacare), which expanded Medicaid and provides federal subsidies for four levels of private insurance coverage—bronze, silver, gold, and platinum. Depending upon which plan you choose you will pay higher or lower premiums, deductibles, and co-payments. Needless to say, as your income fluctuates year to year, the amount of subsidy you receive also changes.

The Trouble with Tying Health Care to Jobs

Unlike every other major country on earth, all of which have universal health care coverage, most Americans continue to get their health care through their jobs. Within employer-based health care, the nature of your coverage depends upon the status of your job, the generosity of your employer, and whether you are represented by a union. There are literally hundreds of different plans—each with different degrees of coverage and cost. If you change your job, which millions of workers do every year, it is likely that your insurance coverage will change. That could mean a different network and different doctors, hospitals, and out-of-pocket costs. Worse yet, you could end up with no insurance at all.

The absurdity of basing health care coverage on one's job became very clear to all during the COVID-19 pandemic and the economic meltdown of 2020. As millions of workers lost their jobs, they also lost their health care coverage. No job, no health care—in the middle of a pandemic, when you need health care the most. That may make sense to someone. Not to me.

For many millions of low-wage workers at companies like Walmart, Starbucks, or the fast-food industry, the kind of coverage that is offered is often useless—because it is simply not affordable. The premiums are just too high for someone earning $10 or $15 an hour. If it's a question of paying for health care or rent and food, it's not much of a choice. You choose what you need tomorrow, having a roof over your head and eating, and hope that you and your kids don't get sick.

The quality of coverage for workers on employment-based health care plans varies widely. Some—but not many—American workers enjoy full and comprehensive coverage completely paid for by their employers. Others end up with junk plans where the coverage kicks in only after a very high out-of-pocket deductible has been paid. In other cases the plans only provide catastrophic care.

Generally speaking, as the cost of health care rises, employers are shifting more and more of the financial burden onto their employees. Most workers now must pay a considerable amount in out-of-pocket expenses—premiums, co-payments, and deductibles. As a result of this growing expense for workers, the bitterest labor disputes are increasingly centered around fights over health care benefits. The fight is always over how much *more* the employer wants workers to pay. Unions are often forced to give up wage increases and other benefits in order to hold on to barely decent insurance coverage.

As someone who has held hundreds of town meetings throughout the country, I have learned about another ugly and destructive aspect of our current health care system. Many workers stay at the jobs they have not because they like them, not because they are happy in their work, but because they *have* to stay in order to maintain decent health care coverage for their families. This reality has a significant impact upon our economy. How many great entrepreneurs, innovative businesspeople, and artists are unable to go out on their own because they will lose the health insurance they need? How many people become embittered, frustrated, and hateful because they are trapped in jobs they want to leave? Americans should not be chained to a job because of health insurance.

Economic Disparities Lead to Diseases of Despair

If we want to extend the lives of Americans, and to ensure that the quality of those lives is improved, it is a moral imperative that we create a universal, high-quality, and cost-effective health care system. Everyone, regardless of income, should have access to the medical treatment they need, as a human right.

But, if we want to create a truly healthy society, that is not enough. We must address the reality that millions of lower-income Americans are dying much too young because they live under enormous, sometimes debilitating, stress. We need to understand that our current economic system breeds massive income and wealth inequality that has a devastating impact on health outcomes.

Rich people in America live much longer lives than poor and working-class Americans. Rich people in America have less chronic illness and pain than poor and working-class Americans. Rich people in America experience less mental illness and addiction than poor and working-class Americans.

We know that a key factor to life expectancy and decent health is easy access to good-quality health care. Yet quality health care is not available to all Americans as a right. Rich people invariably get the care they need. Poor and working-class people don't enjoy that same guarantee. Rich people go to the doctor for regular checkups and screenings. Poor and working-class people often don't. Rich people get immediate medical attention when they feel sick or suffer injuries. Poor and working-class people often don't. Rich people, when they are hospitalized, end up in well-staffed and exclusive hospitals with experienced doctors and the latest technology. Poor and working-class people often don't. Rich people, if they need prescription drugs, can pay whatever it costs for the drugs that will prolong their lives or ease their pain. Poor and working-class people often can't.

It is said that wealth cannot buy happiness. Perhaps that is true. But it is undeniably true that poverty can lead to despair. Millions of Americans are dying young and are suffering from a myriad of diseases—heart disease, cancer, diabetes, asthma—because the conditions under which so many are forced to live, day after day, are counterproductive to good health. They are dying from what doctors refer to as "diseases of despair." People are becoming hopeless with regard to their future and relying on "self-medication" with alcohol and drugs to ease the pain. Far, far too many of them commit suicide.

More than a decade ago, as the chair of the U.S. Senate Subcommittee on Primary Health and Aging, I convened a hearing that asked,

"Is Poverty a Death Sentence?" The testimony that we heard from the panel, mostly physicians, was powerful, enlightening, and heartbreaking. It changed my perspective and led me to focus attention on diseases of despair in the ensuing years. I made these concerns central to my presidential campaigns, and to my service as chair of the Senate Budget Committee, because I knew we could no longer ignore the life-and-death consequences of economic inequality.

Over the years, I have spent a good deal of time with physicians and researchers who have helped me to understand what's referred to as "the physiology of poverty." In other words, poor people, who struggle every day just to survive, live under enormous levels of stress—day after day, month after month, year after year. This never-ending stress impacts not only their psychological well-being, but their physiology as well. Stress makes us sick. Stress kills. It's a factor in heart disease, cancer, high blood pressure, gastrointestinal problems, migraines, obesity, disrupted sleep patterns, and, all too often, alcohol and drug addiction. Wealthy and middle-class people don't worry much about whether there will be food on the table, whether there will be a roof over their heads, or whether they'll be able to get to the doctor when they are sick. Poor people do. Tens of millions of them. Every day is a painful and stressful struggle just to survive.

Imagine the stress that goes with trying to keep ahead of the bills when you are earning just $7.25 an hour. Or even $12 or $15 an hour. It's a daily struggle. How do you get by if you can't pay your electric bill or your phone bill? How do you deal with an unexpected expense, like the need for a medical test or a prescription for a child? What happens if your child is so sick that you have to miss a day of work? Will your boss understand? What happens if the car you use to get to your job breaks down? Will you be fired if you don't show up? Maybe you could work more hours; but how many hours a week can you work, and still be a good parent? Will you be able to stay in your apartment if the landlord raises the rent? If you've got to move, what happens when your child has to go to a new school? The stress keeps building. In desperation, do you take a loan from a payday lender? It's just $500, but the interest rate is 50 percent. How do you make the payments? Will you sink deeper into poverty?

I've had times in my life, especially as a young father in Burlington, when I had to struggle to make enough to pay the bills. But those periods passed reasonably quickly. When I imagine what it might be like to live in such a circumstance permanently, I can feel the tension building within me. There's a sense of hopelessness, and despair.

That's something that other countries strive to alleviate, with social-welfare states—like the ones found in the Scandinavian and Asian nations that lead the world in terms of life expectancy.

America's Declining Life-Expectancy Crisis

In the Senate, I hear my colleagues talk a lot about the cost of health care. But they never get around to discussing the biggest cost of all: the fact that Americans don't live as long as people in the countries with which we choose to compare ourselves.

Life expectancy isn't the only measure of the successes and failures of health care systems. But it's a damn good one. And if we look at the numbers, we quickly recognize that the United States is experiencing a life-expectancy crisis.

Even before the COVID pandemic, which hit the United States harder than other countries because we lack a coherent national health care system, life expectancy in the United States was trailing that of other developed countries. But the loss of more than one million lives to COVID was devastating. Because so many of those who died were essential workers, who were relatively young and often in the prime of their working lives, life expectancy in the United States collapsed from 78.86 years in 2019 to 76.99 years in 2020. In the second year of the pandemic, it kept going down, to 76.6 years, for a net loss of 2.26 years, according to a comprehensive study published in early 2022—the biggest drop for the nation since 1943, the deadliest year of World War II. That decline was horrific. But what was even more horrific was the fact that, as Dr. Steven Woolf, an author of the study noted, "While other high-income countries saw their life expectancy increase in 2021, recovering about half of their losses, U.S. life expectancy continued to fall." That, said Woolf, "speaks volumes about the life consequences of how the U.S. handled the pandemic." It also speaks volumes about the fact that the United States went into the pandemic in a weak position.

For decades, countries around the world have been surpassing the United States when it comes to life expectancy. The average American now lives six years less than the average Norwegian and South Korean, and five years less than the average individual in France, Spain, Italy, and New Zealand. Overall, life expectancy in the United States is four years behind the average of all the comparable nations that the scholars studied.

Think about that. The simple fact that you are an American means that you can expect to live forty-eight months less than someone born and raised in Germany; sixty months less than someone in France, seventy-two months less than someone in Norway. As an average American, you will die 2,200 days earlier than the average South Korean. That's 2,200 fewer days to enjoy retirement, to travel, to spend time with your grandchildren.

"We spend a fortune on medical care and we're a high-income country," Noreen Goldman, a demographer at Princeton University, said after the relative life-expectancy numbers for the United States and comparable countries were published in 2022. "We should be able to do far better."

Goldman's bottom line was blunt: "Shame on us!"

But the shame is not just found in the comparison between our country and others. It can be found within the United States.

Rich People Live, Poor People Die

An enormous and growing gap has opened between how long wealthy Americans live as opposed to low-income and working-class people.

This disparity reveals much more about inequality in America than the usual measures of poverty and economic distress. It's not about what we possess and how much material comfort we have. When it comes to health care and health, the deprivation and struggles and pain of the poor and working class are matters of life and death. If you're rich, you're likely to live a long life. If you're poor, your life will be shorter. Period.

If you are an average man who lives in McDowell County, West Virginia, one of the poorest counties in this country, you will live to be sixty-four years of age. If you are an average man who lives in Fairfax County, Virginia, one of the wealthiest counties in the country, you will live to age eighty-two. A mere 350 miles separate McDowell County and Fairfax County, yet if you live in the wealthier jurisdiction, you get an extra eighteen years of life. If you live on the Pine Ridge Indian Reservation in South Dakota, a very low-income community where I hosted a town meeting in 2016, male life expectancy is just sixty-two years. That's fifteen years less than a non-Native man living eighty miles away in Rapid City, South Dakota.

Huge gaps in life expectancy aren't found only when we compare different regions in the United States. We can find them in different neighborhoods in the same cities. In Washington, D.C., for example, a 2014 study by the Virginia Commonwealth University Center on Society and Health found that the life-expectancy differential was twenty-seven years between those who lived in the Trinidad neighborhood near Gallaudet University as opposed to those living in the Foxhall section of Georgetown. The differential between the Suitland and Tysons neighborhoods in the D.C. metro area was nineteen years. Readers will not be surprised to learn that the Trinidad and Suitland communities are predominantly Black and low-income. Foxhall and Tysons are mostly white and affluent.

In September 2019, at my request, the General Accountability Office (GAO) issued a report on the impacts of income and wealth inequality in the United States. The study examined Americans who were aged fifty-one to sixty-one in 1992 and looked at how many survived the ensuing decades. Fewer than half of the people in the poorest 20 percent of wealth distribution had survived to 2014. Among the richest 20 percent, 75.5 percent were still alive. Overwhelmingly, the wealthy lived, and the poor died.

This truth was starkly illustrated during the COVID pandemic. With a lethal virus taking the lives of hundreds of thousands and spreading rapidly all across the country, millions of workers faced a simple, yet devastating, question: *Do I go to work, interact with others, and run the risk of catching the virus, or do I stay home, isolate myself, and protect my health and life?*

The reality, however, was that not every worker had the luxury of asking that question or making that choice. More than half of American workers live paycheck to paycheck. They didn't have the option of not going to work. In an uber-capitalist system, if you don't go to work, you don't get paid. If you don't get paid, you're unable to feed your family or cover the rent. Millions of Americans sorted out that awful equation by heading to work. They didn't do so with confidence that they would be protected—there were New York City transit workers who were so certain that they would fall ill that they slept in their cars or rented rooms rather than go home and infect their families. These people went to work not by choice but out of desperation. And tens of thousands of them—nurses, airline attendants, bus drivers, postal workers, restaurant employees, factory workers, grocery store clerks—died because they lacked the wealth and privilege that would have allowed them to choose to stay home and stay safe.

The stresses related to economic insecurity play an enormously important role in causing the illnesses that many low-income and working-class people experience. But they are not the only factors wreaking havoc on the lives of working people. Millions of struggling Americans, in both urban and rural areas, live in communities where the air is polluted, the drinking water is unsafe, and the soil and buildings are filled with toxins. It is estimated that some 200,000 Americans die from illnesses caused by air pollution alone, and that number disproportionately comes from low-income and Black communities. Wealthy people don't often live near factories that emit high levels of pollutants into the air. They don't live in neighborhoods with high levels of lead in the water.

Our job, therefore, as we build a new America, is not only to provide health care for all with no out-of-pocket expenses, but to address the root causes as to why our current economic system is so destructive to human health. It is a demand that grows more urgent by the day. Indeed, for millions of poor and working-class Americans, this is a life-and-death mission.

Some of the best answers for how to address the crisis can be found just across the border in Canada.

On the Border Between Life and Death

During my 2020 presidential campaign I wanted to make a point about the high cost of prescription drugs in America. So I took a busload of people from Detroit, Michigan, to Windsor, Ontario. These people were diabetics who needed insulin to stay alive. While on the one-hour bus trip I learned about their lives. One of the people I spoke with was a young man who had played football in college and refused to tell his financially strapped family that he couldn't afford to buy the amount of insulin that he needed. He rationed his insulin, as millions in America do. He became sick and almost died. In Windsor, at a small neighborhood drugstore, he and the others on the bus were able to purchase the same exact insulin products for one-tenth of the price they would have had to pay in the United States. Canada, like every other major country, negotiates prescription drug prices with the pharmaceutical industry. We don't, and we pay as much as ten times what the Canadians do.

The health care situation in our country today is so absurd, so barbaric, that there are people who are extremely ill or who have had major accidents who hesitate to go into a hospital or call an ambulance in an emergency because they fear the unaffordable bills. They worry about what these bills will do to the family budget, and how many years it will take to pay them off. They literally can't afford to be sick or injured. I recently talked to a colleague of mine who mentioned that her niece was billed $1,000,000 for a serious, but not life-threatening, back operation. A million dollars.

And, when we talk about hospital bills within the irrational and wasteful system that we now have, understand that the cost of a medical procedure in a hospital varies widely depending on where you live. The bill you receive for having a baby, an MRI, a colonoscopy, or hip replacement is not primarily dependent on clinical issues but on "hospital market share," location, and the nature of insurance coverage. Even at the same hospital, a *New York Times* investigation found that identical procedures were billed at dramatically different prices for different insurance plans.

The difference in the cost of hospital procedures in the United States compared with other countries, all of which have national health care systems, is off the charts. According to Tom Sackville, chief executive of the International Federation of Health Plans, the United States spends "two or three or five times more than it should, by international standards." The federation found, for example, that "the average cost of an MRI scan (in the United States) was $1,119, compared to $811 in New Zealand, $215 in Australia, and $181 in Spain."

What Happens When Health Care Is Recognized as a Right

Norway is regarded as one of the most advanced countries in the world. What that means, according to the Norwegian government, is that state and local authorities have a responsibility for ensuring that all Norway's inhabitants have access to health care and other essentials of life. Government policy is that "every member of society shall enjoy these benefits; they are not just for rich people and they are not just emergency aid for the poorest people in society."

When I held a livestream discussion in April 2022 with Anniken Krutnes, Norway's ambassador to the United States, several million people heard her explain that "we appreciate a society where we have a safety net, where we know that if our neighbor or families or friends fall, they are OK. We have a lot of trust in society. We know that we don't have to worry about the big things in life, except your own health. Of course health is a worry, but the economy of health is not an issue. We know we have the possibility to give our kids a bright future, with good education, with health care, with childcare. I'm so happy that my three children can go ahead and have babies and they have interesting work and they can develop. That's what they appreciate. At this point, that is more important to us than enormous wealth."

People in Norway understand that they are guaranteed to receive the basic necessities of life for free or minimal cost. That does a lot to reduce stress, and to make people happy. Norway does not just enjoy high life expectancy; it is regularly ranked as one of the happiest countries in the world. Why? "How happy we are with our lives is often tightly connected to how safe we feel, our financial conditions, and our degree of access to meaningful work and social relations," explains psychologist Ragnhild Bang Nes, who studies well-being with the Norwegian Institute of Public Health. "In Norway, we have a welfare system that takes care of us and saves us from a lot of worries. The inequality is low when it comes to the standard of living. We feel safe and free and have a strong sense of belonging."

That sense of belonging equates not just with health but with happiness.

In Denmark, too, studies consistently report that the people are among the happiest in the world. When I asked Danish parliamentarian Dan Jørgensen why he thought this was so, he explained, "The short answer is that it's because of the welfare state. We have free health care, so you don't pay money when you go to your own normal doctor . . . Education doesn't cost you anything. We don't pay tuition in Denmark; actually, if you are a student, you get a grant from the government." Yes, this costs money, Jørgensen explained. "It's true that we do pay a lot in tax, but we also get a lot back. You get the security that you know that if something happens to you, if you lose your job, you get Social Security. If you get sick, you'll get health care. When you look at what you get for the money, most people in Denmark, I will argue, are happy to pay the tax that they do."

Denmark isn't perfect. Jørgensen acknowledges that, for the top 1 percent of people, it might be better to live in the United States. But for the other 99 percent, he told me, Denmark offers higher average wages, better services, more security, and yes, more happiness.

Too often, Americans lack the sense of safety and belonging that people enjoy in countries with a robust health care system that, in every case, is based around a universal health care program. No wonder so many of us succumb to diseases of despair.

What We Don't Know Could Kill Us

The American people are, by and large, unaware of the benefits that major countries around the world provide their citizens. They don't know how far behind we are with regard to childcare, paid family and medical leave, guaranteed vacation time, and other social benefits. Most Americans certainly don't know that we are the only major nation not to guarantee health care as a human right, that we spend far more on health care than other countries, and that, in many respects, the quality of our care is not as good.

This ignorance is not an accident. The less we know about what is available to people in other countries, the less likely we are to demand health care and other services as a right. When people don't even know what to ask for, the ruling class rests easy. In order to counter corporate media blackout with regard to international health care systems, I've done my best to educate Americans about what other countries have achieved. Sometimes I get criticized for making so many international comparisons. But this is a case where knowledge really will set us free.

In November 2017 I traveled to Toronto, Canada, with a number of American doctors, nurses, and media. We met with Canadian physicians, toured a major hospital, and met with the Premier of Ontario. What impressed me most about the visit was how fiercely the Canadians believed that health care was a right, that all people should be treated equally, and that there should be no cost attached to a stay at a hospital or a doctor's visit.

In the United States, there is a lot of intentional disinformation about the Canadian health care system. In their desperation to block efforts to create a universal health care system in America, politicians and many in the media simply carry water for the health care industry and refuse to acknowledge the strength and popularity of what exists in Canada. In other words, they lie.

In March 2014, I invited Dr. Danielle Martin, a Canadian physician, to explain the system in which she practices, at a hearing I chaired with the Senate Health Committee. During the course of the hearing, Senator Richard Burr, a conservative Republican from North Carolina, peddled the usual misinformation about the Canadian system. This time, however, there was a knowledgeable Canadian physician who could respond, and respond effectively. The interaction between Senator Burr and Dr. Martin drew considerable media attention, in both the Canadian and American press. I was stunned when more than 1.7 million people watched the video of the exchange on the website of the advocacy group Physicians for a National Health Program. Hundreds of thousands more tuned in on YouTube and other platforms.

The *Los Angeles Times* posted the video under the headline "Watch an Expert Teach a Smug U.S. Senator About Canadian Healthcare." A CBC radio report in Canada declared, "Canadian Doctor Schools U.S. Senator on Public Health Care." The headline in Canada's *National Post* read, "Toronto Doctor Smacks Down U.S. Senate Question on Canadian Waitlist Deaths."

It was a compelling exchange. Senator Burr asked, "On average, how many Canadian patients on a waiting list die each year?" Dr. Martin replied, "I don't [know], sir, but I know that there are 45,000 in America who die waiting because they don't have insurance at all."

I suspect that many of the millions of Americans who saw my

2022 livestream with Ambassador Krutnes—or clips from it—were surprised to learn that, in Norway, no matter how much time you might spend in a hospital, no matter how many doctor visits you might make, no matter how many prescription drugs you might use, you cannot spend more than $350 a year for health care.

Not one cent more.

We Should Start Listening to Nurses

On May 12, 2022, as chairman of the Senate Budget Committee, I held a hearing on the need to reform health care in the United States and move to a Medicare for All system. One of the panelists at that hearing was Bonnie Castillo, the president of National Nurses United, which with a membership of 225,000 is the largest nurses' union in the country.

Like a growing number of health care professionals, Castillo sees, every day, the frustrations that the nurses she works with experience as they try to provide quality care to patients in a crumbling system.

"In my testimony today," she explained, "I will use the experiences of registered nurses from across the country to illustrate how the current health care system is fundamentally unable to provide the therapeutic quality care that our patients need and deserve. By erecting financial barriers to care, it provides starkly disparate care to different people and communities and, for many, provides no care at all. It is also financially inefficient and wasteful for the country as a whole."

Castillo put the pieces of the puzzle together as she explained that:

> Nurses watch as too many patients forgo needed medications, procedures, or care because they cannot afford the costs. They watch as insurance corporations refuse to cover critical care that is required for the health and well-being of patients. In-

surers override the professional judgment of licensed health care professionals, and nurses can do little about it when our patients do not get the care that they need. Nurses watch as patients finally come to the hospital emergency room with advanced stages of illness or disease that could have been prevented if they had access to treatment earlier. The system we have now is beholden to the corporate interests that determine who gets treatment, and what treatment they get. It is deeply inefficient and unsustainable because it prioritizes short-term financial returns rather than long-term investments in our health. This leads to a system that is unaffordable for our country and for our patients.

Nurses are on the front line of our health care crisis. More than five thousand of them died taking care of us during the pandemic. We owe them an enormous debt of gratitude. We can begin to repay that debt by listening to their arguments in favor of a Medicare for All system where everyone is covered—as a right—by a single-payer, government-administered system similar to what exists in other countries around the world.

Indeed, if we start listening to health care professionals, we will quickly recognize that the movement for a Medicare for All system has already gained widespread support among the people who work in our current health care system.

In addition to National Nurses United, advocates for a single-payer program include Physicians for a National Health Care Program, which has more than twenty thousand members. So does the American College of Physicians. Indeed, according to *Becker's Healthcare*, groups supporting some form of single-payer system include:

American Association of Community Psychiatrists
American Medical Association—Medical Student Section
American Medical Student Association
American Medical Women's Association

American Nurses Association

American Public Health Association

Health Care for the Homeless

Latino Medical Student Association

National Association of Social Workers

National Health Care for the Homeless Council

National Medical Association

Puerto Rican College of Physicians and Surgeons

"There's been a sea change in the way we talk about health care reform," Dr. Adam Gaffney, an instructor at Harvard Medical School and the president of Physicians for a National Health Program, recently told *Time* magazine. Gaffney says that support for Medicare for All is growing among young physicians, nurses, and health practitioners. They know a change has got to come.

Making Medicare for All a Reality

In 1965, President Lyndon Baines Johnson signed the Medicare and Medicaid Act into law, declaring that the time had finally come to end "the injustice which denies the miracle of healing to the old and to the poor." Today, almost six decades later, Medicare is the most popular health care program in America, providing comprehensive health care coverage for all those sixty-five and older. It's also the best model for health care reform in the United States.

In the face of a dysfunctional and failing health care system, the time is long overdue for us to improve and expand Medicare to cover all Americans, and that is what I have proposed with Medicare for All legislation, which would provide comprehensive health care coverage, without out-of-pocket expense, for every man, woman, and child in the country regardless of age, family income, or geographical location. It is a system based on addressing the health needs of the American people, not the profit needs of insurance companies and the pharmaceutical industry.

Under Medicare for All, there will no longer be insurance premiums, deductibles, or co-payments. No more worrying about whether you can afford to see a doctor, no more arguing with insurance agents about the nature of your coverage, no more being hounded by bill collectors for unpaid medical bills, no more worries about going bankrupt from a hospital bill.

This legislation not only expands Medicare to cover all Americans, it also significantly improves upon the services for elderly and disabled Americans who are covered by the existing Medicare program—providing coverage for dental, hearing, and vision care.

Under Medicare for All, there will be no more private "networks," which limit choice as to where Americans can get their medical care. Instead, there will be something we now lack in the United States: complete freedom of choice as to the doctor and hospital you want.

The comprehensive coverage under Medicare for All includes inpatient and outpatient hospital care; emergency services; primary and preventive services; prescription drugs; mental health and substance abuse treatment; maternity and newborn care; pediatrics; home- and community-based long-term services and supports; dental, audiology, and vision services.

This legislation would be phased in over a five-year period. The first year would expand Medicare to cover dental, vision, and hearing, cover all young people under eighteen, reduce the eligibility age to fifty-five, and eliminate deductibles. The second year would lower the eligibility age to forty-five. In the third year, the eligibility age would go down to thirty-five. By the end of the fourth year, everyone would be covered.

The comprehensiveness and simplicity of a Medicare for All system not only benefit individuals and families; they aid the business community and our overall economy by ending the costly and uneven system of employer-based health care. As all Americans would have health care coverage as a right, small- and medium-sized businesses would be free to focus on their core business goals instead of wasting precious energy and resources navigating an absurdly complex system to provide health insurance to their employees. Large corporations would also benefit, as they would no longer be at a disadvantage with competitors in countries where workers are covered by national health systems.

For workers in our economy, Medicare for All means that if you change jobs, you don't have to change insurance plans or worry about losing the coverage you and your family depend upon.

Medicare for All will also significantly benefit health care providers, who can spend more time with their patients and less time doing paperwork. Caring young people will graduate medical and nursing schools knowing that their responsibility is to improve life for their patients—not to argue with insurance companies. A universal health care system will also allow the country to invest more resources in provider education and training. With a rational system in place, we can end the massive shortages we now have in doctors, nurses, dentists, and other providers. We will also make smart investments to adequately staff underserved areas and ensure communities can access the providers they need—especially rural regions that have become "medical deserts" under the current system.

We Can Afford a Healthy America

The major reason the current health care system in the United States is so expensive is that it operates on an uber-capitalist model that is geared to the needs of insurance companies, not patients. Squeezing as much profit out of patients as possible requires an enormously complicated and bureaucratic system that runs up hundreds of billions in administrative costs. In hospitals that often lack an adequate number of doctors and nurses, there are basements full of people who never see a patient. All they do is bill, bill, and bill. During the height of the COVID pandemic, hospitals were shutting down elective medical services because they didn't have enough patients. Somehow, however, the health care industry never shuts down its billing.

Getting rid of all that insurance-industry bureaucracy and all that billing would result in enormous savings for Americans, argues Dr. Gaffney. As he recently told the Senate Budget Committee in written testimony, "In 2017, 34 percent of healthcare spending was devoted to administration in the US—approximately twice the proportion spent on administration in Canada's single-payer national health insurance system. Much of this administrative expense stems from the wasteful bureaucracy inherent to private health insurance. Compared to a public insurer like traditional Medicare, private insurers inflict numerous added costs, including profits for shareholders, bloated executive salaries, product and benefit design, marketing, and burdensome processes for disputing claims (needed to maximize profit)."

Dr. Gaffney went on to say that "reducing insurance overhead for the overall US healthcare system to that of traditional Medicare could unlock enormous savings—funds that can then be used to cover the costs of a generous coverage expansion for all. And indeed, the CBO [Congressional Budget Office] has estimated savings from such a reduction in insurance costs at over $400 billion annually."

Under Medicare for All, doctors and nurses and hospitals could eliminate bureaucratic hurdles that waste tens of billions a year. In the United States, noted Dr. Gaffney, "physician practices spend more than $80,000 annually, per physician, to cover the costs of interactions with insurers—almost four-fold higher than Canada."

Billions can be saved by addressing the profiteering and the bureaucracy associated with the insurance industry. Tens of billions can be saved by taking on Big Pharma. That would happen under a Medicare for All system, which would do what every other major country does: negotiate prices with the pharmaceutical industry. Instead of paying the highest prices in the world for prescription drugs, we could save hundreds of billions over a ten-year period through the plan for tough negotiations with the drug companies that my legislation outlines. Just doing what the Veterans Administration does in terms of negotiating drug prices would cut prescription drug expenditures in half.

All these savings add up.

In 2020 and 2022, the Congressional Budget Office (CBO)—the non-partisan agency that analyzes budget issues for Congress—considered four options for moving to a single-payer system. They found that in all four scenarios a single-payer program would save the American people between $42 billion and $743 billion every year, beginning in 2030.

The option that most resembles the Medicare for All bill that I have introduced would save the health care system $650 billion a year, beginning in 2030, while covering every man, woman, and child with no premiums, no deductibles, and no co-payments. These savings include a $14 billion reduction in administrative costs and a $508 billion reduction in payments to health care providers and pharmaceutical companies—offset by $272 billion in additional spending as a result of an increased use of the health care system.

It's a lie to say that the United States cannot afford to provide quality health care for every American. The truth is that we cannot afford the insurance industry that denies health care to ailing Americans while wasting hundreds of billions of dollars to maintain an unnecessary bureaucracy and to enrich investors.

We Can Overcome an Uber-Capitalist System That Puts Profit Ahead of Health

Despite the massive amounts of money spent to prevent an honest discussion of Medicare for All, despite the buying of politicians from both political parties, despite the corporate media blackout of advocacy for Medicare for All, despite the same media's failure to tell the story of how universal coverage works in other countries, the American people understand, from their day-to-day experiences, that this country's health care system is a disaster and must be changed. Poll after poll shows overwhelming support for Medicare for All. In August 2020, for instance, a Hill-HarrisX poll put the support level at 67 percent.

The fight for Medicare for All is really a fight for our health, and for the rest of our lives. As such, it is an integral part—perhaps the most integral part—of the political revolution that is needed to get this country headed in the right direction. A direction that is no longer dominated by a billionaire class that could care less about the health of ordinary Americans.

Charting the right course, the humane and healthy course, for this country isn't going to be easy. We're battling against the most powerful economic and political forces in the world. But I have no doubt that we will succeed in making health care what it must be: a fully recognized, and fully supported, human right.

On that day, every American will be able to walk into a doctor's office when they get sick and receive the care they need—without having to fill out piles of forms, without having to max out their credit cards.

On that day, Americans will be able to enter a hospital, get the surgery they need and be able to focus on getting well as soon as possible—without the stress of having to worry about whether getting well will bankrupt them.

On that day, Americans, regardless of income, will be able to secure the prescription drugs their doctors prescribe. They will not have to ration pills that cost more than they can afford. And scientists will be freed to concentrate on developing breakthrough drugs, rather than tailoring their research so that pharmaceutical firms can maintain record profits. There will be enough doctors, nurses, and dentists in every part of our country to provide the quality care that our people need, and young people will not have to go deeply into debt because they want to care for their fellow men, women, and children.

On that day, we will have a health care system based on human need, not uber-capitalist profiteering. We will begin to get healthy as a nation—truly healthy—and we will start to live the longer and more fulfilling lives that must be universally understood as our birthright as Americans.

6

WHICH SIDE ARE YOU ON?

*Choosing the side of the working class
in an age of deadly inequality*

Eugene Victor Debs, the railroad workers' union leader who
was the Socialist Party's great organizer and presidential
contender in the first decades of the twentieth century,
declared more than one hundred years ago that "the fruits of labor
must be enjoyed by the working class." Debs has been my hero
since I was a young man, when I took to heart his message that
"the very moment a workingman begins to do his own thinking he
understands the paramount issue, parts company with the capitalist politician and falls in line with his own class on the political
battlefield. The political solidarity of the working class means the
death of despotism, the birth of freedom, the sunrise of civiliza-
tion."

I was so impressed by Debs, his extraordinary life and work, that
I created a short documentary about him in the 1970s when I ran a

small nonprofit media company. The video was sold to colleges and high schools. Folkways Records later released the soundtrack as a recording. I was motivated to do the video because it was distressing to me, although not surprising given the nature of our corporate culture and media, that very few Americans were familiar with Debs.

Debs was a trade unionist who laid the groundwork for the rise of industrial trade unionism in America and the eventual development of the Congress of Industrial Organizations. He was a presidential candidate who received millions of votes and whose platform greatly influenced the New Deal of FDR, and a man of great courage who spoke out against U.S. participation in World War I—which resulted in him being sent to prison for three years. While he has been dead for almost a hundred years, his life, work, and ideology remain enough of a threat to the corporate world that he has been virtually wiped out of our historical consciousness. There is an important lesson to be learned from that erasure.

Debs was a fervent believer in grassroots democracy and opposed to authoritarianism and the cult of personality. "I would not be a Moses to lead you into the Promised Land, because if I could lead you into it, someone else could lead you out of it," he said. I share his view. Real change only comes from the bottom up, when thousands, then hundreds of thousands, and then millions stand together and demand a better deal. Never from the top down. Elected officials should stand in solidarity with workers and do everything they can to empower them. Not "lead" them.

That's my mission. I embrace it with relish.

I have never been neutral when it comes to workers' rights. In the great struggle between the working class and the corporate class, I'm on the side of the workers. No real change in this country can take place unless working people are prepared to fight for their rights. Part of my job, as a mayor, a member of Congress, a senator, and a presidential candidate, has always been to stand with workers who are fighting for economic justice. I don't cross picket lines; I join them. It is a privilege to march with workers who have the courage to take on the powerful special interests that dominate the economic and political life of the country.

But my responsibility doesn't end there. As a presidential candidate and, more recently, as the chairman of the Senate Budget Committee, I've supported the struggles of working Americans in tough times and fought to give them a greater say in controlling their destiny. And frankly, I am frustrated by politicians who talk a good line about workers' rights on the campaign trail but then fail to deliver when they acquire power.

That's bad policy, and bad politics. Democrats made an enormous and far-reaching mistake in the 1990s when President Bill Clinton aligned with Wall Street to approve so-called free-trade pacts, such as the North American Free Trade Agreement (NAFTA). Workers felt betrayed, and it cost the party dearly in the disastrous midterm elections of 1994, when control of the House and Senate shifted to right-wing Republicans who cynically exploited the opening Clinton had given them. Workers understood that you couldn't be both pro–Wall Street and pro-worker. For many working-class Americans, Clinton's choice to side with Wall Street was the end of their allegiance to the Democratic Party, a trend which has only grown over the years.

Democrats should have learned their lesson. But there is very little evidence that this has happened. Too many of them still do not understand that the policies of a party that is supposed to stand for workers must actually do so when in power.

The Inequality Pandemic

While the establishment in both parties may imagine otherwise, there is nothing radical about taking the side of workers. Franklin Roosevelt did so in the 1930s and '40s. It was highly beneficial for the country. It was also extremely good politics for the Democratic Party. I don't mind being radical, in the truest sense of the word, when it comes to addressing the root causes of our problems. We have to forge a future where workplaces are democratized and every American worker has a job that is safe, rewarding, and well-compensated. The billionaire class and the CEOs can complain all they want. As far as I'm concerned, the coming decade must be a time when the power of the elites is overcome, and when the power of the working class is amplified. We need to end the drift toward oligarchy and create a society that works for the many, and not just the few.

As someone who comes from a working-class family, the necessity of economic justice is not new to me. It is my life experience. It's in my DNA. But, in recent years, that struggle has taken on an even greater sense of urgency.

More than any occurrence in modern American history, the coronavirus pandemic exposed the ugliness of modern American uber-capitalism. While billionaires and CEOs sat safely at home, on their yachts, or on their private planes and corporate profits soared, millions of working-class Americans had no choice but to go to work in hospitals, schools, grocery stores, warehouses, and meatpacking plants. Millions of these essential workers got sick. Tens of thousands of them died unnecessarily. We were reminded that, like the kings and queens of past eras, the very rich know nothing about real life, could care less about real people, and firmly believe they have a divine right to rule.

While the pandemic exacerbated the economic crises facing working families, the chaos we saw in 2020 only crystallized what ordinary Americans had experienced for decades.

You won't hear this discussed on CBS or in the pages of *The New York Times,* but one of the biggest stories of our time is how, over the course of the past fifty years, this country has witnessed a massive transfer of wealth from low- and moderate-income families to the very rich. We now have more income and wealth inequality than ever before.

I can tell you as a United States senator that the issue of inequality is barely, if ever, debated on the floors of Congress. While we are very good at renaming post offices and acknowledging Super Bowl winners, we never get around to discussing the reality that, after adjusting for inflation, the average worker in America is making $44 a week *less* today than she made fifty years ago. Think about that. Think about the huge increases in worker productivity that we have seen in the past five decades. Think about the fact that, in 1981, when I became the mayor of Burlington, Vermont, the largest city in my state, we didn't have one computer in City Hall. We didn't have cell phones. We didn't email. We didn't have printers. The same reality existed, for all intents and purposes, in every workplace in America.

With more efficient machinery, the development of the internet and digital communications, automation, robotics, and artificial intelligence, the American economy has become dramatically more productive and the average American worker produces exponentially more than ever before.

The Stolen Promise of Prosperity

From the end of World War II until the late 1970s, according to the Economic Policy Institute, increased productivity and increased pay for workers ran roughly parallel. Since then, the measures have parted ways. Between 1979 and 2020, worker productivity increased by 61.8 percent, while worker pay increased by just 17 percent. What happened? "Starting in the late 1970s, policymakers began dismantling all the policy bulwarks helping to ensure that typical workers' wages grew with productivity," explain the analysts at EPI. "Excess unemployment was tolerated to keep any chance of inflation in check. Raises in the federal minimum wage became smaller and rarer. Labor law failed to keep pace with growing employer hostility toward unions. Tax rates on top incomes were lowered. And anti-worker deregulatory pushes—from the deregulation of the trucking and airline industries to the retreat of anti-trust policy to the dismantling of financial regulations and more—succeeded again and again."

Instead of increased productivity translating into increased pay and shorter workweeks, Wall Street investors made off with the cash in one of the biggest heists in the history of the American economy.

The heist transformed the lives of the very rich, allowing them to pursue their wildest dreams—even if those dreams involved building rockets and flying into space. But for the working families that were left on Earth, horizons narrowed. They had to work harder for less. They live on the margins, struggling to get by. When inflation surged in 2022, many found they could no longer make it. A survey of five hundred parents by the nonprofit advocacy group ParentsTogether Action, found that 41 percent said they've had to get a new job or work more hours to make ends meet. Forty-eight percent said they could no longer afford enough food for their family—and almost half of the working parents in this group said they skipped meals so their children could have enough to eat.

Is it any surprise that, around the same time that the Parents-Together Action survey came out, an August 2022 Decision Lab survey found that a whopping 77 percent of Americans report feeling anxious about their financial situation? For many families, there's a sense that—no matter how hard they work—they'll never catch up. When Americans say our country's best days are behind it, this is what's unsettling them.

When I was growing up in the 1940s and '50s, most American families had one breadwinner who was able to earn enough money to pay the bills. We certainly weren't rich in my family. But my father, who immigrated to this country at seventeen, as a young man who did not speak a word of English, eventually found work as a paint salesman. He never made much money. My mother stayed at home and cared for my brother, Larry, and myself. There were plenty of times when they struggled to keep things together in our 3½-room rent-controlled apartment 2C at 1525 East Twenty-sixth Street in Brooklyn. There were always arguments about money. There were hand-me-down clothes. There were tattered sneakers and baseball gloves. And my mother, who died at forty-six, never achieved her dream of owning her own home. Yet we were never without shelter, never without food, never without the basics of life.

Today, the notion that a family of four could get by in New York City on the earnings of a not particularly well-paid paint salesman is unimaginable.

Economic Injustice Is Killing Us

Talking about grotesque disparities in this country, and the stresses associated with them, is not an academic exercise. We are talking about much more than money and possessions. We are talking about who lives and who dies. We've seen how "diseases of despair" are causing people to turn to drugs, alcohol, and even suicide. It isn't hard to identify the sources of this desperation. Inequality is more than an abstract "fairness" issue, more than an accounting metric. It is something that gets into our hearts and our souls. It hurts. It kills.

Working Americans know that they are living in an immensely wealthy country but not sharing in the wealth. They can literally see the distance growing between their own lives and those of their bosses. In the 1950s, when my dad was selling paint for a living, CEOs made about 20 times more than the average worker. In the 1980s, when I was the mayor of Burlington, CEOs made 42 times more than the average worker. In 2000, ten years into my term in the House of Representatives, CEOs made about 120 times more than the average worker. Today, they are making almost 400 times what the average worker earns.

The Status Quo Isn't Working

Where does it all end? For millions of workers, the answer has simply been to quit jobs that aren't personally satisfying, economically rewarding, or safe. A new phrase entered the language late in 2021, as the economy of the United States was beginning to reboot after the hits it took during the coronavirus pandemic: "the great resignation."

Right-wing politicians claimed that "no one wants to work anymore." But there was more to it than that. People hadn't suddenly become so well-off that they didn't have to work; in fact, many of those who resigned had to deplete their personal savings, tap into retirement accounts, or move in with relatives. Nor had they abandoned the work ethic and suddenly become lazy.

Surveys showed that among those who were quitting jobs, and especially among those who were contemplating quitting—almost 50 percent of all workers—there was a deep frustration with bosses who during the pandemic had called workers "essential" but never really treated them as such. If we were talking about one boss, or even one industry, that would be significant, but as *Forbes* magazine reported, "the great resignation" swept across many sectors of the economy. Hotel and restaurant workers were quitting at particularly high rates. So, too, were grocery and retail store employees. And educators. And nurses and others who had burned out caring for the sick and dying during the worst of the pandemic. What the COVID crisis showed was that American workers were tired of being exploited, tired of sacrificing their lives so that others could become rich.

These Americans weren't done working. For the most part, they intended to find new jobs. As Paul Constant, the co-host of the *Pitchfork Economics* podcast, put it, "The truth about the so-called labor shortage is that nobody wants to work for the low wages and lousy work conditions those employers are offering."

Every indication, from the years leading into the pandemic and from the years since it hit, is that we have reached a critical juncture in the United States, where the future of work is up for grabs. The status quo is not working. We need fundamental change.

Unfettered Capitalism Will Never Make Work Humane

In the media and political culture of today, work is treated as a "given" and rarely discussed in meaningful ways. But it should be. Work, to a large degree, defines who we are, what our social status is, and who our friends are. Many of us spend more time at work than with our families. Work has the potential to make us happy and satisfied, or depressed and anxious. The real debate is not about whether people will work or not. The real debate is whether we will be able to say, "I *want* to go to work" rather than "I *have* to go to work."

I don't pretend to understand everything about human nature but I believe that, very deep in the souls of most people, is a desire to be a part of their community and to contribute to its well-being. People want to be productive and have a positive impact on the lives of their families, their friends, their neighbors, and, ultimately, on their country and their world. Work is a manifestation of this desire. That is true for a janitor. That is true for a teacher. That is true for the president of the United States.

For most Americans, holding a job is about more than "earning your keep." Human beings crave that sense of accomplishment. It gives them self-respect and a deep satisfaction that they are integral parts of their communities.

When I was a young man, in 1963, I spent several months in Israel. I lived and worked at Kibbutz Sha'ar HaAmakim, a small commune that was founded in 1935 by Jewish immigrants from Romania and Yugoslavia. I picked grapefruit as part of an agricultural community that was owned by people, many of them socialists, who had fled poverty and repression in Europe and created a new life in which they shaped their own economic destiny. While the world has obviously changed a lot since that kibbutz was created in the 1930s, and since I worked there in the 1960s, what has not changed is the sense of empowerment that grows when working people are treated not as "employees," but as "owners" who share responsibility for defining the scope and character of their jobs. The sense of community and worker-empowerment that existed there was something that I have never forgotten. It confirmed my view that there are many ways to organize workplaces, and that we have a responsibility to identify the models that respect workers as human beings, and allow them to realize their full potential.

A job has to be more than just a job. As a U.S. senator and a candidate for president I have traveled to workplaces in almost every state in our country. Along the way, I have visited with thousands of workers from all walks of life. What I've learned is that yes, of course, workers want good wages, good benefits, and good working conditions. But I have also learned that working people want more—something that most of them are not getting today. They want dignity. They want respect. They want a voice in the decision-making process. They are human beings and they want to be treated as human beings.

Whether someone is working on a farm, or in an automobile factory, hospital, or school, or delivering mail or writing a book, they want to know that what they do is meaningful and appreciated. They want to have a say about the nature of their work and how it is done. No matter what the job may be, people thrive when they have rewarding work. We feel good about ourselves when we know we are making a contribution to our community, and when we have an opportunity to come up with more creative and effective ways to make that contribution.

But, far too often in the uber-capitalist system that has developed in the United States, people don't get that sense of satisfaction. They feel, correctly, that they are cogs in the machine—exploited, powerless, and disposable. In fact, for major employers like Amazon, Walmart, and the entire fast-food industry, the gross exploitation and discarding of workers is the foundation of their business model. In these corporations the turnover rate is extremely high as desperate workers come in, are worked too hard, earn starvation wages, move on, and are replaced by other powerless low-income workers.

We Can No Longer Treat Workers as Disposable Human Beings

When we discuss deindustrialization in America, we usually refer to statistics—the tens of thousands of factories that have closed since the North American Free Trade Agreement (NAFTA) and Permanent Normal Trade Relations with China (PNTR) were implemented, and the millions of jobs that have been lost. But, too often, we lose track of the human side of the story.

We don't talk about the worker who spends thirty years of his life in a factory and then learns one day that some CEO, in a faraway place, has made a decision to shut down the profitable plant he works in and move that job to Mexico or China, where people can be exploited at a fraction of the wage that he earned. Maybe he'll even be asked to train some of those foreign workers, or actually dismantle the machinery in his factory, travel thousands of miles to another country, and reassemble that machinery for the workers who will replace him. Nobody talked to him about that decision. Nobody asked his opinion. That's just the way the system works when workers have no power. I've talked to workers who've gone through this exact experience. They are outraged and sickened by their powerlessness. This is a life-crushing experience. Many never fully recover.

Here's two months' severance. Have a nice day. What a kick in the gut. You give your whole life to the company. You're making a decent living and planning for retirement. You're producing good stuff. You take pride in your work. Then, through no fault of your own, with no input from you, a decision is made that upends everything in your life. You don't have a paycheck. You don't have health care. And, by the way, if you're fifty years of age or older, you may never have another decent job in your life.

Is it really too much, in the twenty-first century, in the wealthiest country on earth, to begin creating an economy in which people actually have some power over what they do for forty hours or more a week?

The sad reality is that there are many millions of Americans who not only feel powerless as regards their work but are in jobs they actually hate. It's painful to get up in the morning and go to work. They do it for the health care. They do it just to survive. They know they're exploited but they have no alternative. Their lousy job impacts their health and their self-worth. They would like to be able to say, "Take this job and shove it." But the economic reality is that they can't. They need the paycheck.

Dostoevsky was profoundly correct when he wrote, "If one wanted to crush and destroy a man entirely, to mete out to him the most terrible punishment, all one would have to do would be to make him do work that was completely and utterly devoid of usefulness and meaning." And that, tragically, is what life is like for millions of Americans. They feel crushed and destroyed by their jobs. They have no hope for their future.

Economic Rights Are Human Rights

Unfettered capitalism will never accomplish the goal of bringing dignity to work. The American economic system, with its excessive corporate greed and concentration of ownership and power, destroys anything that gets in its way in the pursuit of profits. It destroys the environment. It destroys our health. It destroys our democracy. It discards human beings without a second thought. It will never provide workers with the fulfillment that Americans have a right to expect from their careers. Instinctually, we know this. But we don't talk about it in these terms—the terms that can frame out an argument for something different. Something better.

To get that something better, people have to confront the system itself.

President Roosevelt knew that. That's why, in the 1944 State of the Union address that we referenced in this book's introduction, he made the case for establishing and recognizing economic rights. Unfortunately, because it was delivered in the midst of World War II, FDR's argument never got the attention it deserved. But the point he sought to make then is every bit as relevant today. In his remarks Roosevelt said, "We have come to a clear realization of the fact that true individual freedom cannot exist without economic security and independence."

Americans are proud that our Constitution guarantees freedom of religion, freedom of expression, freedom of assembly, a free press, and other rights. We understand that we can never have political freedom unless we are free from authoritarian tyranny.

But, as Roosevelt explained almost eighty years ago, if we are serious about creating a truly free society, we must take the next step forward and guarantee every man, woman, and child in our country basic economic rights—the right to quality health care, the right to good education, the right to decent and affordable housing, the right to a secure retirement, and the right to live in a clean environment.

And the right to a secure, well-paying, and meaningful job.

Roosevelt's vision influenced the politics of his time, and of the decades that followed his death in 1945. But it never took hold to the extent that he had hoped it would. The neglect of economic rights eventually came to haunt the United States, as unions grew weaker, corporations grew stronger, real wages became stagnant, and ordinary Americans became more and more alienated from a political process that was failing them.

I was inspired to seek the presidency in 2016 and 2020 because I believed that the American people were desperate for a fundamental change in the direction of our economy. The successes that we achieved in those campaigns, I am certain, resulted from the fact that we provided Americans with an alternative vision to a system that wasn't working for them.

In 2016, and to an even greater extent in 2020, the struggle for economic rights was at the heart of my message. I spelled it out in a speech I delivered at George Washington University in June 2019. That speech posed some questions to our nation that are virtually never addressed by the political, economic, or media establishment.

I asked a very simple question:

What does it actually mean to be free?
Are you truly free if you are unable to go to a doctor when you are sick, or face financial bankruptcy when you leave the hospital?

Are you truly free if you cannot afford the prescription drugs you need to stay alive?

Are you truly free when you spend half of your limited income on housing, and are forced to borrow money from a payday lender at 200 percent interest rates?

Are you truly free if you are seventy years old and have to continue working because you lack a pension or enough money to retire?

Are you truly free if you are unable to attend college or a trade school because your family lacks the income?

Are you truly free if you are forced to work sixty or eighty hours a week because you can't find a job that pays a living wage?

Are you truly free if you are a mother or father with a newborn baby but you are forced to go back to work immediately after the birth because you lack paid family leave?

Are you truly free if you are a small business owner or family farmer who is driven out of the marketplace by the monopolistic practices of big business?

Are you truly free if you are a veteran who put your life on the line to defend this country, and now sleep out on the streets?

Since the end of that campaign, I've come to recognize that there are additional questions that must be asked and answered:

Are you truly free if you are forced to work during a pandemic in conditions that may make you sick, or could even kill you?

Are you truly free if you are forced to work in a job where you have no real say about automation schemes that could eliminate that job?

Are you truly free when the most important decisions about our technological progress—in everything from communications to commerce to health care—are made in the boardrooms of multinational corporations that invariably choose quick and easy profits over your well-being?

My answer to all these questions is that Americans are not nearly so free as we think we are, or as we should be.

To achieve the genuine freedom to which we are entitled as human beings, we cannot be satisfied with political democracy alone—especially at a time when democracy itself is under fierce attack. We need economic democracy every bit as much as we need political democracy.

The only way to get it is by breaking the shackles of the old thinking that says there is no alternative to unfettered capitalism. We've got to upend the lie we've been told for decades, the one that says:

This is how the system works. This is how globalization works. This is how capitalism works. This is how employers and employees will always relate to each other.

There's nothing you can do about it.

So just shut up and get back to work.

In a world in which our economy and technologies are rapidly changing, we cannot continue to maintain economic structures that are centuries old. The status quo is not working for the vast majority of our people.

The time is long overdue to address the rampant greed, inequality, and destructiveness that is being caused by the unfettered capitalism we now experience. We need an economic system that serves humanity rather than exploits it. There can be honest debates about how best to achieve that end, but to my view there are at least four steps that must be taken:

The first two of these steps must be made in the short-term, in order to ease the immediate pain of working-class Americans:

1. Create a full-employment economy in which every worker is entitled to a decent job.

2. Strengthen the trade union movement, empower workers, and make unions a genuine counterbalance to corporate power.

The next two, which we'll discuss in the following chapter, are necessary to shape our longer-term approach to work:

3. Remove barriers to worker-ownership and increase the presence of workers on the boards of corporations that are privately owned.

4. Address the reality that technological change is rapidly transforming work in the twenty-first century, in much the same way that free trade did in the twentieth century. New and innovative technology can be a force for good, or it can be extremely destructive. It is imperative that we make certain these sweeping changes to the workforce benefit ordinary Americans, and not just the 1 percent who own the technology.

America Needs a Full-Employment Economy

There was a reason why Rev. Martin Luther King Jr., labor leader A. Philip Randolph, and organizers such as Bayard Rustin and Eleanor Holmes Norton called the 1963 demonstration that would usher in an era of transformational change in the United States the "March on Washington for Jobs and Freedom." They understood the direct connection between racial equality and economic equality, and they knew that Americans needed both equal rights and economic freedom in order to enjoy those rights. "The Negro lives on a lonely island of poverty in the midst of a vast ocean of material prosperity," Reverend King declared from the steps of the Lincoln Memorial, as marchers demanded, in the words of the program issued by the event's organizers, "a massive Federal Public Works Program to provide jobs for all the unemployed, and Federal legislation to promote an expanding economy." Their signs read: CIVIL RIGHTS + FULL EMPLOYMENT = FREEDOM.

I will never forget being one of the 250,000 people who marched in Washington on that extraordinary day. I will never forget that message. There is no real freedom without economic justice. We must address poverty, but we can't stop there. We have to recognize that "full employment for all" and "decent wages for all who work"—as King and Randolph proposed in their visionary 1967 *Freedom Budget for All Americans*—will make the United States a stronger and fairer country.

Of course a full-employment economy would benefit the unemployed. But it would also serve the millions of Americans who hold precarious jobs and are threatened with unemployment. It would benefit young people who are looking for a first job that provides them with the income and experience to improve their lives. And it would benefit the tens of millions of Americans who have secure jobs but are working for inadequate wages.

There are other benefits as well. Dr. King knew that the security that comes from a full-employment economy can ease divisions in society, stabilize communities, and address what the organizers of the March on Washington understood as "the twin evils of discrimination and economic deprivation." The struggle to eliminate those evils became a primary focus of King's last five years of activism, culminating in his announcement of the 1968 Poor People's Campaign.

That campaign had the goal of bringing Black, white, Latino, Asian, and Indigenous Americans together to renew Franklin Roosevelt's call for an Economic Bill of Rights. It also demanded that Lyndon Johnson's War on Poverty be given meaning with concrete programs to provide full employment at a living wage. With increasing urgency in the last months of his life, King called for a movement that would "confront the power structure massively" with demands rooted in an understanding that "if a man doesn't have a job or an income, he has neither life nor liberty nor the possibility for the pursuit of happiness. He merely exists."

The movement King spoke of was for guaranteed jobs. His vision was true. We must renew it.

A Jobs Guarantee Does More Than Put People to Work

In 2020, I proposed a federal jobs guarantee that would establish, once and for all, that every American has a right to a job. For me, this rejection of austerity economics wasn't just a line in a speech, or a casual embrace of populism. It became a major focus of my campaign because I believe that a federal job guarantee will be transformational for our society. Let's be clear: This concept is about much more than just providing work and an income for people who are unemployed, as important as that is. A job guarantee will help us rebuild our country, go a long way to ending economic insecurity, improve mental health, and create a stronger sense of community. It will create a much healthier and happier America.

How would a federal job guarantee work? It's not hard to figure out where to begin:

We need more doctors, nurses, dentists, home health care workers, nursing home attendants, social workers, and other medical personnel—a number that will have to radically increase after we move to a national health program and all Americans can access the health care they need.

We need more childcare workers, teachers, and college instructors, a number that will also increase as we improve the quality of public education in this country, expand educational opportunities, and address our crisis in mental health. And, as the nation ages, we will need millions of additional workers to provide supportive services for seniors to help them age comfortably in their homes and communities, which is where they want to be.

We will require millions of new construction workers as we build large numbers of desperately needed units of affordable housing and as we rebuild our crumbling infrastructure—roads, bridges, water systems, wastewater plants, and public transportation. We will also greatly increase the number of our manufacturing jobs in order to supply all of the products that new housing and infrastructure require.

And, oh yes, there is the slight matter of saving our country and the planet from the devastating effects of climate change and the catastrophic damage that will occur if we do not rapidly move away from fossil fuels.

During the 2020 campaign, and in my work as chairman of the Senate Budget Committee, I have fought for a Green New Deal as outlined by young activists in the Sunrise Movement and a number of us in Congress. If we are serious about moving to energy efficiency and sustainable energy and substantially lowering our carbon emissions, we will need millions of workers to help us make that historic and essential energy transition.

We can meet all those needs—and those that arise in the future—if we create a job guarantee that is sufficiently visionary, and sufficiently funded. "The goal is to eliminate working poverty and involuntary unemployment altogether," explains Darrick Hamilton, an economist at The New School, who has advised me on these issues for a number of years. "This is an opportunity for something transformative, beyond the tinkering we've been doing for the last forty years, where all the productivity gains have gone to the elite of society."

Will a job guarantee cost money? Of course. But failing to invest in our future costs us even more. What is the cost to our nation today of a dysfunctional health care system and childcare system? What is the cost to our country of having one of the highest rates of childhood poverty among the world's industrialized nations? What is the cost to our nation of deteriorating roads and bridges and water systems that fail to provide clean water to residents? And what is the cost if we are not successful in combating climate change and life on this planet becomes uninhabitable? How much is the future of the planet worth?

We Need to Change Our National Priorities

Dr. King recognized in the 1960s that in order to create "new forms of work that enhance the social good," the federal government's budget priorities would need to be reordered. That was true then and it is even more true today.

Take the military budget. We currently spend more than $775 billion annually on our military, over half of the discretionary budget of the United States government. This is more than the next ten countries combined. Yet, despite the enormous size of its budget, the Pentagon remains the only federal agency not to have successfully completed an independent audit. Nobody doubts that within that budget there is a massive amount of waste, fraud, unneeded weapons systems, and outrageous cost overruns. We can cut military spending by tens of billions of dollars a year and use those funds to invest in the social needs of our country, including the creation of a full employment economy.

But it's not just military spending. As we have seen, we have a tax system that is corrupt and regressive. In any given year, large corporations make billions in profit and don't pay a nickel in federal taxes. A fair and progressive tax system could generate an enormous increase in federal revenues, and those revenues could make people's lives better.

In a nation with such extraordinary wealth, don't let anyone tell you that we don't have the resources to maintain a full employment economy and guarantee a good paying job to every American worker who needs one.

But that's just the beginning.

If we are going to create economic justice in America, an economy in which workers have control over their lives and are treated with respect and dignity—and where they have collective power at the ballot box—we're going to have to rebuild the trade union movement.

In Unity There Is Strength

During my 2020 campaign I said that as president I would not only be commander in chief, but also organizer in chief. I would use the office of the president to mobilize the grassroots of this country against corporate greed, support union organizing efforts, and help workers win decent contracts—to shift political power away from the 1 percent and into the hands of workers.

Before I was born, Florence Reece, the wife of a United Mine Workers union organizer in Harlan County, Kentucky, wrote the song "Which Side Are You On?" It told about how the owners of a mine in the county had paid the local sheriff, J. H. Blair, to hire a gang of thugs to threaten union miners. "They say in Harlan County, there are no neutrals there," wrote Florence Reece. "You'll either be a union man, or a thug for J. H. Blair. Which side are you on, boys? Which side are you on?"

Which side are you on? Times have changed, but that question goes to the most profound economic and political issue of our era.

Which side are you on? These days, corporations like Starbucks and Amazon don't hire gun-toting thugs. Instead they hire anti-union consultants and pollsters and politically connected lobbyists—many of them Democrats—to thwart union organizing. But the fundamental premise remains: You're either on the side of workers and organized labor, or you're not.

That is why, when I was a college student in Chicago in the 1960s, I worked for the United Packinghouse Workers of America—one of the most progressive unions of its time. That is why I became heavily involved with the Laborers' Union in Vermont during a prolonged and bitter strike against an anti-union construction company in the 1970s. That is why when I was mayor of Burlington, against the objections of most of the city council, I worked with the municipal unions, not against them. That is why, during my two presidential campaigns, I joined union picket lines in Iowa, New York, and other states and why I held meetings with workers in union halls across the country.

That is also why, after my 2020 presidential campaign ended, I made it a high priority to support striking workers all across the country who were standing up to very powerful corporate interests: John Deere workers in Iowa; Kellogg's workers in Michigan and Pennsylvania; Special Metals steelworkers in West Virginia; Rich Products bakery workers in California; Warrior Met Coal miners in Alabama; Kroger's grocery store workers in Colorado; nurses in California and New York; graduate students at MIT; resident doctors in Vermont.

What struck me every time I joined a picket line, and every time I sat down with workers in a union hall, were five realities:

> 1. The factories, warehouses, and stores where workers were forced to strike were subsidiaries of huge, multinational corporations.
> 2. The owners of these corporations were squeezing their employees unmercifully despite making huge profits.
> 3. The response of workers to that greed was a deep and powerful solidarity. Workers and their families stuck together through the hard times that unfolded during the strikes, making sure that people with chronic health issues maintained their health insurance, that everyone had enough food, and that children of union members got Christmas presents.
> 4. Community after community, no matter in what region of the country, showed strong support for the striking workers.
> 5. In community after community, union after union, a substantial portion of the workers had given up on the Democratic Party and had become Republicans.

My allies and I not only supported workers who were out on strike, we also did what we could to help the growing number of Americans who were organizing their workplaces. In that regard I was delighted to stand with some brave young workers who were successful, for the first time, in organizing unions at Starbucks. That effort, which challenged multibillionaire Starbucks owner Howard

Schultz, began with a few shops in and around Buffalo, New York, and rapidly spread to hundreds of locations across the country. These Starbucks "partners" were underpaid, with poor benefits and unreliable schedules. And, despite intense union-busting efforts, they were successfully fighting back.

The meetings I held with Starbucks workers in Richmond, Virginia; Pittsburgh, Pennsylvania; and Boston, Massachusetts, were immensely inspiring. Young workers were asking the right questions. Why, despite growing profits, was Starbucks unwilling to pay decent wages? Why, if Starbucks was able to afford a $60 million golden parachute for a retiring CEO, couldn't they provide affordable health care benefits? Why, if the company touted itself as being "progressive," were they engaged in a vicious anti-union campaign?

I also traveled to Bessemer, Alabama, in the spring of 2021 to rally with Amazon workers who were engaged in a historic effort to organize a huge warehouse in that so-called Right to Work state. In a closed-door meeting with a number of employees, I learned about the terrible working conditions that existed there, and in Amazon warehouses across the country, and about all the underhanded schemes that Amazon had engaged in to defeat the organizing effort. It later turned out that the anti-union actions of the company were so blatant and illegal that, after the union lost that election, the National Labor Relations Board (NLRB) ordered a new election.

While the organizing project in Alabama did not succeed, an organizing effort in Staten Island, New York, proved that Amazon workers can beat the company's multimillion-dollar intimidation campaigns. In April 2022, I was proud to join in the celebration of the Amazon Labor Union's victory in a union recognition vote at the JFK8 warehouse, a sprawling facility that employs more than 8,300 workers. This was a historic victory. For the first time in the company's twenty-seven-year history, Amazon workers in the United States had organized a union. What was remarkable, and profoundly encouraging, was that grassroots organizers, led by Christian Smalls and Derrick Palmer, had done it on their own. With limited financial resources, an independent union had successfully taken on the most powerful retail corporation in the world. In so doing, they had inspired millions of workers—not just those employed at other Amazon warehouses, but those toiling in oppressive and dangerous circumstances at meatpacking plants, machine shops, and parts suppliers across the country.

Beating Amazon mattered, because Amazon has become the face of uber-capitalism in the twenty-first century.

Amazon and Jeff Bezos: What Uber-Capitalism Is All About

When we talk about uber-capitalism in its rawest form—about greed that knows no limit, about corporations that viciously oppose the right of workers to organize, about the abuses of wealth and power that tear apart our society—we're talking about Amazon, an immensely profitable corporation that is the world's largest retailer outside of China, employing almost one million people in the United States. And when we're talking about Amazon, we're talking about Jeff Bezos.

In 2021, Amazon had revenues of almost $470 billion and made a record-breaking $36 billion profit—a 453 percent increase from where it was before the pandemic. Because of its political power and its ability to take advantage of our regressive tax system, the company paid nothing in federal income taxes in 2017 and 2018. The primary beneficiary of that profiteering is Jeff Bezos, who is now the second wealthiest human being on the planet, with a net worth of $170 billion. That is more than that of most small countries. During the first year of the pandemic, when essential workers, including some at his own warehouses, were literally dying on the job, Jeff Bezos became $65 billion richer—a 57 percent increase in his fortune.

Bezos is the embodiment of the extreme corporate greed that shapes our times. While he becomes richer, his employees struggle to get by.

As I said in an address on the floor of the Senate on April 26,

2022, "Mr. Bezos has enough money to own a $500 million, 417-foot mega-yacht. He has enough money to afford a $175 million estate in Beverly Hills that includes a 13,600-square-foot mansion. He has enough money to afford a $78 million, fourteen-acre estate in Maui. He has enough money to own a $23 million mansion in Washington, D.C., with twenty-five bathrooms. He has enough money to buy a rocket ship to blast William Shatner to the edge of outer space. And yet, even though Mr. Bezos can afford all of those mansions and all of those yachts and all of those rocket ships, Mr. Bezos refuses to pay his workers decent wages, deliver decent benefits, or provide decent working conditions. This is what excessive greed looks like. And this is why Amazon workers have been struggling to organize unions in warehouses across the country.

"From the very beginning of the union organizing effort until today, Mr. Bezos and Amazon have done everything possible, legal and illegal, to defeat the union," I said. "In fact, Amazon cannot even come to grips with the reality that the workers in Staten Island won their union election fair and square. In order to stall the process out, their lawyers have appealed that election result to the NLRB. Their strategy is obviously to use their incredible wealth to stall, stall, and stall. In every way possible, they are refusing to negotiate a fair first contract with the Amazon Labor Union."

How does Bezos get rich? While he piles up money, Amazon continues to misclassify delivery drivers as independent contractors rather than employees in order to evade tax, wage, and benefit responsibilities. The company's inadequate workplace safety policies pose grave risks to workers. According to a *New York Times* investigation, Amazon has a roughly 150 percent turnover rate. Workers come into the warehouses, they are worked as hard as humanly possible, and they leave. And a whole set of new workers comes in to replace them. This is not an aberration. This is the business model that Bezos celebrates. Amazon's workplace injury rates, in some locations, are more than 2.5 times the industry average. In December 2021, six Amazon workers died after they were required to continue working during unsafe weather conditions in a warehouse that did not have appropriate safety facilities or policies.

In April 2022, I held a Budget Committee hearing that featured Chris Smalls, the president of the Amazon Union, and Sean O'Brien, the president of the Teamsters Union. I wanted to get their views as to whether the federal government should provide tens of billions in contracts to corporations who blatantly broke the law in their labor relations. I also sent a letter to President Biden urging him to sign an executive order to prohibit companies that, like Amazon, have violated labor laws from receiving federal contracts paid for by the taxpayers of America.

In my letter to Biden I wrote:

> As you will recall, during the presidential campaign you [President Biden] promised to "institute a multi-year federal debarment for all employers who illegally oppose unions" and to "ensure federal contracts only go to employers who sign neutrality agreements committing not to run anti-union campaigns."
>
> That campaign promise was exactly right. Today, I am asking you [President Biden] to fulfill that promise.

As I write these words some months later, he has not replied.

Rebuilding the Trade Union Movement

For much of the twentieth century, there was a shared understanding of the role unions needed to play, not just in improving the circumstance of workers but in providing a counterbalance to powerful business interests. Democrats like Franklin Roosevelt got it. A North Carolina textile worker famously told a reporter, "Mr. Roosevelt is the only man we ever had in the White House who would understand that my boss is a son-of-a-bitch." During FDR's presidency, the percentage of private-sector workers who were union members rose from 11 percent to 35 percent. The growth of organized labor continued into the 1950s, when a Republican president, Dwight Eisenhower, said, "Today in America unions have a secure place in our industrial life. Only a handful of unreconstructed reactionaries harbor the ugly thought of breaking unions. Only a fool would try to deprive working men and women of the right to join the union of their choice."

Support for unions was not really a debatable point. Strong unions were associated with a strong America.

Tragically, those days ended around the time that Ronald Reagan fired striking air-traffic controllers in 1981.

In the last many decades, unions have been attacked and beaten down so aggressively, and in many cases illegally, that today fewer than 11 percent of Americans are union members—and in the private sector the figure is closer to 6 percent.

This did not happen by accident. The corporate world—the Chamber of Commerce, the National Association of Manufacturers, the Business Roundtable, and other powerful business groups—knew exactly what they were doing. They fully understood that strong unions can put a check on the kinds of greed, exploitation, and unilateral decision-making that exist in non-union companies. These corporate titans knew that a good union contract means that a larger share of corporate profits go to the needs of workers, not just to high dividends for wealthy stockholders, stock buybacks, and outrageous CEO compensation. That's exactly what they did not want to see, and they acted accordingly.

According to data compiled by the Economic Policy Institute:

- When workers become interested in forming unions, 75 percent of private-sector employers hire outside consultants to run anti-union campaigns, 63 percent force employees to attend closed-door meetings to hear anti-union propaganda, and 54 percent of employers threaten workers in such meetings.

- An employee who engages in union organizing campaigns has a one-in-five chance of getting fired.
- Nearly 60 percent of employers threaten to close or relocate their business if workers elect to form a union.
- Even when workers overcome these enormous obstacles and win union elections, more than half of workers who vote to form a union don't have a union contract a year later, and 37 percent still do not have a first contract two years after the election, due to loopholes in labor laws.

By 2022, the United States had lower levels of unionization than at any time since FDR was imagining the New Deal project in 1932. The fifty-seven unions that make up the AFL-CIO now have only twelve million members.

The decline of unions has cost American workers dearly, especially the young and people of color. No wonder so many Americans are frustrated. They are hurting, but they don't have the tools to fight back.

The irony of our moment is that, even though unions are at just about the weakest point in my lifetime, public opinion polls show that they are more popular than at any time in decades. A Gallup survey done in August 2022 found that 71 percent of Americans approved of unions. That was the greatest level of support since 1965, and it was higher than at some points during FDR's presidency. At a time when the middle class continues to shrink, and more than half of our people live paycheck to paycheck, the average American knows that if we're going to rebuild the middle class, we need to rebuild the union movement.

It's not just fierce opposition from the corporate world that makes union organizing increasingly difficult. It's the allies that the corporations have in the political world, where both Republicans and Democrats have pursued an anti-worker agenda.

Over the past fifteen years, Republican governors and legislators in historically strong union states such as Wisconsin, Michigan, and Indiana have adopted so-called Right to Work laws. These measures bar unions from collecting dues from workers they represent, making it dramatically harder for workers to collectively bargain for better pay and benefits and safe workplaces.

In the South, Right to Work (For Less) laws have been on the books for the better part of seventy-five years. The name is a lie. These laws have nothing to do with giving people a right to work. They are designed to make it more difficult for workers to organize strong unions that can bargain good contracts and have a voice in politics at the local, state, and national levels. In effect, they are laws that hold down wages and weaken protections for workers, and their presence on the statute books in southern states can be traced back to the days when segregationist politicians in both parties feared that integrated unions would advance the cause of both civil rights and economic rights. Dr. King said in 1961, "Wherever these laws have been passed, wages are lower, job opportunities are fewer, and there are no civil rights."

The decline of unions not only has a major economic impact, it also harms progressive politics. Unions protect workers on their jobs, while enabling them to band together against corporate interests to elect candidates who represent the interests of working people in general. The establishment of Right to Work laws and the weakening of unions was one of the under-discussed reasons why so many states that Barack Obama won as a Democrat in 2008—including Indiana, Michigan, and Wisconsin—flipped to Trump and the Republicans in 2016, and why they could go for him or another Republican again in 2024.

The imbalance that has developed in our economy and our politics because of the weakening of unions has had an enormously negative impact on working-class Americans. And this destructive process won't change until we get a lot more aggressive about taking on the corporations and the politicians who have made organizing unions in the United States so incredibly difficult.

In America, We Don't Discuss the Reality of Class Warfare

There is a class war going on in the United States. It's never discussed in our media, and rarely mentioned in our political campaigns. That's fine by the bosses. The less discussion of class conflict, the better for them.

Corporate CEOs don't make a lot of noise about their role in the class war. Rarely are they so blunt as Gordon Gekko, the Trump-like character in the movie *Wall Street,* who freely described his corporate-raider approach to capitalism as "trench warfare" and declared that "greed, for lack of a better word, is good. Greed is right, greed works." But, have no doubt, today's CEOs are following the Gordon Gekko playbook. They are engaged in that trench warfare, and they fight ferociously. Yet, because media and political elites avoid mention of the class war—just as they generally avoid using the term "working class"—the conflicts of interest between the owners and the workers are obscured.

Over the past forty years, the ruling class in the United States has gone to war against organized labor and, as part of that war, they have eviscerated the entire concept of class and class consciousness in this country. In America today, we have more income and wealth inequality than at any time in modern history, and there has been a massive redistribution of wealth in the wrong direction. Is it any surprise, therefore, that the people who own this country refuse to even acknowledge—let alone sincerely discuss—the rigid class structure that shapes our society? Not only has the reality of class conflict been removed from public discourse in the media and political world, the ruling class has also been largely successful in writing the working class out of our history. And out of our present.

We regard it as "normal," for example, that corporate media and big business encourage us to identify with the New England Patriots, the Chicago Bulls, or the Los Angeles Dodgers. Millions fervently root for "their" teams—teams that are most often owned by billionaires who would move to another city tomorrow if they could make a few bucks more. We are not encouraged, however, to root for our class—our brothers and sisters who experience the same economic plight that we do and share our hopes and dreams for a better future. Tens of millions of Americans know the names of our great professional athletes—people who are on TV every day. I would be surprised if even 1 percent of the American people know the name of the current AFL-CIO president—Liz Shuler—even though she is the leader of a twelve-million-member organization.

This denial of class consciousness permeates every aspect of our society. Despite the best efforts of historians such as Howard Zinn, history courses in our schools still tend to tell America's story with very little mention of workers or their unions. Newspapers have business sections and cable TV has business channels. Where are the worker sections? The worker channels? There was a time when most newspapers had a "labor beat" and covered the struggles of working people. Not anymore. Even though real wages in this country have been stagnant for fifty years, corporate media meticulously avoids serious discussion about the condition of working people—and the work of unions to improve that condition by giving workers a place at the table.

If you want to maintain the status quo, and the existing power structure, you just don't talk about the crises facing working people, the economic inequality that exists, or how workers' lives could be improved by joining unions and organizing their workplaces. The reality that millions of Americans work for starvation wages, that the middle class continues to shrink, and that large numbers of workers hate their jobs is just not "news" for corporately owned networks like CBS, NBC, ABC, CNN, MSNBC, and, of course, Rupert Murdoch's Fox News.

Labor's Untold Story

I am surely not the first to point out that if we want to understand where we are today, we need to have a sense of history. And that includes the history of the American labor movement.

The United Electrical, Radio and Machine Workers of America (UE), one of the outstanding progressive labor organizations in the country—and, I should add, the first international union to endorse my 2020 presidential campaign—produced a book titled *Labor's Untold Story*. In it, they correctly point out that "fundamentally, labor's story is the story of the American people."

Unfortunately, most Americans don't know much about that story. They don't know about the heroic workers who took on corporate thugs and were sometimes jailed and killed as they fought for decent wages and working conditions. They don't know that there was a time when young children were forced to work in factories and on farms, and that unions were the driving force in eliminating child labor. They don't know that the forty-hour workweek and time-and-a-half for overtime were not gifts from employers but were hard-won victories of the trade union movement. They don't know that the union movement successfully fought to cut down on accidents on the job, forcing employers to eliminate physical and environmental threats in workplaces across this country; or that the trade union movement, with its millions of members, provided the political muscle that brought about Social Security, Medicare, Medicaid, the minimum wage, and a host of other progressive pieces of legislation.

They don't know that progressive trade unions such as the United Auto Workers and the Retail, Wholesale and Department Store Union were an integral part of the civil rights movement and the fight for racial justice—that the chief organizer of the 1963 March on Washington for Jobs and Freedom, the man who invited Dr. King to deliver the "I Have a Dream" speech, was a labor leader, A. Philip Randolph of the Brotherhood of Sleeping Car Porters. They don't know that Dr. King himself was a strong ally of the trade union movement, and that he was assassinated in Memphis, Tennessee, while supporting the American Federation of State, County and Municipal Employees' effort to secure better conditions for striking sanitation workers.

This ignorance of working-class history is not an accident. It's designed to disempower people, to make them believe that there is no alternative to the status quo and unfettered capitalism. It is designed to make them feel helpless.

For the Union Makes Us Strong

It shouldn't have to be this way. Workers shouldn't have to jump through legal hoops and cut through fields of red tape just to secure a say in their workplaces. They shouldn't be worried about losing their jobs because they are pro-union, or be forced to attend compulsory anti-union propaganda meetings. They shouldn't have to deal with threats that their company will shut down or move to China if the union comes.

It isn't like that in the major countries with which we compare ourselves. In most of Europe, Canada, Australia, Japan, and elsewhere, the barriers to organizing are lower and the levels of unionization are much higher. It's easier for workers to negotiate contracts that improve wages, benefits, and working conditions. They also have the power to influence government policy in a way that doesn't exist here. One of the manifestations of a weak trade union is that we are far behind other countries when it comes to national health care programs, free or inexpensive higher education, quality and affordable childcare, strong pension programs, guaranteed vacation time, and paid family and medical leave measures. Simply stated, when unions are strong, governments respond to the needs of workers and the lives of working-class people are dramatically improved.

Some of the most highly unionized countries in the world are in Scandinavia—Denmark, Sweden, Norway, Finland, and Iceland. Not surprisingly, these countries also have the highest standard of living in the world, and experience much less income and wealth inequality than uber-capitalist countries such as the United States.

In Denmark, where 67 percent of workers are unionized, McDonald's employees make more than $20 an hour and, if they are over twenty, the company starts paying into a pension plan for them. They, like all other workers in Denmark, enjoy six weeks of paid vacation each year—and, of course, they're covered by the country's robust and high-quality national health care plan.

Denmark doesn't have a set minimum wage; but it has strong enough unions to assure that workers, even in industries that in the United States pay low wages, are far more generously compensated than American workers. And what's the cost to customers? An *Economist* magazine survey found that a Big Mac in Denmark cost 76 cents *less* than the same item in the United States.

Admittedly, "happiness" is a state of being that is not easily quantified. But there are research projects, like the United Nations–sponsored World Happiness Report, that attempt to do just that on an annual basis. And here's what they found in 2021: The happiest country in the world was Finland, followed by Denmark, Switzerland, Iceland, Netherlands, Norway, and Sweden. In fact, year after year, the Scandinavian countries rank at the top of the list of 146 countries. The United States was nineteenth in 2021.

Obviously, higher pay does not always equate with happiness. Nor does the guarantee of quality health care, free higher education, six weeks' paid vacation, and very strong paid family and medical leave. But it helps. These benefits, available to all, substantially reduce the levels of stress and economic anxiety that impact the lives of so many Americans.

We can be sure that there are at least a few miserable McDonald's workers in Copenhagen. But if Danish workers are unhappy, they've got far greater power to improve their lives—thanks to strong unions and a government and private sector that respect the role of organized labor.

The bottom line is that when you have a strong trade union movement, you have a higher standard of living for workers and less income and wealth inequality. When you have a weak trade union movement, as is the current case in the United States, millions of workers live with inadequate income, health care, educational opportunities, and pensions. And, because of their political weakness, they are powerless to change that reality.

When We Strengthen Unions, We Strengthen America

When that connection becomes clear, the necessary course of action also becomes clear. We don't have to reinvent the wheel. We just have to remember what FDR did during the Great Depression, when he and Democrats such as New York senator Robert Wagner succeeded in passing legislation that struck down the most egregious barriers to union organizing. In 1932, the year Roosevelt was elected, union membership was around 2.8 million. By the time his presidency was finished, it was over 12 million and rising.

FDR's efforts to put government on the side of working people were effective, not just for unions and their members but for the country as a whole. Production increased, and so did prosperity. It can work again.

During the 2020 campaign, I developed a plan for strengthening unions and increasing union membership. I stated, "Declining unionization has fueled rising inequality. Today, corporate profits are at an all-time high, while wages as a percentage of the economy are near an all-time low. The middle class is disappearing, and the gap between the very rich and everyone else is growing wider and wider. There are many reasons for the growing inequality in our economy, but one of the most significant reasons for the disappearing middle class is that the rights of workers to join together and bargain for better wages, benefits, and working conditions have been severely undermined."

To address this reality, I proposed to:

- Double union membership in four years by allowing the National Labor Relations Board (NLRB) to certify a union if it receives the consent of the majority of eligible workers; repealing restrictive sections of the anti-union Taft-Hartley Act; and preventing corporations from gaming the rules by classifying employees as independent contractors.
- Establish federal protections against the firing of workers for

any reason other than "just cause," a change that would make it more difficult to intimidate workers who are engaged in organizing unions and negotiating contracts.

- Enact "first contract" provisions to ensure companies must negotiate a first contract within a reasonable period of time.
- Deny federal contracts to companies that pay poverty wages, outsource jobs overseas, engage in union-busting, deny good benefits, and pay CEOs outrageous compensation packages.
- Eliminate Right to Work (For Less) laws and guarantee the right to unionize for workers historically excluded from labor protections, including farmworkers and domestic workers.

I understand that it may be hard for many Americans to imagine a future where employees are no longer at the mercy of their bosses. Workers and their unions have been so frequently attacked, beaten down, and dismissed that the task of securing a fair shake for the working class seems overwhelming. I don't see it that way. I believe that working-class Americans are more engaged, more energized, and more prepared to pursue economic justice than at any point in my lifetime.

That pursuit will be challenging, but I am convinced the future for the working class holds all the possibility that Eugene Victor Debs foresaw: "Ten thousand times has the labor movement stumbled and fallen and bruised itself, and risen again; been seized by the throat and choked and clubbed into insensibility; enjoined by courts, assaulted by thugs, charged by the militia, shot down by regulars, traduced by the press, frowned upon by public opinion, deceived by politicians, threatened by priests, repudiated by renegades, preyed upon by grafters, infested by spies, deserted by cowards, betrayed by traitors, bled by leeches, and sold out by leaders," he wrote at the dawn of the twentieth century. "But notwithstanding all this, and all these, it is today the most vital and potential power this planet has ever known, and its historic mission of emancipating the workers of the world from the thraldom of the ages is as certain of ultimate realization as is the setting of the sun."

7

FIGHTING FOR OUR ECONOMIC FUTURE

*Workers, not CEOs, must determine
the future of work in America*

The ruling class always comes out on top because they are in a position to determine the future before most Americans even know what's at stake. The wealthiest and most powerful Americans employ teams of analysts and counselors to help them keep tabs on every economic and social trend and then, when they see where things are headed, they start investing in "what's next"—or buying up innovative small firms that have already figured things out. They also get their lobbyists to work on assuring that, when policies and regulations are written, Congress and the state legislatures will agree to those that consolidate their advantages. By the time the average American catches on, the rules have already been rigged so that the rich get richer and everyone else gets left behind.

The ruling class always wins. The working class always loses.

We've got to start playing a differing game.

Working people have to start fighting the fights of the future now, before they are settled against us. To my mind, the fight that matters most will be over control of the technological progress that is transforming all of our lives. We have to make certain that the technological revolution we are experiencing works for workers, and not just for the 1 percent.

Avoiding the Next Race to the Bottom

In the latter part of the twentieth century, the great challenge that American workers faced involved race-to-the bottom trade policies that saw corporations move jobs from place to place in a relentless search for cheap labor, weak unions, and lax environmental regulations.

Initially, jobs were moved from heavily industrialized northern states, where organized labor was strong, to southern states where Right to Work laws undermined unions. Then came the 1990s, when a Democratic president, Bill Clinton, joined with Republicans to approve free-trade deals that rewarded multinational corporations for outsourcing American jobs. By the time most Americans understood what was happening, tens of thousands of plants were dismantled in the United States and shipped off to Mexico and China and Vietnam. Millions of existing and future jobs were lost and communities were devastated. Deindustrialization took hold and the working class of this country was dealt a devastating blow.

When I was campaigning for the presidency, I heard hundreds of stories from workers in Indianapolis and Toledo and Flint about lives that had been ripped apart as factories closed, and about once-great manufacturing centers that were destabilized by an unthinking embrace of corporate-sponsored globalization that treated workers as expendable cogs in the machinery of capitalism.

Let's be clear: We still need to reform our trade policies and move to fair trade as opposed to "free trade." But, in the twenty-first century, workers in the United States aren't just competing with workers in Mexico or China for the scraps that corporations are willing to throw them. Workers are competing with the machines themselves.

In the fall of 2020, *Forbes* reported that "the World Economic Forum (WEF) concluded in a recent report that 'a new generation of smart machines, fueled by rapid advances in artificial intelligence (AI) and robotics, could potentially replace a large proportion of existing human jobs.' Robotics and AI will cause a serious 'double-disruption,' as the coronavirus pandemic pushed companies to fast-track the deployment of new technologies to slash costs, enhance productivity and be less reliant on real-life people." Before the pandemic, *Forbes* featured a report that said automation could eliminate as many as 73 million existing jobs in the United States by 2030. Of course, new jobs will be created in some industries, but the trajectory is toward a future where everything about our working lives is fundamentally changed. And in an uber-capitalist system where there are always winners and losers, those changes are certain to upend the lives of tens of millions of workers.

That's a jarring and disorienting prospect. So jarring that a lot of politicians, journalists, and even some worker advocates choose to look away from an impending upheaval of monumental proportions. But not everybody is avoiding the issue. The multinational corporations investing billions in new technologies that will displace workers and shape the future of a new economy are paying very close attention. Their sole interest is to increase their profits, and they are absolutely committed to seizing every advantage as rapidly as possible.

The working class of this country cannot afford to look away. The changes that are coming will impact every aspect of our society. It is easy to feel overwhelmed. But we have it in our power to shape a destiny where the concerns of working-class people are at the center of decision-making about the future of work.

Congress Is Failing to Define the Future of Work

The changes that are taking place are going to shake up how people work, where they work, what kind of work they will do, and how much they are paid. Yet there is barely any discussion in Congress about industrial policy, or the ways in which our government should relate to the private sector in terms of protecting American workers—and taxpayers—in a rapidly transforming economy.

Here's one example of how weak the federal response has been: In the summer of 2022, Congress passed the CHIPS and Science Act, which included a massive giveaway to the enormously profitable microchip industry. The argument for this legislation was that the future of our economy depended upon microchip production in the United States, and that we had to act because we were falling behind China and other countries.

In a speech on the Senate floor, I acknowledged that "there is no debate that the microchip and semiconductor shortage is a dire threat to our nation. It is costing American workers good-paying jobs and raising prices for families. It is making it harder for businesses to manufacture cars, cell phones, and life-saving medical equipment. It is also putting our national security at risk." Pretty much everyone agreed on that point. But then I added the information that my colleagues did not want to hear. "The microchip industry helped cause this crisis by, over the last twenty years, shutting down 780 plants here and eliminating 150,000 good-paying jobs," I said. "The question before us now is whether these extremely profitable companies will work with the U.S. government on a solution to rebuild the U.S. microchip industry, which is fair to the taxpayers of this country, or whether they will continue to demand a fifty-three-billion-dollar bribe to stay here." With additional tax breaks, that $53 billion later became a $76 billion corporate bonanza.

I wanted to begin establishing policies that benefited workers and taxpayers—not just corporate investors and CEOs. My colleagues wanted to pass a bill and head home for the weekend. So that's what they did, with many of them patting themselves on the back for finally "investing in the future."

As technological change arrives at an ever-expanding rate, this sort of congressional negligence cannot be allowed to continue. Cor-

porate power and influence cannot be allowed to dominate government action about issues as important as this.

The challenge is for Congress to develop an industrial policy that
improves our economy, protects taxpayers, and benefits American
workers. It requires far more than just providing a blank check of $76
billion to powerful and well-connected corporate interests.

It's not just Congress. It's the media, and even some advocates
for workers.

For the most part, we are just letting a revolution in our work life
happen, without considering the implications, without asking what
we might do to make this change beneficial rather than destructive.

Our neglect is cheating the working class and pointing this country toward a "same as it ever was" future where progress is harnessed
to make the rich richer, to squeeze the middle class, and to leave the
poor in even more desperate circumstances.

Machines Should Serve People, Not the Other Way Around

I remember when I was at the University of Chicago in the early
1960s, there was a great deal of discussion about what would happen
when people were only working twenty hours a week because machines would perform so much of the work that humans had historically done. We understood then that machines were not inherently
bad. How could they be? If machines can be employed to do dangerous work, filthy work, drudgery work, is that a bad thing? I don't
think so.

Unfortunately, the dream of a society where machines take over
the most unpleasant and unrewarding jobs, freeing people to work
less and live fuller lives, has not been realized.

How did that happen? Who made the assumption that the primary beneficiaries of advanced technology would be the owners of
that technology—and that the rest of us would have to suffer the
consequences of their decisions?

We have seen a great deal of automation over the past sixty years, and what we have seen is just the tip of the iceberg. Artificial intelligence and automation will impact every aspect of society, and every form of work in this country and around the world. Yet, despite all the promises that this will be for the good, the trajectory we are on is not encouraging.

Automation has replaced some of the most dangerous work and drudgery. But it hasn't necessarily made the lives of workers better. In many instances, it has sped up work so that humans have to keep up with the machines. In what is being referred to as "the new machine age," Americans work some of the longest hours among major countries: fifty-two hours a week, sixty hours a week, even more. Incredible hours. Many professional workers literally take their computers home with them, so that they can respond to work orders from the boss at all hours of the day and night. The promise that new technology would make work-life easier for the vast majority of Americans simply has not been realized.

That's certainly the case at Amazon, where the workers are constantly pressured to work faster and faster in automated warehouses. When workers in Alabama were organizing in 2021, one of the biggest complaints was that they were under such pressure to mimic the machines, they weren't given enough time to go to the bathroom.

But it's not just Amazon workers in Alabama. Across America, and around the world, work is speeding up. In many instances, workers are being told they must keep up with machines that never rest. In many more instances, the machines will simply take the place of the workers.

If you work in a checkout line at the local grocery store, your job will likely be replaced by a scanner.

If you are a bus driver, taxicab driver, Uber driver, or truck driver, your job could disappear as we move into the era of autonomous vehicles.

If you are a factory worker, you face the prospect of being replaced by a robot.

If you are a nurse, you could find yourself monitoring vast wards of patients who are hooked up to machines that replace the human touch with medical algorithms.

Every kind of work will be affected. Whether you're a blue-collar worker in a machine shop or an accountant for the corporation that owns that machine shop, your job is on the line.

Architectural designs are already being done by machines, legal work has gone online, and there are even stories of computer programs that replace journalists. Instead of attending traditional colleges, students are now using apps to find instructors to help them grab "certificates" that will serve the purpose once served by degrees.

And all of this is just the beginning.

How many jobs will be lost as a result of this technological revolution? The estimates are all over the place. While there are those who imagine that every job that is automated will be replaced by some new job, at the same time there are predictions that astronomical numbers of jobs, whole industries, will simply disappear. The McKinsey Global Institute estimates that roughly half of all the work people are paid to do could be automated by 2055. Kiran Garimella, a scientist and author of the book *AI + Blockchain: A Brief Guide for Game Changers*, outlines the prevailing wisdom with a pair of instructive questions and answers:

Q: Will automation, specifically AI-driven automation, eliminate jobs?
A: Yes. Lots of them and in the most unexpected ways and at an unexpected pace.

Q: Will lost jobs be replaced by other jobs, just as it happened so far throughout history?
A: Only to a limited extent; there will be a massive net loss of jobs. I know many scientists and thought-leaders whom I respect a lot are predicting a huge increase in AI-related jobs to more or less compensate for the losses. I think this time they are wrong. When jobs were lost to mechanization, jobs for the mind opened up. What will happen when jobs for the mind become unnecessary or uneconomical?

We should heed the neglected counsel of the Obama administration from 2016, when its final report on automation declared, "Accelerating artificial intelligence (AI) capabilities will enable automation of some tasks that have long required human labor. These transformations will open up new opportunities for individuals, the economy, and society, but they have the potential to disrupt the current livelihoods of millions of Americans. Whether AI leads to unemployment and increases in inequality over the long-run *depends not only on the technology itself but also on the institutions and policies that are in place.*"

A Future Of, By, and For the Working Class

There must be a sense of urgency in progressive messaging about the challenges and the opportunities that are ahead of us. The British parliamentarian Yvette Cooper, a Labour Party MP and a former secretary of state for work and pensions, channeled it well in an op-ed for *The Guardian* in late 2018:

> The robots are coming, artificial intelligence is expanding, yet no one is doing enough to make sure workers benefit rather than losing out. According to a new survey, a quarter of the workforce think their job won't be needed in future. Many of us expect the technological revolution to be as disruptive as the industrial revolution. This could bring amazing opportunities and emancipation, but also new forms of exploitation, deeper inequalities, injustices and anger. Trades unions and communities can't just stand by and hope for the best. If we want technological change to benefit everyone rather than widening inequality then we need to start preparing now. It took decades for new legislation, the growth of trade unions and the emergence of the welfare state to tackle some of the injustices of the industrial revolution and start harnessing the benefits for everyone. We cannot afford to wait that long this time.

The British circumstance is different from the American one in many ways. But the sense of urgency should be the same. In this country, where so much of Big Tech is headquartered, and where so many of the pathologies that extend from it are felt most profoundly, we have the power to shape a future that puts the benefits of social, political, and technological progress to work for the working class. The challenge now is to seize that power. Here are the steps I propose:

1. START PLANNING FOR OUR FUTURE

Needless to say, if we're going to effectively address the sweeping and enormously consequential changes that our technological transformation will bring, we need to immediately begin planning for the future.

Unfortunately, as Rep. Ro Khanna, a California Democrat who co-chaired my 2020 campaign, has wisely noted, the United States tends to avoid the sort of planning that would prepare us for these changes. In European countries there is a broad understanding—by parties on the left and right—that it is vital to use data and forecasting to prepare for economic changes that extend from technological progress, climate change, migration patterns, and social demands. Countries such as Germany maintain carefully plotted industrial policies that allow them to prepare for the future. The United States hasn't done that in the past.

But we can't afford to be so neglectful in the future.

The pace and direction of technological change cannot be left to the market if there is to be hope for a fair distribution of the benefits of that change. This does not mean that the state must manage every aspect of change. But it must be openly and aggressively engaged in determining the direction of that change, with an eye toward supporting research projects, investments, and policies that assure an equitable distribution of the benefits.

In order to avoid duplication and turf wars, we should create a new cabinet-level agency that would deliberately focus on the future

of work, and on the future of workers and their families, in a transforming economy. The challenges are too great, and the time is too
short, to permit bureaucratic blundering to get in the way of proper
planning and implementation of policies.

I share the view of Annette Bernhardt, the director of the Low-
Wage Work Program at the UC-Berkeley Center for Labor Research
and Education, who argues that "our collective task is to develop a
transparent public policy framework for assessing the impact of
emerging technologies, mitigating negative effects where they occur,
and prioritizing innovation that truly contributes to the social good.
Of particular importance will be to include the interests of workers
and their communities—especially low-income communities and
communities of color—in the development of that framework. A
public policy response to new technologies need not be anti-
innovation; automation and displacement are not the only path and
our goal should be to leverage technology to build an economy that
works for everyone."

2. BREAK 'EM UP!

In order to assure that public health, public safety, and consumer
and environmental protections are not just retained but adapted to a
new economy, and that workers are protected in that economy, we
have to step up anti-trust regulation and prosecution. Law professor
Zephyr Teachout, an expert on corporate monopolies and the author
of the book *Break 'Em Up,* told the House Judiciary Committee's
Subcommittee on Antitrust, Commercial and Administrative Law in
2020 that "Amazon, Google, and Facebook play a grossly outsized
role in the basic public functions of our society and have become
unelected, unaccountable, and self-serving heads of a planned
economy—planned by them."

Power over the future of our economy should not be ceded to a
handful of tech giants. Teachout warns that "the highly concentrated
big data market, and the existing abuses of big tech enabled by their
dominant positions, pose a major democratic threat." And that con-

centration will only increase as AI-driven automation reshapes the ways in which we work, and in which we trade in goods and services.

Facebook, Google, and Uber are often seen as potential targets for anti-trust action because of the disruptive impact of their companies on politics, communications, and transportation. But there is a deeper, more fundamental argument to be made about the need to set standards with regard to not just these firms but the corporate conglomerates that have yet to emerge in an era when billionaires like Elon Musk are buying up companies such as Twitter. The corporations that come to define how we utilize digital platforms, robots, and artificial intelligence may be already-existing tech or manufacturing firms, or they may evolve from them; they may in rare instances appear on their own. But firms that profit from advancements in artificial intelligence could grow exponentially faster than traditional corporations, and quickly obtain exponentially more power than the market-dominating behemoths about which Americans are already justifiably concerned. That's why I believe future presidents and Congresses must be prepared to govern as trust-busters and regulators in the public interest.

3. Tax the Robots

If workers are going to be replaced by robots, as will be the case in many industries, we're going to need to adapt tax and regulatory policies to assure that the change does not simply become an excuse for race-to-the-bottom profiteering by multinational corporations.

Microsoft's Bill Gates—not someone I regularly agree with—proposes that governments levy a tax on the use of robots by corporations. "For a human worker who does $50,000 worth of work in a factory, the income is taxed," says Gates. "If a robot comes in to do the same thing, you'd think that we'd tax the robot at a similar level." Gates argues that the "robot tax" revenues could be used to pay for the retraining of people whose jobs are eliminated or downsized due to automation. In particular, Gates suggests, the retraining could focus on preparing people to work at jobs "where human empathy and understanding are still very unique"—such as "[care for the] elderly, having smaller class sizes, helping kids with special needs."

A variation on the idea has been proposed in South Korea, one of the most rapidly automating countries in the world. Last year, the Korean government developed a tax reform plan that reduces tax credits for investment in automation technology.

In San Francisco, former supervisor Jane Kim's Jobs of the Future initiative proposed a study of what *Bloomberg News* described as "the viability of a statewide payroll tax on employers across the state of California that replace a human employee with a robot, algorithm, or other form of automation." Kim's plan imagined a scheme where companies that replace human beings with robots would still be required to pay a portion of the payroll taxes they had been providing into a fund that would cover the costs of retraining displaced workers as well as invest in emerging industries that might provide additional employment—for humans.

In an important article for the *Harvard Law & Policy Review,* published in March 2021, Ryan Abbott and Bret Bogenschneider made an even more far-reaching argument with regard to tax policy and automation. "The tax system incentivizes automation even in cases where it is not otherwise efficient," they explained. "This is because the vast majority of tax revenues are now derived from labor income, so firms avoid taxes by eliminating employees. Also, when a machine replaces a person, the government loses a substantial amount of tax revenue—potentially hundreds of billions of dollars a year in the aggregate. All of this is the unintended result of a system designed to tax labor rather than capital. Such a system no longer works once the labor is capital. Robots are not good taxpayers."

Abbott and Bogenschneider suggest that existing tax policies must be radically reformed. "The system should be at least 'neutral' as between robot and human workers, and automation should not be allowed to reduce tax revenue," they explain. "This could be achieved through some combination of disallowing corporate tax deductions for automated workers, creating an 'automation tax' which mirrors existing unemployment schemes, granting offsetting tax preferences for human workers, levying a corporate self-employment tax, and increasing the corporate tax rate."

4. SHORTEN THE WORKWEEK AND MAKE JOBS MORE FLEXIBLE

"If the robots are indeed taking our jobs, shouldn't we all probably be working less?" asks the tech magazine *Gizmodo*. The answer from progressives around the world is: "Yes."

The British Trades Union Congress (TUC) has proposed that, in response to the digital and automation revolutions, the number of hours spent at work during the average week should be cut. "In the nineteenth century, unions campaigned for an eight-hour day. In the twentieth century, we won the right to a two-day weekend and paid holidays," explained Frances O'Grady, TUC's outgoing general secretary, at the federation's 2018 conference. "So, for the twenty-first century, let's lift our ambition again. I believe that in this century we can win a four-day working week, with decent pay for everyone. It's time to share the wealth from new technology, not allow those at the top to grab it for themselves."

O'Grady summed things up with an observation: "Jeff Bezos owns Amazon, now a trillion-dollar company. He's racking up the billions while his workers are collapsing on the job exhausted."

John McDonnell, the veteran U.K. Labour Party parliamentarian who served as former party leader Jeremy Corbyn's shadow chancellor, led a successful drive to make a four-day workweek without a pay cut part of the party's national platform. "With millions saying they would like to work shorter hours, and millions of others without a job or wanting more hours," he said, "it's essential that we consider how we address the problems in the labor market as well as preparing for the future challenges of automation."

McDonnell endorsed a report from the British think tank Autonomy, "The Shorter Working Week: A Radical and Pragmatic Proposal," which proposed a transition to a four-day workweek by 2025.

"We should accept automation as something that does increase productivity and recognize that that's a good thing in an economy," Aidan Harper, the report's editor, and a researcher at the New Economics Foundation, told *Gizmodo*. "It's just that the proceeds of automation should be shared evenly—in the form of a working time reduction. Machines should liberate us from work, not subject us to this ever-increasing inequality."

German trade unions have gone even further, striking successfully for a twenty-eight-hour workweek. And a number of industries have embraced the change. As Britain's *New Statesman* magazine suggests, "The left is resurrecting one of the classic socialist critiques of capitalism: that it makes humans unfree."

But this is not just a socialist initiative. A New Zealand firm, Perpetual Guardian, which allowed its employees to work four days a week while being paid for five, found the experiment was so successful that it began looking to make the strategy permanent. Workers reported significant improvements in their work/life balance and told researchers that the extra day off made them more energetic and efficient when they returned to their jobs.

The world is not quite where John Maynard Keynes imagined in his 1930 essay "Economic Possibilities for Our Grandchildren," which predicted that economic and technological progress would by the early twenty-first century lead to a fifteen-hour week. But if we make the right choices and investments, we might get to the place where, as Keynes suggested, "for the first time since his creation, man will be faced with his real, his permanent problem—how to use his freedom from pressing economic cares, how to occupy the leisure, which science and compound interest will have won for him, to live wisely and agreeably and well."

5. MEDICARE FOR ALL, FREE COLLEGE EDUCATION, AND EXPANDED SOCIAL SECURITY MUST BE GUARANTEED

European countries, which have far better developed social-welfare states than the United States, are already developing plans for how to expand and enhance programs that provide health care, education, and pensions so that they can keep up with the new economy. In the United States, this time of economic transition can also be a time for catching up—and perhaps even getting ahead of the rest of the world when it comes to providing for basic needs.

Medicare for All, free college education, and expanded Social Security, along with other universal guarantees, are good ideas in and of themselves, as is explained in other sections of this book. But they are dramatically more necessary in a transition period from an old economy to a new one.

The best models for that new economy will include strong unions and well-defined workplace protections. But the definition of the workplace will change radically, making guarantees to workers unpredictable as the economy is transformed. The availability of health care and education—as human rights—will be essential. If people do not have access to them, they will be forced to work harder for less. Inequality will continue to increase and our political debates will grow more desperate.

That doesn't have to be our future. By embracing Medicare for All, as well as plans to expand Social Security, we can ensure that working-class people—many of whom will find themselves self-employed or working in the gig economy—will not be left in the lurch because they do not have a steady employer that provides health benefits and a pension. And in an era where people will need more training and expertise than ever before, free college education should be a no-brainer.

Give Workers Control over Their Workplaces

If we're talking about a new economy, shouldn't we also be talking about new ways to empower workers? As jobs are remade by digitalization, automation, and advances in AI technology, we are constantly told that the workplace will be transformed. But there's one aspect of the old workplace that corporations cling to even as they talk about embracing innovation: the structures that keep control in the hands of billionaire owners and Wall Street investors rather than the people who actually do the work.

Unions give workers a voice on the job, and in society. But they don't provide most employees in most industries with the level of control that is needed to establish genuine workplace democracy. For that to happen, workers need to have the option of collectively owning and operating their factories, warehouses, offices, and stores.

In Germany and other countries, union representatives don't just negotiate with major corporations. They sit on the boards of those businesses. They're in the room where the decisions are made and, while they're in the minority, they have access to information and options for intervening in deliberations over everything from working conditions to decisions about whether to shutter or maintain existing operations. In 2018, Senator Tammy Baldwin of Wisconsin released a report produced by her staff, which determined that:

- Companies with worker representatives on their boards created 9 percent more wealth for their shareholders than comparable companies without board-level worker representation.
- Communities that are home to companies with worker representation distribute income more equally and provide their citizens greater economic opportunity.
- Wages in countries that require worker representation on corporate boards are 18 to 25 percent higher than wages in the United States.

Arguing that broadening the base of corporate decision-makers is likely to "yield more shared economic prosperity in the United States," Baldwin introduced the Reward Work Act, which I was proud to cosponsor. The legislation proposed a requirement that one-third of the directors of each public company be elected by its employees. Polls found the plan was popular with Democrats, Independents, and Republicans in every region of the country.

When I was campaigning for the presidency in 2020, I argued

for the creation of a system like that of Germany, where the law requires that corporations maintain two separate boards, one of which would be organized along more traditional corporate lines, the other representing the interests of shareholders and workers. During a Fight for $15 town hall discussion in the fall of 2019, Tanya Herrell, a McDonald's employee from Gretna, Louisiana, asked me, "How would you use the power of your office to help bring workers to the table to talk with workers like me?" My answer was that she and her fellow workers needed "a seat at the table." I explained the German model and said, "If forty percent of McDonald's board was composed not of CEOs of other large corporations but of working people, trust me, you would be making today at least fifteen dollars an hour, and there would be vigorous efforts to protect workers from sexual harassment and violence, because workers would be reflecting the needs not just of workers who want stock buybacks, but representing the needs of workers who want decent wages and decent working conditions."

Clearly, we need laws that promote workplace democracy. To that end, as a senator, I have proposed legislation to require that 45 percent of the board seats of corporations that are publicly traded, or bring in more than $100 billion in annual revenues, be elected by their employees. That's a higher percentage than some of my colleagues have proposed, because I think it is necessary to provide workers with a genuine voice in decision-making—and to assure that the diversity of workforces at these massive corporations is represented in boardrooms that have historically been dominated by older white men.

This is a big deal. If you have just one worker on the board, you begin to overcome the powerlessness that employees feel when decisions are made behind closed doors by corporate CEOs who may be genuinely uninformed about what happens in the workplace. In a responsible corporation, it's a way to get good ideas to the top. In an irresponsible corporation, at the very least, the workers have a way to get information about what's being done before the pink slips start arriving.

Why Not Let Workers Be Their Own Bosses?

Improving corporate governance is important, but we must go further.

While a voice in the corporate boardroom is vital, employees need more than that. In order to fundamentally shift the wealth of the economy back into the hands of the workers who create it, we have to give workers an ownership stake in the companies that employ them. And we have to make it easier for workers to establish employee-owned businesses that can compete at the national and global levels. We also have to support small business owners and small farmers, who struggle to hold their own against multinational corporations that have rigged the playing field to favor one-size-fits-all conglomerates.

These are issues that have interested me since the early 1980s, when as the mayor of Burlington I organized a town meeting on empowering workers. That was a time when there was a great deal of talk in the United States about employee stock-ownership plans (ESOPs), which allowed workers to earn a stake in their workplaces. At the same time, there was a growing consciousness of the successes of international initiatives along these lines, such as the Mondragon federation of worker cooperatives based in the Basque region of Spain.

Founded in the 1950s, Mondragon now employs more than eighty thousand people, working in what has become the seventh-largest business in Spain. It has done this while abiding by the standards of the International Cooperative Alliance, which requires them to operate "based on the values of self-help, self-responsibility, democracy, equality, equity and solidarity."

The town hall in Burlington was packed. People were really engaged with the issue, and over the succeeding years a number of worker-owned companies were developed in Vermont. We've now got around forty companies that are at least partially employee-owned, according to the Vermont Employee Ownership Center, and they employ more than three thousand people. Nationwide, there are roughly seven thousand companies with ESOPs, with more than ten million employees and $1.4 trillion in assets. Every year the Vermont ESOPs get together and I meet with them. The morale among the workers is much higher than in traditional, shareholder-controlled corporations. Absenteeism is lower. Productivity is great—for all the right reasons. If the ideas of workers are heard, if they have a vote on how the company is run, and if they get a share of the profits, why wouldn't they work hard?

That's not just my observation. Research by the Institute for the Study of Employee Ownership and Profit Sharing at Rutgers University has found that employee ownership boosts company productivity by 4 percent, shareholder returns by 2 percent, and profits by 14 percent.

This is a case where discarding the old uber-capitalist models and trying something new is good for workers and good for business. That's one of the reasons why I made employee ownership a big issue in my second presidential campaign. Under the plan that we developed during the campaign—and which I have since used as a basis for legislative proposals—corporations with at least $100 million in annual revenue, as well as all publicly traded companies, would be required to provide at least 2 percent of stock to their workers every year until the company is at least 20 percent owned by employees. This would be done through the issuing of new shares and the establishment of Democratic Employee Ownership Funds.

These funds would be controlled by a board of trustees directly elected by the workers, and that board would have the right to vote the shares in the best interest of company employees—in the same way that other institutional shareholders vote their shares. The shares would be held in permanent trust for the workers, and so, while they would increase in value, they wouldn't be sold to speculators. But employees would benefit from the increased value through dividends paid directly to them. When we released this plan in 2019, we calculated that 56 million workers in over 22,000 companies in the United States would benefit from it. An estimate based on data from over a thousand companies showed that directing 20 percent of dividends to workers could provide an average dividend payment of over $5,000 per worker every year.

That's a pretty good deal. A share of the profits and a real say in the direction of the company—since, as Elon Musk, Carl Icahn, and other corporate raiders have shown us, a 20 percent stake makes you a major player in even the largest corporations. But how do we make sure that employees can get a share of the companies they work for, and build new companies that are worker-owned? Should workers have to go to the big banks on Wall Street and ask for loans? I don't think so. If we're talking about establishing new economic models, we shouldn't be indebted to the guardians of the old models. So I have, with support from Senators Kirsten Gillibrand (D-NY), Patrick Leahy (D-VT), Maggie Hassan (D-NH), and Jeanne Shaheen (D-NH), introduced two pieces of legislation to help workers around the country obtain the funding they need to form employee-owned businesses.

One bill, the WORK Act, would provide more than $45 million to states in order to establish and expand employee ownership centers, which would provide training and technical support to people who want to take control of their workplaces. The other would create a U.S. Employee Ownership Bank to provide $500 million in low-interest loans and other financial assistance to help workers purchase businesses that would be operated under an employee stock-ownership plan or as worker-owned cooperatives. The argument I made for this legislation when I introduced it in 2019 was that expanding employee ownership and participation would create stronger companies, prevent job losses, and improve working conditions for struggling workers. It would also be good for the communities where worker-owned companies are located, especially those involved in manufacturing. Why? Because when employees have an ownership stake in their company, they will not ship their own jobs to China to increase their profits. They will choose to stay where they are located, find ways to be more productive, and keep the profits in their hometowns.

That's not the way uber-capitalists run companies these days. But that is the way that working Americans would run things if they had the authority and resources necessary to take charge of their own futures. That's not capitalism as it has operated in this country in recent years. That's economic democracy as Franklin Roosevelt envisioned it when he declared after his first term, "I should like to have it said of my first administration that in it the forces of selfishness and of lust for power met their match. I should like to have it said of my second administration that in it these forces met their master."

An Economy That Serves the Working Class

Discussions about the future of work, especially when they force us to consider the role that automation and artificial intelligence will play in defining that future, can be daunting. These discussions get even more demanding when we begin to discuss who should be in charge of workplaces, industries, and the broader economy. But we don't have to be overwhelmed by the debates that need to be had. We can keep the challenges in perspective by understanding that, while the technology may change, the basic economic and political and moral questions remain:

Will we treat workers with respect?
Will we give workers a real say in their workplaces?
Will we invite them into the debate about how those workplaces evolve?

These aren't new questions. They are the same questions that Eugene Victor Debs asked when he won almost a million votes in 1920 as the Socialist Party candidate for presidency, in a campaign he waged from an Atlanta jail cell—where he was imprisoned because of his opposition to the war profiteering and slaughter of World War I. The machinery may have changed, but the imbalance between economic elites and the working class has not. Nor has the injustice that extends from that imbalance.

It is time, finally, to set things right.

Progressive activists, trade unionists, and all who believe in dignity for workers must build a strong and visionary movement to remake our working life. To do that, we need a politics that is prepared to advance the cause of that movement. Only then can we ensure that the too-frequently wretched existence of today's exploited and exhausted workers will be transformed, and that the future will be forged by an emboldened and empowered working class.

8

EDUCATING CITIZENS, NOT ROBOTS

*Children should be taught to think—
not educated to be cogs in the machine*

The trouble with debates about public education in the United States is that they rarely have anything to do with education— let alone establishing the habits of analytical thinking and civic engagement that give us the freedom to be more than just cogs in the machinery of corporate America.

For the most part, in recent years, education debates at the national level and in communities across this country have been proxy wars for right-wing strategists who see schools as vehicles to advance their divide-and-conquer agenda. Cynical Republicans like Florida governor Ron DeSantis want to argue about whether students and teachers should be required to wear masks during a pandemic, about whether LGBTQ kids should be treated with respect, about whether educators should be allowed to teach the actual history of the United

States—as opposed to a truncated version in which fundamental issues are ignored and critical thinking is disregarded.

Amid all the political infighting over mask mandates and Critical
Race Theory, about test scores and funding mechanisms, we're losing our focus on what matters most in education: the encouragement
of students to explore big ideas, to learn how to assess what makes
sense and what does not, to become engaged and active citizens who
live happy and fulfilling lives. For education to get focused on the
real needs, and the real possibilities for students in the twenty-first
century, we have to break out of the mentality that considers our elementary and secondary schools merely training grounds for workers. There needs to be a recognition that Nelson Mandela was right
when he said, "Education is the most powerful weapon which you
can use to change the world."

The Great Equalizer

In a time of tremendous turbulence in the United States, when the
world was rocked by economic chaos and the rise of fascism, Franklin Roosevelt said, "Democracy cannot succeed unless those who
express their choice are prepared to choose wisely. The real safeguard of democracy, therefore, is education." Implicit in Roosevelt's
observation was the understanding that every American had a right
to a high-quality education, and that with this education, America
would forge a more humane and prosperous country. We certainly
didn't live up to the promise of universal high-quality education in
FDR's time—when school segregation was accepted not just in the
South but in much of the North—and we still don't today.

But under the influence of pioneering educational theorists such
as John Dewey and Mary McLeod Bethune, we began to recognize
that education could be about more than just job training. It could
help us realize our own promise as creative and engaged citizens
who, in turn, are able to make our democracy and our society work
for all of us. It could take children from difficult backgrounds and

give them opportunities that their grandparents and parents had been denied. It could realize the potential that the great abolitionist and education reformer Horace Mann outlined in the nineteenth century when he said, "Education, then, beyond all other divides of human origin, is a great equalizer of conditions of men—the balance wheel of the social machinery."

The education I got in the post–World War II era played a huge role in giving me the background that allowed me to become a mayor, a member of Congress, a U.S. senator, and a candidate for president of the United States. I came from a working-class family. I went to public schools in Brooklyn, P.S. 197 and then James Madison High School, the same school that graduated Ruth Bader Ginsburg and Chuck Schumer. The kids I went to school with didn't have a lot of money, but in the post–World War II era, we were encouraged to see college as a way up, and I certainly did. After a year at Brooklyn College, I transferred to the University of Chicago and started studying political science. There I had the opportunity to do a great deal of reading about economics, sociology, history—you name it, I read it.

I want my grandchildren to have the same opportunities I did. But I'm not so nostalgic, or so naive, as to believe that a replication of the education I got in the 1950s and '60s will be sufficient for the times in which they will come of age. I want them to have an education that prepares them for the twenty-first century. At the heart of that education, however, must be a set of values that help us to learn from the mistakes of the past and start getting things right. I know, from meeting with students and parents and teachers across this country, that there is a passion for making public schools better than they have ever been. And I know from talking with experts on education in this country and countries around the world—including Finland, which will figure prominently in this chapter—that there are great ideas for how to get the job done.

But, for that to happen, progressives have to renew their understanding that education policy is central to progress for society. Historically, progressives were at the forefront of education debates, battling to establish free public education, to open schools to all students, to build great schools in urban and rural areas, and to fully fund them. There was a forward motion to our activism.

Over the past several decades, however, right-wingers have warped the debates to such an extent that most of our fights these days seem to be defensive ones. We've been forced to push back against privatization schemes, against anti-teacher sentiment in general, and specifically against the efforts by Republican governors, such as Wisconsin's Scott Walker, to disempower teachers' unions, against cuts in funding for rural schools, against those who see diversity as a problem rather than a strength, against efforts to dumb down curriculums, against campaigns to take over school boards by right-wing zealots. It's overwhelming. And it gets us off course. When we are always fighting against those who would take us backward, it's hard to find time to make the arguments for what needs to be done to go forward.

We've got to reclaim this debate because the fight for universal, high-quality education at the primary and secondary levels, and for free college, is about more than just maintaining public schools. It is about making them stronger, more accessible and more engaging than they have ever been. It is about making our society better. And it is vital to the struggle that we defeat the threat of authoritarianism. Students and teachers recognize this. As Randi Weingarten, the president of the American Federation of Teachers, has said, "The fight to safeguard democracy begins in America's classrooms and schools, where we both embrace America's diversity and forge a common identity. Our public schools are where young people develop the skills they need to be engaged and empowered citizens—voice, latitude and the ability to think for oneself. Teachers must have the freedom to teach these skills—which may not be measured on standardized tests, but which are the measure of a vibrant citizenry."

This is not just a fight that teachers can or should fight on their own. We should be at their side, raising up the best ideas and ensuring that they have the resources and the support, the freedom and the flexibility, that are needed to renew public education's promise as both the great equalizer and the great champion of democracy.

Start by Listening to Students and Teachers

During my 2016 and 2020 presidential campaigns, the media tended to reduce my advocacy on education issues to two words: "free tuition." I didn't entirely mind that. I knew that we were remaking the debate about how to fund higher education at a time when more and more young adults were being saddled with student debt—and when too many of them were giving up on their dreams because they no longer believed they could afford to follow them. But, as a senator and presidential candidate who earned much of my support from young voters, I have never limited my discussions and my advocacy to one rung on the education ladder, or to one set of issues facing educators and their students.

For a dozen years in Vermont, I have sponsored a "State of the Union" essay contest that asks Vermont high school students to submit essays about major issues facing the country and to offer proposals for how to solve them. Over the years, more than 5,300 students have entered the annual competition, and I've had many chances to sit down with these remarkable teenagers. Some of the best discussions I've had about public policy have occurred in these gatherings—and in town meetings I've held with middle school and high school students over the years. They've given me a lot of ideas about how to make schools more responsive to their needs. The same goes for the town hall meetings I had on education with high school and college students, parents and teachers, during my presidential bids.

In Iowa, I heard again and again about the crisis facing underfunded rural schools where too many students have been left on the losing side of the digital divide, which has opened up because of a failure to extend high-speed broadband internet to every corner of this country. In Nevada, I heard about deteriorating schools that had begun to crumble as a result of this country's failure to invest in infrastructure. As I was traveling across the country in 2018 and 2019, I heard from a lot of teachers like Jay O'Neal, an eighth-grade history instructor at Stonewall Jackson Middle School in Charleston, West Virginia. Jay was one of the key organizers of a 2018 teachers' strike in West Virginia that, along with similar actions in so-called red states that year, drew national attention to the fact that low pay was forcing teachers to struggle just to support their own families. I was moved by the courage of these teachers— and by their deep commitment to public education in general and to their students in particular. "We were afraid to go on strike," explained Jay, who like other teachers in the Right to Work state of West Virginia faced the prospect of losing his job if he struck for better pay and better schools. "I remember talking to my wife like, 'Is this a risk I want to take? I might be fired.' But circumstances are just getting to that point where it's pushing a lot of us to that place where we finally have got to stand up no matter what the consequences are."

The teachers in West Virginia had tried negotiations. They had asked state officials to listen to their pleas for better pay and better school-funding formulas. Instead of a response that prioritized education, they were met with proposals from the state for increased health insurance payments. Things were heading in the wrong direction and state senator Richard Ojeda, a Democrat who represented the rural coal country of southern West Virginia, warned his fellow legislators in January of 2018, "We're not listening to our teachers. You're sitting on a powder keg." He was right.

The teachers walked out on February 22, 2018, wearing the red T-shirts that gave rise to the slogan RED FOR ED, and they quickly won the support of students and parents. Crowds at the state capitol grew so large that media outlets across the country began to take notice. So, too, did West Virginia legislators and the governor. On March 6, 2018, after nine days of protests in Charleston and around West Virginia, headlines announced: "West Virginia Teachers Win 5 Percent Pay Raise as Massive Strike Comes to an End." It was a remarkable victory, and a powerful inspiration for teachers and supporters of public education across the country. The movement spread beyond the borders of West Virginia to other states—Arizona, Colorado, Kentucky, North Carolina, and Oklahoma among them—and led to a number of victories for teachers and their unions.

I was enthusiastic about what Jay O'Neal and other educators were doing. "The courage of the teachers is reverberating all across the country," I declared in speeches as I launched my 2020 presidential bid. Our campaign produced a video featuring Jay. In it, he said, "Somebody has got to do something and I guess that somebody is me. It's up to us. Nobody else is going to make the change."

I understood the sense of isolation that many of these teachers felt, and I resolved to make the cause, and big thinking about the future of public education, central to the campaign.

An Education Agenda That Puts Students and Teachers First

In May of 2019, on the sixty-fifth anniversary of the U.S. Supreme Court's *Brown v. Board of Education* ruling that racial segregation in public schools was unconstitutional, our presidential campaign announced a comprehensive vision for a fundamental overhaul of schooling in America. We called it the "Thurgood Marshall Plan for Public Education" out of respect for former U.S. Supreme Court Justice Thurgood Marshall, who as the head of the NAACP Legal Defense and Educational Fund had served as chief attorney for the plaintiffs in the *Brown* case.

The plan took on a lot of powerful interests and I knew it would be controversial. But I did not mince words in announcing it:

> The United States, as the wealthiest country in history, should have the best education system in the world. Today, in a highly competitive global economy, if we are going to have the kind of standard of living that the people of this country deserve, we need to have the best-educated workforce. But let me be very

honest with you, and tell you that, sadly, that is not the case today. Our nation used to lead the world in the percentage of young Americans with college degrees. We were number one. Today, we are number eleven, behind countries like South Korea, Japan, Canada, Ireland, the United Kingdom, and Australia—and that is not acceptable. And here is the simple truth: Forty or fifty years ago, in California and Vermont, virtually any place in America, if you received a high school degree, the odds were pretty good that you would be able to get a decent paying job, raise a family, buy a house, buy a car, all on one income. That was the world forty or fifty years ago. But that is not the world we live in today. The world has changed, the global economy has changed, technology has changed, and education has changed.

Misplaced priorities and a failure to focus on the future have, I argued, robbed tens of millions of students of educational opportunities, as states made savage cuts to education funding that were having a profound impact on the quality of education. "Among the thirty-five countries that are members of the Organization for Economic Cooperation and Development, the United States ranked thirtieth in math and nineteenth in science," I said. "Reading scores for our students are not much better. The United States ranked twenty-fourth when compared to other highly industrialized countries such as Singapore, Canada, and Germany."

That was bad enough. Worse yet was the reality that this decline in education standings hit hardest at students of color, low-income students, LGBTQ students, students with disabilities, and underserved students in rural schools.

Start with the Basics: Fund Schools, Pay Teachers, Feed Kids

The plan I campaigned on, and that I continue to promote as a member of the Senate, was comprehensive. It proposed to:

- **Combat racial discrimination and school segregation.**
  To undo the damage done by Betsy DeVos, Trump's education secretary, I argued that we needed initiatives to increase
  federal funding for community-led strategies to desegregate
  schools. I also promised to execute and enforce desegregation
  orders and to appoint federal judges who would enforce the
  1964 Civil Rights Act in school systems. In addition, I said,
  we needed to establish a dedicated fund to create and expand
  teacher-training programs at Historically Black Colleges and
  Universities, and at tribal colleges and universities, to increase educator diversity.
- **End the unaccountable profit motive of charter
  schools.** I said that we needed to ban for-profit charter
  schools, and support the NAACP's moratorium on public
  funds for charter school expansion, until a national audit
  could be completed to determine the impact of charter
  growth in each state. I also called for halting the use of public
  funds to underwrite new charter schools.
- **Guarantee equitable funding for public schools.** I outlined a plan for establishing a national per-pupil spending
  floor for all schools, ensuring that schools would have the
  funding needed to maintain art, music, and foreign language
  education. I also called for providing rural and Indigenous
  communities with equitable funding; providing schools with
  the resources needed to shrink class sizes; reducing reliance
  on standardized testing; and providing $5 billion annually for
  career and technical education to give students the skills they
  need to thrive once they graduate.
- **Strengthen the Individuals with Disabilities Education
  Act (IDEA).** The federal government once promised to fund
  40 percent of the cost of special education. That promise was
  broken, and I argued that the time had come to provide man-
  datory federal funding of at least 50 percent of special education costs. I also argued that officials could, and should,

guarantee children with disabilities an equal right to high-quality education by enforcing the Americans with Disabilities Act.

- **Raise teacher pay and empower them to teach.** The federal government should work with the states to set a starting salary for teachers at no less than $60,000, with adjustments for areas with a higher cost of living. I also said it was time to protect and expand collective bargaining rights so that teachers could advocate for their own rights—and for their students.

- **Expand after-school/summer education programs.** In order *to* guarantee that all students can get the academic, social, and professional skills they need to succeed, I called for new funding for after-school and summer-learning programs. While the Trump administration had actually cut funding for these vital programs, I proposed to spend $5 billion annually to expand them.

- **Provide universal school meals.** As a morally and practically necessary intervention in a country where, prior to the pandemic, one in every six kids went hungry, I pledged to deliver year-round, free universal school meals. I also proposed incentives for sourcing food from local sources. When the pandemic hit, Rep. Ilhan Omar and others got the federal government to provide funding for just such programs. Unfortunately, they were allowed to lapse. We need to restore them.

- **Develop sustainable community schools.** I advanced a plan to deliver $5 billion in annual funding so that public schools could serve not just as places of learning, but as community centers that build the health and well-being of students. The concept here was to promote the recognition of our education system into a high-quality public good that connects education, health, and social services to young people.

- **Invest in school infrastructure.** The plan I outlined would completely close the gap in school infrastructure funding so that we could renovate, modernize, and green the nation's schools.
- **Make schools a safe and inclusive place for all.** In the interest of equity and common sense, I argued that we had to protect the safety of all students by enacting comprehensive legislation to guard against gun violence; enforcing Title IX protections against harassment, discrimination, and violence in educational institutions; ensuring that immigrant children and their parents are free from harassment and surveillance at school, regardless of their immigration status; and enacting protections for LGBTQ students. As I said at the time, "Our schools must be safe for all students. Period. It is disgusting that our children must face the terrifying reality of being at risk of being killed in their own schools, and that school districts must resort to measures like this to try to keep kids safe. We must ensure LGBTQ students can attend school without fear of bullying, and work to substantially reduce suicides."

Utopian? Not at all, if we care about the future of our children and grandchildren. Too ambitious? Only by American standards. Much of what I proposed in 2019 has already been implemented in other countries, which rank far above the United States in terms of educational achievement. We were falling behind before the coronavirus pandemic hit, which only put us further behind—as schools were forced to shutter and students struggled with distance learning. I want to catch up. But then I want us to take the next step that will put the United States at the top of the rankings.

To get there, we have to start by recognizing why the United States is having a hard time keeping up. Mike Colagrossi, who writes frequently about education issues for the World Economic Forum, suggested several years ago that, "despite calls for education reform and a continual lackluster performance on the international scale, not a lot is being done or changing within the educational system. Many private and public schools run on the same antiquated systems and schedules that were once conducive to an agrarian society. The mechanization and rigid assembly-line methods we use today are spitting out ill-prepared worker clones, rudderless adults and an uninformed populace."

That's a tough but reasonably sound assessment of the challenges we face. And Finland—a country that Colagrossi and others point to as a model—offers us ideas for how to respond to them.

What We Can Learn from Finland

Finland is a small Scandinavian country that is very different from the United States in very many ways. But I believe it has a lot to teach us in terms of education, and I'm not alone in this regard.

Finland's education system is regarded as one of the best in the world. Over just the past five years, it has earned steadily high rankings from the international Organization for Economic Co-operation and Development's Better Life Index, *The Economist*'s Worldwide Educating for the Future Index, and the World Economic Forum's Global Competitiveness Report. These rankings shift from year to year, but Finland's are always near the top and often number one.

The bestselling author William Doyle, teaching at a Finnish university as a Fulbright Scholar a few years ago, enrolled his seven-year-old son in a rural public school there. He wrote an essay on the experience that began, "I have seen the school of tomorrow. It is here today, in Finland.

"I found Finland's school system to be an absolute inspiration, and a beacon of hope in a world that is struggling, and often failing, to figure out how to best educate our children," wrote Doyle, who explained that the secret of Finland's success is that it has developed "a whole-child-centered, research-and-evidence based school system, run by highly professionalized teachers. These are global education best practices, not cultural quirks applicable only to Finland."

Like me, Doyle rejects the notion that Scandinavian countries such as Finland are too small or too distinct from the United States to provide instruction for Americans on how to improve schools. "Some skeptics dismiss Finland's schools as being the product of its demographics, but they ignore the fact that its population size and poverty rate are similar to over two-thirds of American states, and in the United States, education is largely run at the state level," he observes. "Finland's schools are the product of a unique culture. But so are the public schools of Canada, Singapore, Shanghai, Denmark, South Korea, Australia and Japan, as are the private schools attended by the world's political and business elites. To automatically dismiss critical insights from any nation or school is a mistake. We can all learn from each other."

With that in mind, I arranged a conversation with Li Sigrid Andersson, who became Finland's minister of education in 2019. The thirty-five-year-old mother of a one-year-old daughter, Li is the leader of the Left Alliance, a democratic socialist party that has for decades argued that democratic institutions must be strengthened in order to resist the overwhelming influence of global capitalism on economics, politics, and society. It's a party that says, "We want everyone to receive sufficient income, extensive public services, and secure, excellent health care and nurture. We are building a society where every child can access quality pre-schooling and elementary education, where everyone can get to the doctor when they need it, possesses an equal opportunity to obtain a decently priced home, and enjoys their work." Anyone who is reading this book knows that these are values that I share. So, though Li and I live in different countries and are about forty-five years apart in age, we found we had a lot in common.

Li began by explaining her view that, for progressives the world over, education must be a focus not just in and of itself but as part of a broader struggle to create a freer and more equal society. I agreed and we got down to business. Then she described what she referred to as "a few cornerstones of Finnish education policy." In particular, she emphasized that Finland:

- **Trusts teachers.** "I've said we have a trust-based system, not
  a control-based system. Our teachers are all educated at university, which means that you have to have a master's degree
  for teaching children from the first years all the way, of
  course, to upper-secondary level.

  "The teaching profession is still quite an attractive and valued one, societally. Teachers' salaries are fairly good, which
  means that we have been able to [attract talented young people]
  to the profession. It also means that we've been able to build a
  system where teachers get a lot of autonomy in their work."

- **Rejects standardized testing in its primary education
  system.** "We trust our teachers and their professional compe-
  tences and give them the autonomy to decide on the issues
  themselves in the classroom in their own schools.

  "Compared to Anglo-Saxon countries, which are heavily
  control-based, and where (even at the elementary school
  level) they start teaching and students start studying just for
  these standardized tests, in Finland there is an effort to focus
  on the joy of learning, on learning how to learn."

- **Believes every school must be a great school.** "We don't
  have any lists of the best schools in the country. We have a
  system based on public education, so each student can trust
  their closest neighborhood school in their own area of the city
  or their own municipality. They can trust that school to be
  one of the best in the world . . .

  "The differences between schools in learning outcomes
  are among the smallest of all the countries in the world—
  even the smallest of all the Nordic countries—which we
  think is largely based on the fact that we have highly educated and competent teachers, so we've managed to build a
  structurally strong system when it comes to education."

- **Maintains an overwhelmingly public education system.**
  "Almost all of our primary education is public. There are
  some private education providers, but they are not allowed to

make profits. It's forbidden in the Finnish education law. So this means there is no market for private companies. That's why we have quite few private actors in primary education, and they are mostly, for example, Montessori [schools] that want to emphasize a different kind of [learning]."

- **Believes education must be free.** "Education is free of charge from primary education all the way up to university education. We also introduced a system with free school meals as early as 1948, which is sometimes a factor that's quite overlooked in education policy debates, but actually very important for equality and also for good learning outcomes, especially for students that come from less advantaged backgrounds. To get a good, free, warm meal in school every day during studies is important."

- **Gives everyone the option to further their education.** "We strive for structural equality, which means that no matter what path you choose after primary education—whether you choose vocational education and training or general upper-secondary education—you have the possibility to apply to university studies afterwards. So you don't close any doors if you choose vocational education.

   "This is something I think is important from a leftist perspective because it also means that, even though you go and study to become a carpenter or a chef or a car mechanic, you need and you will study languages. You will study mathematics. You will study civics. And you will have the right to apply for university later on, if you want to."

How do they pay for all this? Not like we do in the United States, where most K–12 education is funded by property taxes—meaning that wealthy school districts tend to have far more money for teacher pay, new buildings, and ambitious curriculums than working-class districts. In Finland, municipalities all around the country receive funding from the national government on a per-student basis. Mu-

nicipalities can add to the amount if, for instance, they want to
provide more kindergarten programming for low-income neighborhoods. But no school in Finland can fall below the baseline of funding that is determined to be necessary to provide an outstanding
education.

There's constant concern about inequality creeping in, explained
Li: "We work hard on the local level, making sure that we don't get
segregated cities with certain areas for the poorer families and certain areas for the richer families. And we're also working with something that we call needs-based funding, or equal-opportunity funding,
which means that schools or kindergartens that are located in more
disadvantaged areas will get additional financial resources for more
teachers, or extra teaching or for smaller classes."

Let Kids Be Kids

The economics are important, and the emphasis on equality is vital.
But what really struck me was the education minister's emphasis on
making sure that kids get to be kids.

While Finland competes with countries that have far more rigid
education systems—including ours in the United States—Li suggested that one of the reasons why the Finnish system succeeds
when others stumble is its flexibility. And its emphasis on maintaining a balance between schoolwork and fun.

"I think compared to many other educational systems, Finnish
children start school quite late. Primary education starts at age seven,
and our school days are not that long," she said. "In many Asian
countries, for example, you will have very long hours and very long
days, and then you'll have extracurricular activities afterward. We
focus on making sure that there is a balance between schoolwork
and leisure. There's also a lot of focus on leisure and play during the
school day. We try and remember that well-being is as important for
learning as good teaching."

The well-being of parents is also a focus of the Finnish system.

Finland, which was once a very poor country, has in the post–World War II era developed one of the most advanced social-welfare states in the world. People are guaranteed health care as a right. New parents are given a year of paid leave so they can stay home and care for their baby. Moms and dads usually divide the time off. Li had a baby while serving as education minister. "I was away for half a year, then I came back, and now a colleague of mine from the Greens was away for half a year. She came back. And then our husbands have been at home for half a year after us," she explained. When both parents are back at work, families can take advantage of a childcare system that is one of the best in the world. And one of the most affordable, with fees minimal for working-class children and capped at less than 300 euros a month for better-off families.

When children start school at seven, they enter a system where teachers see it as part of their job to ensure that every child succeeds. That's true of many American teachers, as well. But in Finland, teachers are given the resources and the time to do the job. School days are short. There's plenty of time for after-school clubs and sports in centers that are funded by the state. Schedules are arranged so that there's lots of time for individual attention to the needs of students who might otherwise fall through the cracks. Teachers are given immense flexibility so that they can find their right approaches. "I think this idea about investing in teachers, investing in that profession, in trusting them, is something that is a policy," said Li. "You can address it as you need to from your own country's perspective, but I still think that this whole idea of the role of the teaching profession is my main message from Finland."

That idea pays enormous benefits for individual young people, who can pursue their dreams in a higher education system where college is free, and government grants and loans are provided to assure that college students can concentrate on their studies. Instead of graduating with massive amounts of student debt, young Finns are free to be creative and contribute to society rather than struggling to manage overwhelming debt burdens.

Teaching Young People That They Really Can Save the World

Finns don't simply train young people to be good workers—although the country has a global reputation for its innovative and productive workforce—they teach them to be good people. And good citizens.

"There is a lot of emphasis on democratic citizenship," Li told me. "We don't want our children just to know how society functions—how a law is made, for example; what are the powers of each institution. We also want children to know how they can make a difference. If you want to change something in society, how do you do it? What are the different ways that you have, as a citizen, to make the change?"

Curriculums are organized so that students can examine complex societal problems—such as climate change—in all of their classes, as well as in clubs and after-school activities. The point is to give young people a sense of the role they can play in solving those problems. "As a minister, I've emphasized the importance of really getting everybody involved, by creating democratic processes that will engage all students in the classroom, so that we are not used to the idea of always just electing officials that will then go on and deal with these issues for us. We want to encourage each child to think about how they could make a change in society if they want to."

Instead of telling young people to be quiet, and discouraging dissent, Finland encourages them to recognize their roles as leaders in the society they will inherit.

"It's something that we need to work on all the time," Li told me. "If you look at the climate movements and Greta Thunberg, I think it's a good example of what I'm talking about. Our school students doing school strikes for the climate I think is a sign that our school system is doing something right, because it means that we have been able to teach our students about the enormous impact that the climate crisis will have on our society, what a huge and important issue it is for all of us—and also we're encouraging them to engage in active citizenship."

Think about that. Students being taught about problems, and

then being taught they can solve them—indeed, that they should take the lead in resolving them. I know there are dedicated teachers in the United States who try to do this every day, and sometimes they succeed. But I also know that, too frequently, our best teachers are overwhelmed. They lack the resources they need to do their jobs. They are forced to manage all the crises that arise when students are hungry, or lack access to housing, health care, and transportation.

Why Shouldn't American Schools Be the Best?

The Finns didn't try to suggest that they had all the answers. Like any good progressive, Li talked to me about all the things she still wanted to do—provide more support for rural schools, guard against privatization, help schools better prepare students for the changing future of work.

But I was struck during our conversations by her optimism and enthusiasm. She didn't see education as a problem or a mess or a crisis to be "dealt with"—as so many policymakers in the United States do. She saw schools as places of hope and opportunity. She recounted their successes, and delighted in talking about the connections between those successes and Finland's rank as one of the happiest countries in the world.

Yes, the United States and Finland are different. But there is no reason why the United States can't have the best schools and, yes, the happiest students and teachers, parents and citizens, in the world. In fact, there is every reason why we should make it our immediate goal. Our children and grandchildren deserve no less.

9

CORPORATE MEDIA IS UNDERMINING DEMOCRACY

Political reform requires alternatives to a for-profit media system that dumbs down and diminishes debate in America

As someone who has won more than a dozen election campaigns, and lost a few along the way, I understand as well as anyone that the media plays an enormously important—often definitional—role in our entire political process. But the influence of media on our lives goes far beyond campaigns and elections. Media shapes our public consciousness. It determines the "news of the day" and the issues that we are supposed to consider "important." It shapes our thinking about what is realistic, and what must be dismissed as unobtainable "pie-in-the-sky" pipedreams.

Media does not merely determine the range of "acceptable" options that are available to Americans when it comes to tackling the major challenges of our times. Media, in many instances, determines the range of options that are available for living our lives. Through the constant bombardment of corporate advertising, media shapes our culture and our value systems and tells us what is necessary in order to live "the good life" in an uber-capitalist society. The advertising tells us what coffee we must drink in order to be cool, what cars we must purchase in order to be prestigious, and what credit cards we must obtain in order to pay for all that stuff. While kids who watch television may not know in what century the Vietnam War was fought, they surely do know what sneakers they must buy in order to be in with the "in" crowd.

There is a widespread illusion in this country that, because we have access to hundreds of cable channels and can go just about anywhere on the internet; because we've got Twitter and Facebook and YouTube and TikTok; because we still see dozens of newspapers and magazines on newsstands, that we are a nation with many media outlets that are independent and separately owned. Among a great many Americans, there remains a lingering faith—or perhaps it is just a hope—that our "free press" system gives us a wide diversity of options when it comes to gathering the information that is needed in order to govern our own lives.

Unfortunately, that's not the case.

Billionaires Own the Media, and It Shows

Today, roughly 90 percent of all U.S. media is controlled by eight major media conglomerates—Comcast, Disney, Warner Bros. Discovery, Netflix, CBS, Facebook, Fox News, and Hearst—and that concentration of ownership has become tighter and tighter over the years as a result of multibillion-dollar media mergers and acquisitions. Options aren't expanding, they're contracting, as we saw in the spring of 2022, when the sale of CNN by one media conglomerate, AT&T, to another, Warner Bros. Discovery, was followed by reports that the new owner would shut down the much-heralded CNN+ streaming service and either remove or "rein in" hosts who were seen as too critical of Donald Trump.

The bottom line is this: A handful of huge media conglomerates, owned by the wealthiest people in the United States, maintain overwhelming control over what we see, hear, and read. It would be absurd to imagine that these billionaire owners expend substantial fortunes to buy and maintain massive media conglomerates as a public service. They have agendas—rooted in a desire to expand their wealth and power—and those agendas have nothing to do with bettering conditions for America's working families.

If the corporate agenda were advanced openly and unapologetically on an individual television network, that would be one thing. Many countries have business-friendly news outlets that answer every question about policy with a proposal to "let the market decide." But that's not how it works in the United States. In this country, a cable television viewer can flip from one station to another and still be viewing the "product" of the same media conglomerate.

So it is that, in the United States, you can change the channel from NBC to MSNBC to CNBC to Telemundo to the Peacock streaming service and you'll still be watching news shows that are produced, written, reported, and anchored by employees of one company: Comcast. Tired of the news and want some entertainment? You can watch USA Network, Syfy, Oxygen, Bravo, G4, and E! and always remain on a network owned by Comcast. You watch a movie from the Universal Pictures studio, or a feature developed by DreamWorks Animation, Illumination, or Universal Animation Studios, and, again, you'll be in the warm embrace of Comcast, which owns all those studios.

Comcast, which had assets of $276 billion at the end of 2021, is the biggest multinational telecommunications conglomerate in the United States, the biggest pay-TV company, the biggest cable TV company, the biggest internet service provider for homes in the United States, and the third-biggest home telephone service provider. Its reach extends to more than forty states and the District of Columbia. And with all of that said, we're just scratching the surface of a media landscape packed with digital distribution, streaming services, and ad-tech firms owned by Comcast.

Where Comcast leaves off, Disney picks up. The animation firm that brought you Mickey Mouse now owns ABC and a $200 billion empire that includes major stakes in ESPN, A&E, The History Channel, Lifetime, "local" television and radio stations across the country, and entertainment producers such as Touchstone Pictures and the *Star Wars* franchise at Lucasfilm Ltd.

Then there's Rupert Murdoch's Fox Corporation, which owns the Fox Broadcasting Company, Fox News, Fox Business, Fox Nation, Fox Sports, the Big Ten Network, Fox News Talk, and twenty-eight local television stations in major markets across the country. Its Fox New Radio operation supplies national news reports to more than five hundred local AM and FM radio stations nationwide, while at the same time feeding programs to SiriusXM satellite radio. Its Fox News Talk project produces right-wing talk radio programming for Sirius and for broadcast radio stations nationwide. Fox's "sister corporation," News Corp—a pet project of Murdoch and his family—owns newspapers and magazines, as well as radio and pay-TV outlets in the United Kingdom. News Corp is particularly influential in Murdoch's native Australia, where the firm's newspaper holdings have historically played a critical role in influencing coverage of politics. But its influence in the United States may even be greater. Here, News Corp owns Dow Jones & Company, the publisher of the nationally circulated *Wall Street Journal,* as well as major financial publications and news sites such as *Barron's* and MarketWatch. Since 1976, Murdoch and News Corp have owned the *New York Post,* a daily newspaper that has played an outsized role in the politics of New York City, the metropolis that produced Donald Trump.

Fox faces "competition" but less and less scrutiny these days from CNN, which is owned by the newly formed Warner Bros. Discovery conglomerate. In February 2022, AT&T spun off its media holdings in a $43 billion deal with the Discovery Channel that moved CNN, and other "media properties" it had owned, under the umbrella of Warner Bros. Discovery, a firm that also owns HBO, Cinemax, the Turner Broadcasting System, Warner Bros. Entertainment

Inc., the Warner Bros. Pictures Group, the Warner Bros. Television Group, and the Warner Bros. Home Entertainment Group.

The Same Wall Street Firms Own "Competing" Media Conglomerates

If you think that it is dangerous and anti-democratic for a handful of major media corporations to own most of the major media outlets in the United States, I've got bad news for you. It's even worse than you think. Today in America, three Wall Street firms control assets of over $20 trillion and are among the major institutional investors in the vast majority of American companies. That includes media companies. In other words, at a time when the handful of giant conglomerates own hundreds of newspapers, television channels, radio stations, internet outlets, movie production companies, book publishing firms, and magazines, these giant corporations themselves are at least partially owned by even larger entities on Wall Street.

Vanguard Group is the largest institutional investor in Fox Corporation, and BlackRock is the fourth largest. Vanguard is the top institutional investor in Warner Bros. Discovery, and the second-largest institutional investor is BlackRock. The biggest institutional investors in Disney are Vanguard and BlackRock. Vanguard is the top institutional investor in Comcast, with 402,080,815 shares as of January 29, 2022—or roughly 9 percent of the company—while Black-Rock was the second-largest investor, with 320,503,107 shares, for around 7 percent ownership. And that's not even counting the major investments by mutual funds, such as the Vanguard Total Stock Market Index Fund, the Vanguard 500 Index Fund, and the Vanguard Institutional Index Fund, in Comcast.

It's Not Just Conglomerates

Not all major media companies are owned by conglomerates. Some are owned directly by individual billionaires. Jeff Bezos, the second-wealthiest person in the world, bought *The Washington Post* in 2013.

John Henry, a billionaire who owns the Boston Red Sox, is the owner of *The Boston Globe*. Patrick Soon-Shiong, a biotech entrepreneur, owns the *Los Angeles Times* and *The San Diego Union-Tribune*. Michael Bloomberg, former New York City mayor, former presidential candidate, and one of the wealthiest people in the country, owns Bloomberg News. The late billionaire Sheldon Adelson, a major Republican Party contributor, owned the *Las Vegas Review-Journal*. Glen Taylor, the owner of the Minnesota Timberwolves, owns the *Star Tribune* in Minneapolis. And of course, Rupert Murdoch, while not the owner of every Fox and News Corp share, still calls the political shots—along with his like-minded son, Lachlan Murdoch, who serves as CEO of both Fox Corporation and News Corp—when editorial decisions are being made.

It matters when very rich men own the largest and most influential newspapers and news networks. It also matters that their employees, the anchors and hosts at those networks, are themselves wealthy, collecting salaries that are in the millions per year. For instance, Fox's Sean Hannity banks a salary of more than $40 million annually and has a net worth of $250 million. Hannity may play a populist on TV, but he's actually a quarter-billionaire with a major stake in serving his own interests and those of his billionaire benefactors.

Most working journalists struggle to get by. That's especially true for reporters and editors on regional dailies that have been gutted by distant owners who are more interested in maximizing profits than in making sure communities are covered. But media elites work in a rarefied atmosphere where they have far more in common with their employers, the wealthy and the powerful, than they do with the working class. And let us not forget: At the end of the day, these well-known media personalities are nothing more than well-paid employees. Giant conglomerates write their paychecks.

In terms of political coverage, my main concern with corporate media has not been so much about the accuracy of the reporting. Donald Trump, surprise, surprise, is wrong when he says what's reported by major media outlets is "fake news." That's not the case. He's just upset that the media often exposes his own pathological lying. For the most part, my experience has been that reporters are serious and hardworking people who try to get their facts straight. I've been in politics for a long time, and I can tell you that I've rarely been misquoted.

Why Doesn't the Media Talk About Class Issues?

The problem with the corporate media is not "fake news" or inaccurate reporting. It's what, because of ownership pressure, the media chooses to cover and emphasize, and what they choose to ignore and downplay. This is what Noam Chomsky, the linguist and activist who is widely recognized as the greatest public intellectual of our time, refers to as "manufacturing consent." In our corporate media today, with its thousands of television stations, radio stations, newspapers, magazines, and websites, there is a virtual blackout when it comes to issues of class and power in the United States. Not surprisingly, the people who have the wealth and power are not interested in publicly discussing their wealth and power and how they exercise it. They know that's better dealt with behind closed corporate doors, because if Americans understood how multinational corporations really operate, they would face overwhelming outrage.

Without deep discussions and honest analyses of corporate power, it is extremely difficult for citizens to understand what goes on in the country, and why. And it is almost impossible to know who should be held to account. How can anyone make an intelligent critique of power if they don't know who is making the decisions that shape our lives? But how can we get that information from the corporate media when the owners of that media benefit from our ignorance? The bottom line is that the billionaire owners of corporate media aren't going to open up national debates about growing income and wealth inequality, about the ways in which their lobbyists wield power in Washington, or about how the effective tax rates they pay are lower than for the people they employ. Because we don't have those national debates, there is growing alienation on the part of the American people from the political process.

And, by the way, in terms of reporting on important issues, how often have you seen discussions on our major media outlets about who owns the media?

Faith in democracy itself has been undermined. If Americans are not offered honest reporting on the reality of their lives, if they do not see their lived experience in what they read, see, and hear, politics becomes irrelevant to them and they give up on government—not only as a vehicle for solving their own problems but as a force for good in society. Some people embrace conspiracy theories and anti-government extremism. Many more simply check out. Election turn-out in the United States, even in presidential years, is only a fraction of what is seen in European and Asian democracies. Our local elections, especially in communities where media systems have collapsed, are so neglected that turnouts as low as 25 percent are celebrated as "good."

Over many years, as a member of the U.S. House of Representatives and the U.S. Senate, and as a presidential candidate, I have appeared on every major Sunday news show—ABC, CBS, NBC, CNN, Fox—numerous times and have done thousands of TV interviews. Yet, in all those interviews, I have *never* been asked about some of the most important and profound issues facing our country. Never! And it's not just me. There are issues of enormous consequence that are almost totally ignored by corporate media. Here are a few of the questions that I have never been asked:

Question: What does it mean, morally, economically, and politically, that three multibillionaires own more wealth than the 160 million Americans who make up the bottom half of our society? Why do we have more income and wealth inequality today than at any time in the past century? What does it mean that, in an economy supposedly based on free enter-

prise and competition, three Wall Street firms—BlackRock,
Vanguard, and State Street—manage over $20 trillion in as-
sets and are major shareholders in more than 96 percent of
S&P 500 companies?

Question: Why does the average American worker today, in
inflation-adjusted wages, earn less than he/she did fifty years
ago—despite an explosion in technology and worker productivity? Why, in the richest country on earth, do 60 percent of
our people live paycheck to paycheck, while millions are
forced to work for starvation wages?

Question: Why are we the only major country on earth not to
guarantee health care for all people? Why do we pay twice as
much per capita for health care as any other country, and yet
have 85 million Americans who are uninsured or underinsured?

Question: Scandinavian countries—Sweden, Finland, Denmark, and Norway—have made enormous progress over the
years in providing a high quality of life for their citizens and,
according to international surveys, are generally at the top of
the list in terms of human happiness. What can we learn
from these countries in terms of social policy?

Question: The scientific community, for many decades, has
made it crystal clear that climate change—and all the dangers
it poses in terms of drought, floods, extreme weather disturbances, and disease—is the result of carbon emissions from
the fossil fuel industry. And yet, despite all of this evidence,
the oil companies spent millions of dollars lying about this reality and about their responsibility. What should Congress do
to hold the fossil fuel industry accountable for the enormous
destruction it has caused to the planet?

There can be honest differences of opinion as to the answers to
these questions. But it is unconscionable and dangerous for our democracy that they are virtually never asked. These questions are not

posed to me. They are not posed to other elected officials. They're not asked of anyone in power. A vibrant democracy cannot flourish while the most important issues facing it are largely ignored because of the enormous conflicts of interest inherent in a corporately controlled media.

Most Political Coverage Is Gossip

Instead of focusing on the vitally important questions that impact our society, including the impact of wealth and power on decision-making, corporate media most often focuses on gossip, trivia, and personalities—especially when it is covering campaigns and elections. Is it important for citizens to know about the lives of those who seek public office—their honesty, experience, health, family, and history of personal relationships? Yes it is. But at the end of the day, elections have to be about a lot more than personality contests. We're not going to get any kind of progress in this country if the media remains obsessed with the "issues" of who is more "likable" and whom we would most like to have a beer with.

I suspect that we will not be soon returning to the three-hour Lincoln-Douglas debates of 1858, but the focus of campaigns must be about what candidates stand for, and what they will do to improve our lives and the world we live in. Elections must center around the needs of the people, not the petty personal fumbles of the candidates. The focus on personalities unlinks politics from the major issues we face, dumbs-down serious discussion, and deflects attention from the role that corporate interests and the billionaire class play in impacting the lives of the great mass of Americans. This, in turn, narrows the frame in which governing is reported and constrains the range of options that Americans believe are available. The issues that matter most to working-class Americans—a dysfunctional health care system, low wages, poverty, deindustrialization, the abandonment of working-class communities, and growing inequality—are neglected, and only grudgingly addressed when they cannot be avoided.

This has long been the case. But as media ownership consolidates, and as corporate influence expands, a bad circumstance is getting worse.

During my years in politics, I have witnessed a profound decline in the amount of attention devoted to issues of consequence. It started with television and radio stations, which often were more interested in quick takes than in-depth reporting, but soon newspapers joined in focusing on "the horserace." Today, corporate media generally covers politics as entertainment with more and more attention to personality foibles, gaffes, polls, petty disputes between candidates, and whatever else is sufficiently sensational to pass for "news." In media analysis of candidate debates, the focus is more often than not on who got in the best "zinger" and who "won" the debate, not on the ideas the candidates advanced.

Calling Out Corporate Media on the Debate Stage

This is a point I made on the Democratic presidential debate stage in Detroit in the summer of 2019, when I called out the corporate media on live TV when the CNN moderators Jake Tapper, Dana Bash, and Don Lemon were asking the presidential contenders about health care reform. I made my pitch for a single-payer system, telling the moderators and the crowd, "If you want stability in the health care system, if you want a system which gives you freedom of choice with regard to a doctor or a hospital, which is a system which will not bankrupt you, the answer is to get rid of the profiteering of the drug companies and the insurance companies, move to Medicare for All."

At each turn in the debate, I made the case for a Medicare for All system: "Right now, we have a dysfunctional health care system: eighty-seven million uninsured or underinsured, five hundred thousand Americans every year going bankrupt because of medical bills, thirty thousand people are dying while the health care industry makes tens of billions of dollars in profit." I explained what was possible, noting that "five minutes away from [the debate stage in Detroit] is a country, it's called Canada. They guarantee health care to every man, woman, and child as a human right. They spend half of what we spend. And by the way, when you end up in a hospital in Canada, you come out with no bill at all. Health care is a human right, not a privilege. I believe that. I will fight for that."

When my rivals on the stage challenged these arguments, I was ready to counter them. In one of the more talked-about exchanges of the debate, Ohio congressman Tim Ryan tried to suggest that union members could lose benefits under Medicare for All. I countered that they would get better care. "Medicare for All is comprehensive," I explained. "It covers all health care needs. For senior citizens it will finally include dental care, hearing aids, and eyeglasses." Ryan interrupted, saying, "But you don't know that—you don't know that, Bernie." I replied, "I do know it, I wrote the damn bill."

What was unusual about that evening in Detroit was not the debate with my rivals. Nothing unexpected there. What made the clash in Detroit interesting was that I wasn't just debating with my opponents. I was debating with the moderators.

Within seconds of my response to Ryan, Jake Tapper jumped in to press the congressman's point, claiming, "If Medicare for All is enacted, there are more than six hundred thousand union members here in Michigan who would be forced to give up their private health care plans." He demanded to know if I would "guarantee those union members that the benefits under Medicare for All will be as good as the benefits that their representatives—their union reps—fought hard to negotiate."

Suddenly CNN was worried about union contracts. But, of course, that wasn't the point. The worry was that the case for Medicare for All was being made, and that voters were embracing it. That didn't fit the narrative that CNN or its advertisers wanted on a night when one of the two major parties was beginning to decide who it might nominate for the presidency. But I wasn't about to back down. After explaining that workers would indeed be better off under a system that would protect their families from going bankrupt if a child got sick, I said, "What I am talking about and others up here are talking about is no deductibles and no co-payments. And, Jake, your question is a Republican talking point."

The audience, which included many supporters of candidates other than myself, exploded in applause.

"And by the way," I added, "the health care industry will be advertising tonight on this program."

The applause grew louder.

Tapper cut me off and tried to move to another candidate and another line of questioning. I refused to let up.

"Can I complete that, please?" I asked.

"Your time is up," snapped Tapper. But I had the crowd with me and he finally said, "Thirty seconds."

I didn't need that much time to make my point.

"They will be advertising tonight with that talking point," I said.

Sure enough, they did. During the breaks in the debate, ads from pharmaceutical and biotech companies proliferated. An ad from the "Partnership for America's Health Care Future" (PAHCF), a corporate group funded by insurance companies, hospital owners, and pharmaceutical giants, featured "average Americans" delivering the industry talking point: "We don't want to be forced into a one-size-fits-all government insurance system."

I don't want to be too hard on Jake Tapper. I have known him for years and like him. He is a knowledgeable and serious journalist who does a better job than most. The exchange we had on that night in July 2019 could have occurred during any of the debates and with any other moderator—or in any of the other town halls, forums, and interviews on cable news shows.

When *The Washington Post* Brought the Hammer Down

In politics, one of the important functions of the corporate media is to tell us who the "serious" candidates are that we should support, and which candidates are "fringe" and unworthy of much attention.

You will not be shocked to learn that, in my first presidential campaign, I was not considered by the establishment media to be one of the "serious" candidates. At least, not initially.

In 2016, the political and media establishment believed that their candidate, Hillary Clinton, was a shoo-in for the party's nomination. She had been a powerful force in Bill Clinton's presidential administration, a U.S. senator, and secretary of state. And she was the darling of Wall Street and the Democratic elite. She had the support of a large number of Democratic members of the Senate and House, as well as governors around the country. She would've been the first woman president of the United States. What was not to like?

I, on the other hand, was described as a *firebrand, rabble-rouser, radical, loud, gadfly, rude, unkempt*—and worse. I had almost no political support from prominent Democrats, and certainly not from the corporate world. I was many things, but certainly not a "serious" candidate. After all, by definition, how could someone with my anti-ruling-class political views be considered "serious"?

A funny thing happened on the way to the Democratic National Convention in Philadelphia. Voters disagreed with the assessment of the corporate media. We drew larger and larger crowds at our rallies, and our poll numbers, starting at 3 percent, rapidly improved. In the first-caucus state of Iowa, I tied with Clinton. In the first primary state of New Hampshire, I won a landslide victory.

That shook the establishment and the media they own. How could things have gone so wrong? Why were so many Americans, especially newly energized young people, voting for Bernie Sanders? And what could they do to halt the momentum of a political revolution?

The Washington Post had an answer.

The *Post,* in many ways, is the media embodiment of the corporate establishment. For decades the paper was owned by the Graham family, a pillar of the inside-the-Beltway elite. The paper has certainly taken some liberal stands over the years, and its reporters have done some groundbreaking work—especially during the Watergate era—but it has always been an institutional presence in the nation's capital. Firmly within the circles of power, it might object to the excesses of Richard Nixon or Ronald Reagan, but it was never going to challenge the economic status quo. That appealed to Jeff Bezos, the billionaire owner of Amazon, who purchased the *Post* in 2013.

The influence of the *Post* cannot be measured merely in terms of the impact it has on its own readership. It is one of the primary conveyors of the establishment perspective in American media. Its reporters and editors appear frequently on national television, its stories are amplified across media platforms, and its approach to issues has a huge influence on how other newspapers and news networks cover America and the world. The paper's enthusiastic support for the disastrous war in Iraq, for example, helped to "legitimize" that tragic military adventure in the eyes of media outlets that lacked the *Post*'s global reach and resources. So it is that, when the *Post* is wrong, the American discourse—and American policymaking—can quickly go off-track.

By the time I decided to run for president in 2016, I was well aware that the *Post* had little use for me or the ideas I was promoting. But I had no idea just how deep the antipathy ran until our campaign began to take off. After we tied in the caucus results from Iowa and then won the New Hampshire primary, the calculations of the political and media elites were upended. It was clear that we would go all the way to the convention in Philadelphia, and there was open speculation that I might actually defeat Hillary Clinton as the party's nominee. That was a prospect that the *Post* was not prepared to entertain.

On March 6 and 7, at the height of the campaign, just after we had won contests in Colorado, Kansas, Maine, Minnesota, Nebraska, Oklahoma, and Vermont, and as a key primary vote was looming that week in Michigan, the *Post* unleashed an attack on our campaign that revealed the extremes to which media outlets will go when they want to crush candidates and ideas that challenge their worldview and their economic interests. In one twenty-four-hour period, through a series of sixteen articles, they managed to imply that I was a racist, a sexist, a gun-lover, and an intellectual fellow traveler with right-wing ideologues like Donald Trump and Ted Cruz. Here is what Fairness & Accuracy in Reporting, a media watchdog group, wrote on March 8, 2016:

> In what has to be some kind of record, the *Washington Post* ran 16 negative stories on Bernie Sanders in 16 hours, between roughly 10:20 PM EST Sunday, March 6, to 3:54 PM EST Monday, March 7—a window that includes the crucial Democratic debate in Flint, Michigan, and the next morning's spin:
>
> - March 6, 10:20 PM: Bernie Sanders Pledges the US Won't Be No. 1 in Incarceration. He'll Need to Release Lots of Criminals
> - March 7, 12:39 AM: Clinton Is Running for President. Sanders Is Doing Something Else
> - March 7, 4:04 AM: This Is Huge: Trump, Sanders Both Using Same Catchphrase
> - March 7, 4:49 AM: Mental Health Patients to Bernie Sanders: Don't Compare Us to the GOP Candidates
> - March 7, 6:00 AM: 'Excuse Me, I'm Talking': Bernie Sanders Shuts Down Hillary Clinton, Repeatedly
> - March 7, 9:24 AM: Bernie Sanders's Two Big Lies About the Global Economy
> - March 7, 8:25 AM: Five Reasons Bernie Sanders Lost Last Night's Democratic Debate
> - March 7, 8:44 AM: An Awkward Reality for Bernie Sanders: A Strategy Focused on Whiter States
> - March 7, 8:44 AM: Bernie Sanders Says White People Don't Know What It's Like to Live in a 'Ghetto.' About That . . .

- March 7, 11:49 AM: The NRA Just Praised Bernie Sanders—and Did Him No Favors in Doing So
- March 7, 12:55 PM: Even Bernie Sanders Can Beat Donald Trump
- March 7, 1:08 PM: What Bernie Sanders Still Doesn't Get About Arguing With Hillary Clinton
- March 7, 1:44 PM: Why Obama Says Bank Reform Is a Success but Bernie Sanders Says It's a Failure
- March 7, 2:16 PM: Here's Something Ted Cruz and Bernie Sanders Have in Common: And the Piece of the Argument That Bernie Doesn't Get Quite Right
- March 7, 3:31 PM: 'Excuse Me!': Bernie Sanders Doesn't Know How to Talk About Black People
- March 7, 3:54 PM: And the Most Partisan Senator of 2015 Is . . . Bernie Sanders!

All of these posts paint his candidacy in a negative light, mainly by advancing the narrative that he's a clueless white man incapable of winning over people of color or speaking to women. Even the one article about Sanders beating Trump implies this is somehow a surprise—despite the fact that Sanders consistently outpolls Hillary Clinton against the New York businessman.

The one-day tsunami of attacks against me from *The Washington Post* was an extreme example of the establishment's response to a candidate who stood for transformational change. But in their enmity to my campaign, Bezos's paper was not alone.

In December 2019, at a time when I was either leading in the polls or running a close second, *The New York Times* went through its endorsement process. As the *Times* had decided to endorse two candidates, each member of the editorial board was given two votes. In total, there were thirty votes cast. I received one of those votes. One. The initial editorial-board tally made public was: Warren: 8,

Klobuchar: 7, Booker: 6, Buttigieg: 4, Biden: 3, Sanders: 1, Bloomberg: 1.

Oh, yes. Then there is Rupert Murdoch's *Wall Street Journal*. I haven't researched this, but I think it's fair to say that there is no member of Congress, not one, who has been on the receiving end of more attacks from the editorial page of that paper than I have. Like almost every day. There are hundreds of daily newspapers in America. In 2016 I won the endorsement of one major metropolitan daily paper. Thank you, *Seattle Times*.

Here's another twist from the corporate media coverage of my campaign. In 2015, when our presidential race was taking off, we were running roughly as well in the polls on the Democratic side as Donald Trump was in polls on the Republican side. Yet an analysis of TV network coverage of the campaign found that they had given twenty-three times as much coverage to Trump's campaign as they had to ours. "The network newscasts are wildly overplaying Trump, who regularly attracts between 20–30 percent of primary voter support, while at the same time wildly underplaying Sanders, who regularly attracts between 20–30 percent of primary voter support," observed Eric Boehlert of Media Matters, in a report that relied on data from media analyst Andrew Tyndall. "Obviously, Trump is the GOP front-runner and it's reasonable that he would get more attention than Sanders, who's running second for the Democrats. But 234 total network minutes for Trump compared to just 10 network minutes for Sanders, as the Tyndall Report found?"

A Crisis for Journalism Becomes a Crisis for Democracy

The crisis in American media is not just about corporate control and the establishment's hostility to those of us who are fighting for transformative change. It goes deeper and broader. The function of a corporation is to make as much money as possible, and when a company is not making sufficient profits, for whatever reasons, it cuts back. It disinvests. It goes out of business. And that's what media companies are doing in local communities all across the country. Owning media conglomerates like Comcast or Disney may be extremely lucrative, but, for a wide variety of reasons, it is increasingly difficult for locally owned newspapers and radio stations to make a decent profit.

All of this raises a simple question: How do you maintain a democracy and representative government if local media disappears and residents are not receiving information and news as to what's taking place in their communities? A vibrant democracy requires a vibrant media—at all levels of society. And, in many parts of our country, that local media is disappearing.

In my travels around America in the late 2010s and early 2020s, I heard more and more complaints about the death of local media. Television stations covered weather, sports, and crime but no longer found time—or had the staff—for reports from the city council meeting or the school board, and you could forget about investigative reporting that might upset the corporations that bought ads before, during, and after their newscasts. Radio stations had been bought up by conglomerates such as Clear Channel, which replaced local programming with syndicated right-wing shows hosted by the likes of Rush Limbaugh and Sean Hannity. Newspapers that had once been important sources of information for small towns and cities had laid off so many editors and reporters that there was little content to fill the few pages that rolled off the presses. In a growing number of communities, the papers had simply folded, leaving no newsrooms to cover vast stretches of Middle America.

On a personal level, I can tell you that when I was the mayor of Burlington, Vermont, in the 1980s, the press conferences I held were usually attended by seven or eight local media outlets—radio and TV stations, the local daily newspaper, the weekly paper, and perhaps the Associated Press. These outlets also covered the city council, the school board, and other municipal agencies. Today, when I do a press event, half that number show up. Further, many of the radio interview shows that covered local politics are gone.

Yes, of course, people have the internet. They can check out pronouncements from national figures and "influencers" in Washington and New York and Los Angeles. But they can't get the straight story on what's happening in their hometowns—at the city council, the school board, the mayor's office.

As regional daily newspapers have shuttered, as local newspapers have downsized, as local radio hosts have been replaced by syndicated "content," and as old lines of distinction between broadcast and print and digital media ownership have been blurred, communities across the country have been left in the lurch.

The Great American News Desert

The crisis is so severe that Margaret Sullivan, one of the country's ablest media observers, noted in *The Washington Post* in the summer of 2022 that "every week, two more newspapers close—and 'news deserts' grow larger." If trends continued, Sullivan warned, "one-third of American newspapers that existed roughly two decades ago will be out of business by 2025."

Sullivan was reflecting on the 2022 "State of Local News" survey from Northwestern University's Medill School of Journalism's Local Media Initiative. That study reached a number of sobering conclusions. Four of them stood out to me:

> **More than a fifth of the nation's citizens live in news deserts—with very limited access to local news—or in communities at risk of becoming news deserts.** Seventy million people live in the 208 counties without a newspaper, or in the 1,630 counties with only one paper—usually a weekly—covering multiple communities spread over a vast area. Increasingly, affluent suburban communities are losing their only newspapers as large chains merge underperforming weeklies or shutter them entirely. Most communities that lose newspapers and do not have an alternative source of local news are poorer, older, and lack affordable and reliable

high-speed digital service that would allow them to access the important and relevant journalism being produced by the country's surviving newspapers and digital sites. Instead, they get their local news—what little there is—mostly from the social media apps on their mobile phones.

The surviving newspapers—especially the dailies— have cut staff and circulation significantly as print revenues and profits evaporated. This has sharply reduced their ability to provide news to communities, further exacerbating an information gap not only in rural areas, but also in suburbs surrounding a city. Since 2005, when newspaper revenues topped $50 billion, overall newspaper employment has dropped 70 percent as revenues declined to $20 billion. Newsroom employment has declined by almost 60 percent, with on-staff photographers declining by 80 percent.

Digital alternatives remain scarce, despite an increase in corporate and philanthropic funding. Over the past two years, the number of new digital-only state and local news sites, 64, slightly exceeded the number of sites that went dark. In 2022, there are 545 digital-only state and local sites; most employ six or fewer full-time reporters. Each state has at least one digital-only outlet. However, even established local digital news organizations often fail to attract the monthly traffic of television and local newspaper sites, somewhat diminishing the impact of the stories they produce. Four out of ten local sites are now nonprofit, supported by a combination of grants, sponsorship, and donations. But whether nonprofit or for-profit, the vast majority of those sites are located in larger cities, leaving much of the rest of the country uncovered.

The disparity between communities that have strong news organizations and those that don't is primarily

**the result of market demographics, ownership struc-
ture, and available funding.** Whether print or digital, local
news organizations that have entrepreneurial owners, and are
in affluent and/or growing communities with diverse sources
of funding, are much more likely to establish and maintain a
successful for-profit, nonprofit, or hybrid enterprise. Economically struggling and traditionally underserved communities—
where residents need journalists providing transparency and
oversight of local government and business decisions—are
the ones most likely to lose a news organization and be overlooked by funders looking to invest in both for-profit and nonprofit news operations. That loss of local journalism
exacerbates political, cultural, and economic divisions between and within communities.

You don't have to be a rocket scientist to see what's happening.
Media companies are abandoning local journalism because they
aren't making the profits they demand. Consolidation of media ownership at the national level is mirrored at the local level, where most
of the daily newspapers still in existence are now owned by chains
that owe their allegiance not to the communities they are supposed
to serve, but to hedge-fund managers who have no interest in journalism.

As advertising, which historically made media outlets highly
profitable, has gone digital, says media scholar Robert McChesney,
the funding model for local and regional journalism has collapsed.
Advertisers "no longer need to support a local newspaper to reach
their target audience. They no longer need to use conventional news
media." Without the profits derived from ad revenues, he says, "no
one's investing to do traditional journalism anywhere if they're out to
make money. They might be doing it because they have a political
edge they want to push. They might be doing it for this reason or
that. But it's lost all its commercial value. It is no longer profitable.
The capitalist class has basically abandoned journalism altogether.

The only people buying up media outlets today are these hedge funds and equity funds that are buying them to strip them for parts. They don't care about journalism. That's the only people in the market. You can't find an investor to buy papers to do news or to buy news media to do news if they want to make a profit on their investment."

"Journalism," says McChesney, "is no longer profitable."

This has profound consequences for society in general and democracy in particular. Unfortunately, policymakers keep coming up with "solutions" that are the equivalent of putting a Band-Aid on a gaping wound. They propose small tax credits for media conglomerates that keep journalists on the job, but they continue to suggest that, somehow, "the market" will come up with a solution. Or that enlightened billionaires are going to make up the difference. That's not going to happen.

A New Deal for Journalism

As more and more newspapers go out of existence and vast stretches of the country become news deserts, we need to rethink how local media is maintained in order to guarantee that Americans can access the information they need to cultivate a vibrant democracy.

In my view, there has to be significant public funding for diverse, competitive media at the national, regional, and local levels.

That's not a radical idea. At the founding of the United States, the first Congresses provided massive postal subsidies to printers so that they could distribute newspapers. The subsidies went to all sides in the great debates of the early United States, and they fostered media diversity and discussion so intense that the French philosopher Alexis de Tocqueville determined, after touring the young country in the 1830s, that newspapers were an essential underpinning for "Democracy in America." Even now, almost two hundred years later, our largest media outlets enjoy massive subsidies. The public owns the airwaves of this country, yet media conglomerates claim exclusive use of those airwaves for their own economic benefit.

Once they have obtained a license, they can bank whatever profits come to them from owning television and radio stations; and, with the loosening of standards and regulations initiated by the Telecommunications Act of 1996 and industry-aligned members of the Federal Communications Commission, they have generally done so with little or no accountability.

As a young man, I made a meager living writing for newspapers in Vermont. I believed then, and I believe now, that freedom of the press means that the government must never be allowed to tell journalists what to cover—or how to report on what they encounter. But I also believe that it is possible to create systems of support for media outlets that allow them to speak truth to power, and to survive.

The place to begin is with a radical rethinking of the role of public and community media in the United States, and a major infusion of public funding to sustain independent, not-for-profit media—and the robust local, state, and national democracy that extends from it. Think of it as a New Deal for Journalism.

Other countries, like Germany and Norway, have made this sort of investment, with considerable success. It's time for the United States to do the same, as part of a broader media reform strategy that seeks to promote genuine competition. Yes, we should break up media monopolies that have stifled honest and expansive discourse at the national level. We should promote more diverse ownership of major media, and a more serious exchange of ideas, by making the FCC a champion of debate and discourse, not of consolidation and profiteering. But just as important, and perhaps even more urgent: We must renew journalism at the local level in communities that have been abandoned by corporate media.

Robust Public Media Generates Robust Democracy

The way to do this is by making a significant investment in public media.

University of Pennsylvania media scholars Victor Pickard and

Timothy Neff have identified a clear connection between funding of public media and democracy. In their 2022 study "Funding Democracy: Public Media and Democratic Health in 33 Countries," Pickard and Neff determined that "high levels of secure funding for public media systems and strong structural protections for the political and economic independence of those systems are consistently and positively correlated with healthy democracies."

Unfortunately, the United States does not provide high levels of support for public media. It starves public television, public radio, and community outlets that are already in existence, and it has not begun to develop a plan to address the news deserts that are emerging all across the country.

How severe is the underfunding?

According to Pickard, the United States government allocates roughly $1.40 per capita annually—0.002 percent of the Gross Domestic Product—to public broadcasting. That's less than an iced coffee at Starbucks.

Compare the U.S. commitment to public media with that of Norway, the country that ranks No. 1 on both the Economist Intelligence Unit's Democracy Index and the Reporters Without Borders' World Press Freedom Index. Norway spends $110.73 per person to sustain a public media system that comprises four main national services, with extensive local coverage for even the most remote regions of the country. Germany, a much bigger country than Norway, maintains the largest television market in Europe, and it ranks relatively high on the Democracy Index of "full democracies" (No. 15) and the World Press Freedom Index (No. 16). How does it do this? By spending $142.42 per person annually on public media. Under a system designed after World War II with strong support from General Dwight Eisenhower, Germany sustains nine regional public broadcasting systems that produce content for viewers nationally and in their individual states. These networks provide intensive national, regional, and local coverage of news, culture, and sports. The networks maintain dozens of local newsrooms, which provide thorough reports for communities across Germany. There are additional public stations at the national level, and in particular localities, that provide special programming and extend the reach of these public services to rural areas and ethnic communities.

Norway, Germany, and other countries that pour significant resources into public and community media are among the freest countries in the world. They face challenges, to be sure. But their democracies remain robust and dynamic. The same cannot be said for the United States, which ranks No. 26 on the Democracy Index, putting it in the "flawed democracy" category with countries such as Hungary and Brazil. It ranks even worse in the World Press Freedom Index: No. 42, right behind Moldova and Burkina Faso. "After four years of President Trump constantly denigrating the press, President Biden signaled his administration's desire to see the US reclaim its global status as a model [for] freedom of expression, thus reinstating regular White House and federal agency press briefings," explained the Reporters Without Borders analysis. "Despite these efforts, many of the underlying, chronic issues impacting journalists remain unaddressed by the authorities—including the disappearance of local news, the polarization of the media or the weakening of journalism and democracy caused by digital platforms and social networks."

Bringing News Deserts Back to Life

Clearly, we've got a lot of work to do if we want to get information flowing in America's news deserts.

Pickard and Neff argue that, "given the systemic market failure that's driving US local journalism into the ground, a public media safety net is especially urgent now." They make the case that even a modest investment in public media could do a great deal to shore up local media and increase media independence. "To reach its full democratic potential, public media must be politically and economically independent. This goal requires closing the federal funding gap, as well as ensuring that adequate financial support is guaranteed well into the future, shielded from political whims and interference," they explain. If the United States simply spent as much proportionally as the United Kingdom does on the BBC, that would allow us to spend $35 billion for public media nationwide.

What could be achieved if an annual commitment of $35 billion—a good deal less than what senators added to President Biden's Pentagon budget in 2022—was made to develop and maintain public media in the United States? McChesney argues that a well-organized "Local Journalism Initiative" could support newsrooms in every one of the nation's more than three thousand counties, effectively eliminating news deserts and establishing a democratic governance system where people at the local level would have a say in directing resources to competing newsgathering operations. These newsrooms would be primarily digital, reducing costs and extending their reach, but would have lots of room for innovation to identify models and platforms that best serve their communities.

Pickard suggests that federal funding could be used to develop community-based "Public Media Centers" that would operate as news cooperatives. They'd be managed by the journalists who work for them and directly responsive to the communities they serve. "As a new community anchor institution alongside schools and hospitals, PMCs could serve as primary building blocks for a post-commercial media system that's both democratizing and impervious to market failure."

Pickard acknowledges that this may sound a little "utopian" to Americans. But the experience of countries where media culture is more dynamic than in the United States, and where democracy is far healthier, has shown that federal support for initiatives of this kind can work.

What We Can Learn from Norway

I understand that Norway is a small country. Nonetheless, there is much we can learn from a nation that is broadly recognized for having some of the freest and most democracy-enhancing media in the world.

The Norwegian Media Authority has since 1969 provided subsidies to local print and, more recently, online news operations to maintain competition at the local level. Awarded in proportion to a newspaper's circulation and online appeal, these subsidies have not only maintained competing local newsrooms but fostered robust debate in some of the smallest Norwegian communities. They have allowed ethnic and linguistic minorities to develop distinctive news operations, and they have sustained journals that highlight the perspectives of dissenting political movements. In addition to the subsidies, Norwegian publications are exempt from taxes on newspaper sales.

While the subsidies sustain local competition, Norway has taken a number of steps since the late 1990s to prevent concentration of media ownership at the national level. It's not a perfect system. There are still chains of newspapers and media conglomerates that critics say are too powerful. Media outlets still struggled during the early days of the coronavirus pandemic, although they got quick assistance in the form of a special pandemic press-support scheme and new funding for innovation. Unions representing reporters and editors still find plenty to complain about. Politicians still object to how they are covered. But the Norwegians have maintained a media system, for the most part, that is muscular enough to resist the pressures posed not just by right-wing fake news but by hedge-fund profiteering. By comparison to the system in the United States it's thriving.

I don't think it's utopian to suggest that the wealthiest country in the world could have a media system as innovative, intellectually diverse, and inclined toward addressing major issues as that of Norway—or Germany, or any of the more than forty countries that rank ahead of us on freedom-of-the press indexes. In fact, I believe that recognizing quality journalism as a public good that must be available to all—and that can be enhanced and extended by significant investments in public media, especially at the local level—is critical to ending our country's embarrassing status as a "flawed democracy."

My faith in the power of well-funded, speak-truth-to-power journalism is sufficient to make me believe that it can play a critical role in making the United States what it should be: a "full democracy." That's a fight I'm ready to wage—along with the tens of millions of Americans who are right to worry that, unless we act, news deserts will become democracy deserts.

10

THIS IS A CLASS WAR. IT'S TIME TO FIGHT BACK!

We must stop being afraid to call out capitalism and demand fundamental change to a corrupt and rigged system

L et's talk about politics. Real politics.

Not the politics that gets talked about on CBS, ABC, NBC, CNN, and the rest of the corporate media. Not the gossip that passes for politics, with its relentless ruminations on personalities, strategies, polls, focus groups, gaffes, ad buys, sensationalism, the "news of the day," scandals, and all the pleasant things that Democrats and Republicans say about each other.

Let's talk about politics as if it mattered to the lives of ordinary Americans, because, of course, it does. Let's talk about politics as a process that can make the lives of working people dramatically better—or dramatically worse. Let's stop blathering and start focusing on how to make our political system more democratic and inclusive, so that we can finally address the real issues that concern working families and the dispossessed—decent wages, health care, hunger, housing, education, bigotry, and the need to save the planet from the ravages of climate change.

Real politics recognizes the truth of what is going on in our country and how the current economic system destroys the lives of countless Americans.

Real politics identifies the root causes of our problems. It does not shy away from the challenges posed by uber-capitalism. It dives in and sorts them out.

To do this, real politics asks the hard questions that mainstream politicians and the corporate media avoid like the plague:

> How does massive income and wealth inequality—and the corporate power that extends this inequality—impact the whole society?
>
> What kind of "democracy" are we when billionaires are allowed to buy elections?
>
> Why has there been a massive transfer of wealth from the middle class to the 1 percent over the last fifty years?
>
> Why do we spend twice as much per capita on health care as other nations and have so little to show for it?
>
> Why do we accept childhood poverty in a land of plenty, and what does that mean for the future of a country that keeps failing its next generation?
>
> Why is there so much money available for mega-mansions, gated communities, and super-yachts, and so little to address homelessness and hunger?
>
> Why do we allow a handful of corporate media conglomerates to control our political discourse?
>
> What does it say about our political system that the last two major American wars, in Vietnam and Iraq, were based on establishment lies; and why do we spend more on the military than the next ten nations combined?
>
> Why have we allowed the fossil fuel industry to keep destroying the planet?

Real politics seeks to lay bare our problems, and to develop concrete solutions to the crises we face—without concern about whether doing so will offend the powerful or negatively impact the bank accounts of the wealthy.

Above all, real politics recognizes the need for *systemic* change, not tinkering around the edges of social policy. It understands that unless we make bold changes to our uber-capitalist system, life will never significantly improve for the vast majority of our people. It understands that the greed of the ruling class today is not only destructive to the lives of ordinary people, it threatens the literal survival of the planet. This understanding underpins the essential premise of real politics: that power over the economic and political life of the country must rest with the majority of people, not a tiny minority.

Real Politics Starts with Organizing

Real politics is about recruiting and training working-class candidates at the local level to win elections for city council, the school board, and state legislative seats. It's about electing those candidates with people-powered campaigns that knock on doors to register "nontraditional" voters. It's about helping workers form unions and get decent contracts from their employers. It's about joining picket lines when union members are on strike, and demanding a living wage for all workers. It's about standing with tenants who can't afford outrageous rent increases, and parents who want decent schools for their kids. It's about marching for racial justice, women's rights, and against all forms of bigotry. It's about demanding, with people all over the world, that the planet we leave future generations is healthy and habitable.

One of the important lessons I have learned from history is that real change never takes place from the top on down. It always comes from the bottom on up. The great abolitionist Frederick Douglass was right when he stated, "Power concedes nothing without a demand. It never did and it never will." Fundamental change is not going to happen because of fundraisers at wealthy people's homes. It's not going to happen because of clever TV ads or the scheming of inside-the-Beltway political consultants and pollsters. It's going to happen when millions stand up and demand that change. And the progressive movement intends to be at the center of that struggle for change.

Real politics is about knowing our history, and recognizing its power as an organizing tool. Every new generation of Americans must be reminded of the great battles for transformational change that have been fought and won, and will continue to be won, against overwhelming odds. When someone says that it is impossible to take on uber-capitalism, we have to answer them with lessons from our past. Creating unions and ending child labor and the uncontrolled, ruthless exploitation of workers was not easy. Abolishing slavery and legalized segregation was not easy. Ending the poll tax was not easy. Standing up for the rights of Native Americans to control their own lands was not easy. Winning women the right to vote and establishing abortion rights protections so that they could control their own destinies was not easy. Enacting legislation that protects civil rights and women's rights, and provides minimal protections for the poor and working people—Social Security, Medicare, Medicaid, a minimum wage, clean air and clean water standards—was not easy. But those fights were won, and those victories inspire us to wage the great struggles of the twenty-first century.

Real politics is about rejecting the establishment's determination as to what is "possible," "achievable," and "acceptable." It is about declaring, unapologetically, that we will not allow American oligarchs and their legions of publicists to shape our vision as to the kind of world we want to live in. That's our decision.

Real politics sees through the disempowering lies that are told by the establishment. It understands that in the wealthiest country in the history of the world, we must reject the austerity economics that attacks the needs of working families in order to keep taxes low for the rich. It recognizes that we have the capacity to build a humane society in which all people can live with security and dignity. Real politics knows this is not utopian, pie-in-the-sky thinking. It is simply the conscious rejection of an age-old hierarchical system based on oppression and exploitation. Real politics recognizes that the technological revolutions of our time are already transforming society, and that the benefits of that revolution must improve lives for the many, not create more wealth for the few.

Real politics is about understanding that the economic elites will never support policies that threaten their wealth and power. They are waging class war against working people, and they are winning. According to the RAND Corporation, over the past forty-seven years $50 trillion in wealth has been redistributed from the bottom 90 percent to the top 1 percent—primarily because an ever-increasing percentage of corporate profits has been flowing into the stock portfolios of the investor class.

Real politics recognizes that the corporate elite are not nice guys, no matter how much they contribute to charity or how many awards they receive from universities and hospitals to which they have donated buildings. They are ruthless, and day after day they sacrifice human life and well-being in order to protect their privilege.

In the face of a politically powerful billionaire class and its corporate allies, real politics recognizes that progressives must be smarter and more strategic than ever before. We need to think big, not small, and we need to introduce questions of morality into the political debate by challenging the greed, irresponsibility, and brutality of the ruling class. There are many ways to kill people and injure them. Yes. It is morally wrong for a thief to take out a gun and shoot somebody. But it is also morally wrong for monopolistic drug companies to charge outrageous prices that result in people not being able to afford lifesaving medicine—and leaving them to die. It's morally wrong for insurance companies to deny treatment to sick people who will die without that care. Yes, it is morally wrong that so few have so much, while so many have so little.

Real politics is about recognizing the systemic injustices that crush working families. It is about breaking the vicious cycles perpetrated by those systems, so that we can renew our faith in Lincoln's vision of "government of the people, by the people and for the people."

Real politics fights for real choices. Progressives must make it clear that there are two sides in this fight. On one side are the wealthy few who will cede nothing to the many. On the other side are the many, who must demand what is rightfully theirs.

Taking On Uber-Capitalism

The truth is that no struggle for justice and human rights has ever been easy. But if we are honest with ourselves, we must admit that the struggle against uber-capitalism will be harder than any other because *all* the forces of greed and power will be arrayed against us. We're taking them all on, and they will respond in kind.

The corporate elite will use their unlimited resources to maintain a rigged economy of unprecedented income and wealth inequality. The status quo is working very well for them and their families, and they are determined to maintain it. They will do everything in their power, legally and illegally, to prevent workers from joining unions. They will enact anti-worker trade policies. They will oppose wage increases. They will use their politicians and lobbyists to generate new tax breaks and more corporate welfare.

American oligarchs will use their media to ignore or trivialize the major issues facing working families and do their best to deflect attention away from those concerns. While millions of Americans live in abject poverty and are experiencing declining life expectancy, and while the middle class continues to decline, the corporate media will continue to "entertain us to death."

Finally, the Big Money interests and their super-PACs will spend billions to own and control our political system. They will steer obscene sums of dark money into campaigns to elect the candidates of their choice and, of course, to defeat those they see as a threat. The campaign finance situation is so absurd that billionaires and corporate CEOs often donate directly to *both* major parties, and to candidates of both parties in the same election cycle. It doesn't matter to them who wins, so long as their corporate interests are protected. In the 2022 Democratic primaries, for example, billionaire-funded super-PACs spent tens of millions trying (sometimes successfully) to defeat progressive candidates for Congress who represented the needs of working families. The wealthiest people in America, many of them active Republicans, were meddling in Democratic primaries to throttle opposition to their agendas. And, of course, to elect their own political agents. Once elected, the main function of corporately funded politicians is not only to protect the interests of their sponsors but to remind us, over and over, why we can't bring about the kinds of changes that ordinary people want and need.

Real Politics Is Smart Politics

When we talk about *real* politics and addressing the long-neglected needs of the working families of our country, we're not talking about complicated strategies that are developed by pollsters and focus groups to sell unpopular ideas. We're talking about creating a simple, straightforward, and progressive agenda that can transform lives and is widely supported by Americans from all backgrounds. In practical political terms, it's an agenda that can create grassroots excitement, overcome racial and ethnic divisions, and win elections.

As a practitioner of real politics, let me put things in perspective.

In August 2022, a USA Today/Ipsos poll found that I had the highest overall favorability rating of nearly two dozen prospective 2024 presidential candidates from both major parties. The accompanying article observed that "[Sanders's] 46% rating—not exactly stratospheric but better than the others—is thanks to his strength among Democratic voters (78%) paired with his crossover appeal. He is the highest-rated Democrat among Independents (at 41%) and

among the highest-rated Democrats among Republican voters (at
18%)." The poll showed me with a 46–41 favorability rating, with
Biden and Trump tied at 43–52.

Polls go up and down, and tomorrow I will probably be at the
bottom of some other survey, but what is important here is not just
my 78 percent favorable rating from Democrats, but my 41 percent
support from Independents and 18 percent from Republicans. What
this shows me, and I hope it tells others, is that if you fight for the
working class of this country, you can win support across the political
lines that seem so intractable these days. Whether voters are Democrats, Republicans, or Independents, they know that the current political system is corrupt and the economic system is rigged against
them. And they want change.

I have been to nearly every state in the country, held meetings in
almost all of them, and personally spoken with many thousands of
Americans from all political perspectives. In order to restore the confidence of the people in their government and their democracy, we
need an agenda—and the ability to implement that agenda—that
will change lives *now*. And if powerful corporate interests hate us for
moving forward on that agenda, all the better. People will know that
what we're doing is real and meaningful. Remember what President
Roosevelt said in a 1936 campaign speech about the powerful corporate forces that opposed his New Deal and wanted to defeat him in
that year's presidential election. "They are unanimous in their hate
for me," FDR declared, "and I welcome their hatred." He went on to
win a landslide victory. It turned out that there were many more
working-class voters than corporate bigwigs.

The same is true now. But, just as in Roosevelt's day, we need to
present a clear program for change. The following agenda and set of
principles are not meant to be comprehensive and all-encompassing.
But they are a start in laying out a program that addresses the long-
neglected needs of working families, strengthens democracy, and
helps to save the planet from climate change. Poll after poll shows
that these ideas are popular, and are supported by Democrats, Re-

publicans, and Independents of every race and background, by people living in urban America and in rural areas. The enactment of this agenda will do more to bring Americans together, unify this country, and restore confidence in our democracy than anything I can think of. Here is some of what that agenda and set of principles should include:

Get money out of politics. There is no way that any government can represent the interests of working people when billionaires are able to buy candidates and elections. Whether you are right-wing, left-wing, or somewhere in the middle, people understand that if we are going to have a vibrant and representative democracy, we need major campaign finance reform. We need to overturn the disastrous Supreme Court decisions in *Buckley v. Valeo* and *Citizens United v. FEC*—by any means necessary, including a constitutional amendment—and we must establish public funding of elections.

Guarantee voting rights. By pushing the big lie that he won the election of 2020 and that his victory was "stolen" from him, Donald Trump and his right-wing supporters have waged an all-out war against the basic foundations of American democracy: free and fair elections. In the process, in Republican state after state, governors and legislatures, under the guise of "voter fraud," have worked overtime to make it harder for people of color, low-income Americans, people with disabilities, and young people to participate in the political process. We have got to fight back with an honest assessment of what's really going on. Republicans don't want everyone to vote. We do. Republicans want to erect obstacles to voting. We want to tear them down. Republicans want to follow the lead of European right-wing authoritarians like Hungary's Viktor Orbán. We want the United States to have the most vibrant and inclusive democracy in the world. Republicans want to rig the boundary lines of voting districts in their favor. We want to end extreme gerrymandering so that every American has the representation they're entitled to.

Make the Constitution relevant to the twenty-first century. The American constitution, as it was written in 1787, was a transformational document. For its time. But this is 2022, and that document must be updated if our democracy is to be renewed.

Abolish the Electoral College. It is absurd to maintain a political system where a presidential candidate receives millions more votes than his/her opponent, and yet loses the election. It is equally absurd that modern presidential elections center around a dozen "battleground" states that are competitive, while thirty-eight states—including many of the most populous states in the country—are largely ignored because they are considered to be reliably "red" or "blue."

Rethink the United States Senate. It is equally hard to believe that, in a democratic society, it is appropriate for Vermont, Wyoming, and Alaska to have equal representation in the Senate with California, a state that has sixty times more people than each of these small states. Democracy is about one person, one vote and equal representation, and that has never been the case with the U.S. Senate.

Rethink the U.S. Supreme Court. Of course we need checks and balances, and the judiciary plays an important role in providing them. I trust, however, that few people would dare to suggest that today's Supreme Court consists of nine non-political justices who make their enormously important decisions based on their honest and exhaustive interpretation of the Constitution and case precedents. This is a court where right-wing judicial activists have eliminated campaign reforms, gutted the Voting Rights Act, and overturned the 1973 *Roe v. Wade* decision and put abortion rights at risk in states across the country. Simply stated, it is unacceptable and anti-democratic that a handful of unelected lifetime appointees exert the kind of political power that they do.

Revitalize American media. A vibrant democracy cannot exist without a vibrant media. It is not acceptable that, because of corporate disinvestment, tens of millions of Americans now live in "media deserts" and no longer have access to news and information about their local communities. We need to learn from other countries and greatly increase funding for public, non-partisan, nonprofit media at the national, state, and local levels.

End all forms of bigotry. My father came to this country not only to avoid poverty, but to escape the anti-Semitism that existed in Poland. He got out, but much of his family died in the Holocaust. I know what extreme white nationalism is, and I know it poses a threat in the United States that cannot be ignored. From its inception, this country has been afflicted by racism, anti-immigrant xenophobia, sexism, homophobia, and other forms of bigotry. In recent years we have made progress but, obviously, much more needs to be done. It will not be easy but our goal must be to identify the systemic under-pinnings of bigotry and undo them so that the United States lives up to its promise that all men—and women—are created equal.

Treat workers' rights as human rights. Today, in the wealthiest country on earth, more than half of our workers are living paycheck to paycheck and millions more are falling deeper into debt as they try to survive on starvation wages. Unbelievably, despite huge increases in worker productivity, with real inflation accounted for, wages today have barely budged from where they were almost fifty years ago. At a time when there is an enormous amount of work that needs to be done, we must make certain that all Americans who are able to work are guaran-teed employment. The "minimum wage" must become a living wage. No full-time worker should be living in poverty. Every worker, full-time or part-time, traditional or gig, must be able to exercise their constitu-tional right of free association, join a union, and bargain a fair contract. And, as part of that contract, they should be able to demand and receive pension benefits so that we can address the injustice of a country where roughly half of older working-class Americans retire with no savings.

Democratize the future of work. As technological change is upending everything about our work lives, we need to prepare for the profound changes that will take place as artificial intelligence and robotics eliminate many millions of jobs. Technology can have posi-tive or negative impacts. We must ensure that workers—not just tech-company CEOs—enjoy the benefits of progress.

Health care is a human right. Period. I'm not talking about expanding the Affordable Care Act and providing more subsidies to the insurance companies that maintain—and profit immensely from—an incredibly wasteful, bureaucratic, and cruel system. I'm talking about all Americans being able to walk into a doctor's office or a hospital and get all the health care they need with no out-of-pocket costs. I'm talking about replacing a wildly inefficient system in which we spend over $12,000 per person every year, almost twice as much as any other major country, while 85 million Americans are uninsured or underinsured and sixty thousand a year die because they don't get to a doctor on time.

I'm talking about a Medicare for All system.

The establishment—the corporate world, the politicians, and the media—tells us that this is a "radical" idea. Totally impractical. It just can't be done. It's not even worth discussing—not in the halls of Congress, not on radio or TV, not in most medical schools.

Really? If this is such an impractical idea then why, in one form or another, has every other major country on earth already accomplished the goal of providing health care for all—and at a fraction of the cost that we're paying? On a recent trip to London, I chatted with a Conservative member of Parliament who told me how proud she was of the free health care the government provided. That's a Conservative speaking!

Will Medicare for All solve all our health care problems? Of course not. But think about the profound impact it will have when the burden of devastating health care expenses is lifted from the shoulders of working families. Think about what it will mean when no American hesitates to walk into a doctor's office because of the cost. Think about what it will mean when no one goes bankrupt because they have a serious illness. Think about what it will mean when Americans can change jobs and not worry about losing health coverage.

A new business model for the pharmaceutical industry. Despite what drug company TV ads say, the prime function of the pharmaceutical industry today is not to come up with new drugs that will save lives and alleviate pain. And it is certainly not to make sure that all Americans can afford the drugs they need. Simply stated, the function of the major drug companies is to charge the highest prices they can get away with in order to enrich their investors.

Drug researchers tell us that innovation has the potential to cure or, at the very least, alleviate the worst impacts of terrible illnesses—cancer, heart and respiratory disease, COVID, strokes, Alzheimer's, diabetes, and Parkinson's, to name just a few. Americans know millions of lives can be saved. But to do that, this country needs a pharmaceutical industry that is 100 percent engaged in research and development to discover those cures, not one that spends billions on lobbying, campaign contributions, and advertising in order to maintain huge profits and CEO compensation packages.

The U.S. government already has a very significant relationship with the pharmaceutical industry. But it is a totally one-sided relationship. Through the funding of the National Institutes of Health (NIH), other government agencies, and grants to universities and research institutes, the taxpayers of this country are paying for the research that has created some of the most important lifesaving drugs on the market. Unfortunately, the results of that research are simply given over to the drug companies with no strings attached. The companies then turn around and charge us, by far, the highest prices in the world for the prescription drugs that we helped develop.

As president, Donald Trump did not have many good ideas. But in creating Operation Warp Speed to develop a vaccine for COVID, he actually got something right. He directed the industry to come up with vaccines as quickly as possible and gave them the resources they needed to get the job done. And, within a reasonably short period of time, they delivered. (That Moderna and Pfizer ended up making billions in excessive profits, and tried to block efforts to make vaccines more affordable, is another sad but predictable story.)

The U.S. government should be prepared to generously fund the research needed to develop breakthrough drugs, and pharmaceutical companies should be able to earn reasonable profits. But not excessive profits based on monopolistic practices. In return, Americans must be able to buy those drugs for an affordable price, not the exorbitant prices we are now charged. In short, we need an entirely different relationship between our government and this essential industry.

Protect our children. You have heard it a million times, and it is obviously true: *Children are the future of our country.* How does it happen, therefore, that in the richest nation on earth we have the highest rate of childhood poverty of almost all major countries—disproportionately impacting Black and Brown families—and that millions of American children face food-insecurity?

How does it happen that we are almost the only country on earth not to provide paid family and medical leave? Psychologists have made it abundantly clear that the first four years of human life are determinative in shaping our futures. Yet low-income and working-class moms are often forced back to work only weeks after giving birth, and are denied the opportunity to bond with their baby.

How does it happen that, at a time when most families now require two breadwinners, we have a totally dysfunctional childcare system—a system that is wildly expensive, in which there is a scarcity of openings in day-care centers, and that pays most staff totally inadequate wages?

How does it happen that in many parts of the country public schools perform so poorly? Why are so many classrooms overcrowded and teachers underpaid? How does it happen that higher education is unaffordable for many, and 45 million have been forced into student debt?

Clearly, we need revolutionary changes in how we approach the needs of our children and young adults. We cannot continue spending almost $800 billion a year on the military, provide massive tax breaks for the rich and multinational corporations, and then claim that we are too poor to adequately meet the needs of our children and their parents.

Protect the elderly and disabled. As a society that is rapidly aging, the needs of seniors will become ever more apparent in the coming years. To forestall major crises, we must take action now.

Today, half of Americans over sixty-five are living on incomes of $25,000 or less, and 10 percent of older women live in poverty. Millions of older Americans cannot afford such basic necessities as dental care, hearing aids, eyeglasses, or prescription drugs.

Social Security benefits must be increased. Luckily, we can do that—and assure the long-term solvency of the program—simply by lifting the cap on taxable income for the wealthy. We have to recognize that, when someone making $100,000,000 a year pays the same amount of taxes into Social Security as someone making $140,000, we have a system that is too regressive to protect the elderly and people with disabilities. In addition to securing the program's funding, we have to address desperate shortages in senior housing, assisted living facilities, and nursing homes by renewing our commitment to home care. When we know that millions of elderly and disabled people would prefer to live out their lives with loved ones at home, we have to give them that option—just as we have to pay a living wage to the people who provide their care.

The United States will never be a "great" nation if we turn our backs on the weak and vulnerable. Our parents and grandparents, the people who raised us, who built and defended this country, have the right to a secure and satisfying old age. This is what a civilized society is all about.

Provide affordable housing for all. Communities across the country are facing a major housing crisis. While the cost of housing is soaring, some 600,000 Americans are homeless, and millions more teeter on the precipice—as nearly eighteen million households are spending 50 percent or more of their limited incomes on housing. Not only should we build millions of units of low-income and affordable housing, we also need to greatly expand concepts like community land trusts, which keep housing perpetually affordable. We should also support those communities that want to move forward with rent control to protect their tenants.

Break up monopolies. Today, the ownership of our economy is more concentrated than at any time in the modern history of this country. A handful of giant corporations control what is produced and how much we pay for their products. Just three Wall Street firms (BlackRock, Vanguard, and State Street) control assets of over $20 trillion and are the major stockholders in more than 96 percent of S&P 500 companies.

We are told every day that the American economy is based on free enterprise and competition. That's a lie. Today, our economy is dominated by a handful of huge, multinational corporations that enjoy astronomical profits, engage in price gouging on a regular basis, and exert enormous influence over our political life. This is uber-capitalism on steroids. This dangerous concentration of ownership must be ended.

Neither Democratic administrations nor Republican administrations have had the courage to break up these corporations. But that's exactly what we must do.

Make billionaires pay their taxes. Despite massive income and wealth inequality, the wealthiest people and most profitable corporations in this country refuse to pay their fair share of taxes. And the federal government lets them get away with it. It is unacceptable that billionaires now pay a lower effective federal income tax rate than nurses, firefighters, and construction workers and that, in any given year, many of our large profitable corporations pay nothing in federal income taxes.

We need a tax system that is based on ability to pay, that raises the funds we need to support strong social programs for working people, children, and the elderly. We need to move aggressively against the grotesque level of income and wealth inequality that currently exists by creating a truly progressive tax on wealth.

We must save the planet. For decades now, scientists all over the world have been telling us that unless we act quickly and boldly, climate change will wreak havoc with our planet. There will be more heat waves, more drought, more flooding, more extreme weather disturbances, more acidification of the oceans, more forest fires, and more disease. And that is exactly what has been happening.

The choice that the United States, and every other country on earth, faces is whether we rapidly transform our energy systems away from fossil fuels and into energy efficiency and sustainable energies, or continue to allow the planet to become more and more unhealthy and uninhabitable. If we care at all about our children and future generations, that doesn't seem like much of a choice. The United States must act, and act now, in leading the world to environmental sanity. Quite unbelievably, uber-capitalism is willing to sacrifice the future of the planet for its short-term profits. We cannot allow that to happen.

Which Way, Democrats?

Real politics makes it clear that uber-capitalism is wrecking not just our economy but our society. And it presents an alternative to a miserable future in which billionaires and CEOs decide our fate. The polls leave no doubt that the American people want that alternative. The job of progressives is to demand that the Democratic Party be that alternative.

Over the last several decades, we have seen American politics take an ominous turn. The Democratic Party, which under FDR, Harry Truman, John Kennedy, and Lyndon Johnson was clearly identified as the party of the working class, has increasingly come to be seen as the party of better-educated and better-off Americans. A *Nation* magazine article in the summer of 2021 asked, "Have Democrats Become the Party of the Rich?" A *New York Times* article, published a year later, more or less accepted the premise and asked, "How Can Democrats Persuade Voters They're Not a Party of Rich Elites?"

It's no secret that, since Donald Trump came on the national scene, with his disruptive approach to politics, Democrats have made significant gains in affluent suburban communities that historically had voted Republican. But it is also not a secret that the Republican Party, the traditional home of the bankers, investors, and CEOs, has been attracting steadily more working-class support— especially, but not exclusively, among white workers in smaller cities and rural areas. The labor-farmer coalitions of the past, which gave Democrats steady control of the Congress for most of the time from the Great Depression to the 1990s, have crumbled in states across the country. In 2022, John Fetterman won back some voters in rural areas, small towns, and small cities, and that made a major difference in his successful bid for Pennsylvania's U.S. Senate seat. But in Ohio and Wisconsin, rural counties went overwhelmingly for the Republicans, and Democrats failed to flip seats in equally critical Senate races.

In 2020, only 28 percent of white working-class men voted Democratic, while 36 percent of white working-class women did so. That represented a modest improvement over 2016, but there were still plenty of troubling trend lines for Democrats. The 2020 presidential election saw notable movement in a number of regions by Latino working-class voters, a traditional base of support for Democrats, toward the GOP. Among the people who had historically provided Democrats with their greatest support, Black working-class voters, there has been a smaller but still significant shift toward the Republicans—especially among men. The Democratic Party still runs well in urban areas. But it finishes *very* poorly in rural areas. In fact, in the predominantly white rural regions of the Great Plains and the Mountain West, media reports describe a crumbling Democratic Party infrastructure. In some states, the party barely exists. In Wyoming, the Republican Party now has an 8-to-1 registration advantage. In Idaho, it's 4-to-1. In South Dakota and Oklahoma, registered Republicans outnumber registered Democrats by roughly 2-to-1 margins. Those are all states that not so many years ago elected Democratic governors and U.S. senators. Indeed, South Dakota sent former Senate majority leader Tom Daschle to Washington until just two years before I was elected to the Senate.

When you look at maps charting election results nationwide, the weakness of the Democratic Party is so profound that it is hard to make a case that it should be considered a national party. In large stretches of the country, in county after county, the map shows nothing but red. Yes, Democrats can still win the presidency and, in a good year, the party can even take the House and Senate. But at the local level, in many parts of the country, the trend shows clear and growing Republican support. Democrats picked up two governorships in 2022, but the days when Democrats dominated state legislatures and local offices across the country are long gone.

Why is this so? It's a long story, but it has everything to do with a party that has largely turned its back on the working class of this country. Too many working Americans feel abandoned by the party they once trusted. And they're angry. After the 2020 presidential election, I talked with legislative candidates from across the country. A candidate from West Virginia told me, "When I talk to the people at the doors they like everything I stand for. But then they ask me, 'What party are you from?' When I say 'I'm a Democrat,' they say, 'Get out of here.'"

The Democratic Establishment Strikes Back

Let me offer a few personal observations that get at the crisis facing the Democratic Party. During the presidential primary season, it is common for state Democratic parties to schedule events to hear from the competing candidates—and, in the process, to raise money for their fall campaigns. I attended a number of these functions in 2016 and 2020. If I was going to be in a city on a given day to attend a Democratic Party dinner or evening event, our campaign would often schedule a rally in the same city to get supporters together.

I was constantly struck by the enormous differences between the rallies we held, usually in the afternoon, and the state Democratic Party events that I attended a few hours later. Yes, they were both "political" gatherings. But that was the only similarity between them.

Our events usually brought out diverse, raucous crowds of thousands of people. There were a lot of young people. The people who showed up were mostly working-class. Some were in college; some had degrees but many did not. What united them all was a dissatisfaction with the status quo and a fervent desire for change. They wanted the government to work for them, not just for the people on top.

The state Democratic Party events were pretty much the opposite. The turnouts were small and the people who attended were older, whiter, and wealthier. A significant number of them—lawyers, professionals, and businesspeople—were "major donors." Compared to our campaign rallies, the energy level was almost nonexistent.

Here's another personal observation. During the last several years, I've been involved in a number of strikes involving locals from some of the largest unions in the country. I have always been deeply impressed by the decency of the workers on strike, their courage, and their sense of solidarity. In speaking to the leaders of these local unions I was shocked and disturbed to learn that a strong majority of their members were now voting Republican.

These realities, which I have personally observed, explain the challenge facing the Democratic Party. How do you succeed politically now, and in the future, if you can't attract young people, the future of the country, into the party? How do you win elections if you are losing support from working-class voters, the majority of Americans?

The key question facing the Democratic Party is not complicated. Does the party want to open its doors and welcome into its ranks working-class Americans, people of color, and young voters who could shake things up? Is the party willing to listen to people who want to fight for fundamental change? Is it ready to be the party that demands that the promise of economic and social and racial justice be made real? Or does it want to maintain a tired status quo that poses no real threat to politics as usual? In other words, does it want to be a working-class party fighting for change, or a corporately dominated party protecting the well-off? In the vast majority of states I visited, the answer was that the party establishment was not just satisfied with the status quo, but fiercely determined to preserve it.

In February 2017, this conflict came to a head when it was time to elect a new chairman of the Democratic National Committee. On the eve of the 2016 Democratic National Convention in Philadelphia, Florida representative Debbie Wasserman Schultz had been forced to resign as DNC chair. It became apparent that she had improperly used her position to support Hillary Clinton's campaign against me, and even Clinton's backers knew that she had to go. Donna Brazile, a longtime party activist, replaced her on an interim basis during the fall campaign and worked hard to pull the party together for the race against Trump. But after the election, it was time to pick a new permanent chair.

Progressives supported congressman Keith Ellison, a dynamic young Black representative from Minnesota and one of the first members of Congress to back my candidacy. Keith wanted to open up the party by moving it away from its embrace of Big Money and toward a more grassroots-oriented model. He wanted the party to be organizing in every state and down to the precinct level. South Bend mayor Pete Buttigieg was also mounting an energetic campaign for the chairmanship. But the party establishment, including former president Barack Obama, supported Obama's former labor secretary Tom Perez. Perez talked about opening the party up, but there was little evidence that he was serious about moving away from status quo politics or fundraising models. Perez won by a 235–200 margin. Despite having just lost the presidency to the least qualified candidate in modern American history, despite having lost a thousand legislative seats since 2009, despite hemorrhaging working-class support all across the country, the Democratic leadership voted to continue in the same failed direction in which it had been headed before the disastrous 2016 election.

The Politics of Resentment

When we ponder the future of the Democratic Party, a simple question has to be asked: How does it happen that the Republican Party—which supports tax breaks for the rich, attempted to deny 32 million Americans the health care coverage they had under the Affordable Care Act, wants to cut Social Security, Medicare, and Medicaid, opposes legislation to lower prescription drug costs, and resists efforts to raise the minimum wage or to make it easier for workers to join unions—now has the support of a substantial and in many regions a growing number of working-class voters?

And what does that mean for the future of our country?

The answer to this all-important question is complicated. In some parts of the country, especially southern and border states where Democrats remained viable into the 1990s, the answer has to do with long-standing racism and resentment on the part of white working-class voters at the gains Black Americans have made over the decades. In some parts of the country, social conservatives have sought to use homophobia, and in recent years transphobia, to divide working-class voters against one another. And anyone who has been paying attention knows that Trump and his Republican allies have made xenophobia and the fear of immigrants central to their politics.

It's not just extreme right-wing Republicans who promote division. The GOP's senior leadership and strategists have for years been playing the politics of resentment with an eye toward pulling working-class voters—especially white working-class voters, but in recent years a growing number of Latino and Black voters—away from the Democratic fold. They use all sorts of disingenuous tactics to attract people to their cause. And they have become very good at pressing the buttons at election time.

But there is something more to this discussion, and it goes far beyond voting blocs and elections and what Trump and reactionary Republicans do. And that is that the Democratic Party, over the years, has helped create the political vacuum that allows these issues to fester. It has done so by turning its back on the American working class. What this means is that, even when the party does better than the Republicans, as it did in 2020 and 2022, it only does so by the narrowest of margins. It doesn't register the sort of transformational victories that could make way for the next New Deal or Great Society. The coalitions Democrats pull together these days are slimmer and more vulnerable than they should be. They lack the multi-racial, multi-ethnic, multi-generational heft that is needed. Why? Because the party, in too many cases and in too many places, has lost touch with working Americans. It doesn't know how to speak to them because it doesn't know what is going on with them.

The fact is that working people in this country are angry. There's a reason for this.

Tragically, the Democrats have ignored this anger, and ignored the pain and frustration that cause it. Working people want to know why they're falling further and further behind, and why their kids are even worse off. They want their elected officials to recognize their distress and their fears. And, most important, they want their elected officials to stand up and fight for them. That's not what Democrats have done. A *Washington Post* poll in late September 2022 showed that, by 17 points, Americans trusted the Republicans on economic issues more than they trusted Democrats.

Workers have a right to be angry because, despite huge increases in productivity, their wages have been stagnant for fifty years. They are angry because they lost good-paying jobs when their companies shut down and moved to China. They are angry because they are working for starvation wages and the federal minimum wage has not been raised since 2009. They are angry because they can't afford health care or prescription drugs. They are angry because they are spending too much for housing and childcare and their kids lack the money to go to college or a trade school. They are angry because they can't retire with security. They are angry that during the pandemic they had to go to work in unsafe conditions, while their bosses worked comfortably at home. They are angry that despite record-breaking profits, companies are cutting back on wages and benefits and their bosses make hundreds of times more than they do.

If the Democratic Party of today is to be successful, it must have the courage to recognize that anger. And it must speak to it in the way that FDR did in 1937, when he began his second term by ac-knowledging that there was much his New Deal had not yet accom-plished. He looked out at the country, saw the suffering, and spoke to it—and promised to address the pain that he witnessed. He was not afraid to tell the truth. This is what he said:

> In this nation I see tens of millions of its citizens—a substan-tial part of its whole population—who at this very moment are denied the greater part of what the very lowest standards of today call the necessities of life.
>
> I see millions of families trying to live on incomes so mea-ger that the pall of family disaster hangs over them day by day.
>
> I see millions whose daily lives in city and on farm con-tinue under conditions labeled indecent by a so-called polite society half a century ago.
>
> I see millions denied education, recreation, and the op-portunity to better their lot and the lot of their children.
>
> I see millions lacking the means to buy the products of farm and factory and by their poverty denying work and pro-ductiveness to many other millions.
>
> I see one-third of a nation ill-housed, ill-clad, ill-nourished.

Democrats have to learn the lesson that Roosevelt taught.

Have the honesty to acknowledge the suffering that working peo-ple are experiencing.

Have the courage to take on the special interests in order to im-prove their lives.

Republicans Have Mastered the Art of Exploiting Working-Class Frustration

Republicans understand just how widespread working-class frustration has become, and how volatile it is. They have made it their mission to exploit that frustration in starkly divisive terms. Republican officials, and their powerful media echo chamber, go out of their way to provide working people with an "explanation" for their angst. It's built on a foundation of lies. But these Republicans are extremely sophisticated in playing the blame game and attacking everyone—women, immigrants, Blacks, Muslims, transgender people, teachers, and union leaders—for the challenges facing the nation. Like every demagogue of the past, they smear everyone except the people who are actually responsible for what's gone awry—the people with the wealth and power.

The Republican lies have been carefully developed, using focus groups and polling. Here's some of what they claim at election time:

- **Immigrants are the problem.** Donald Trump, as a candidate and then as president of the United States, regularly attacked immigrants from Mexico, claiming that "they're sending people that have lots of problems, and they're bringing those problems [to] us. They're bringing drugs. They're bringing crime. They're rapists." That's a lie.
- **Black people are the problem.** Republicans have long criticized programs that seek to address systemic racism by claiming that these programs discriminate against whites. Their attacks on affirmative action programs have gone to such extremes that Senator Roger Wicker (R-MS) claimed that Justice Ketanji Brown Jackson, one of the most qualified nominees ever for the U.S. Supreme Court, was simply "the beneficiary of this sort of quota." That's a lie.
- **LGBTQ people are the problem.** Florida governor Ron DeSantis, a leading contender for the 2024 Republican presidential nomination, went so far as to promote a so-called

Don't Say Gay law that made it illegal to teach young people about sex and sexuality. Dismissing education that respects transgender kids and others as "woke gender ideology," DeSantis announced that "it's not something that's appropriate for any place, but especially not in Florida." That's a lie.

- **Muslims are the problem.** Portraying Muslims as potential terrorists and a threat to the United States, Donald Trump tried as president to block Muslim immigration and threatened to close down mosques, claiming that "I think Islam hates us." Representative Marjorie Taylor Greene (R-GA), called a Muslim colleague, Rep. Ilhan Omar (D-MN), "bloodthirsty," "pro–al Qaeda," and "basically an apologist for Islamic terrorists." Another Republican House member, Lauren Boebert (R-CO), claimed that Omar—who has been an international leader in dialing down sectarian tensions— was a member of "the jihad squad." That's a lie.

- **Teachers are the problem.** Even though it's not taught in K–12 schools, Republicans have been crusading against Critical Race Theory, portraying honest education about slavery, segregation, and systemic racism as "indoctrination." That's a lie.

- **Discrimination against white men is the problem.** As Republican politicians and media outlets such as Fox News have picked up on elements of the alt-right "Great Replacement Theory," a 2022 Yahoo News/YouGov survey found that most Republicans now believe that white Americans face as much discrimination as Black Americans, and a Pew survey recently found that almost 40 percent of Republican men believe progress toward women's rights has come at the expense of men. It's a fact that 40 percent of Republican men do believe this. But what they believe is a lie.

And on and on it goes.

Republicans are constantly on the watch to exploit grievances.

And what of Democrats? Do they counter the GOP strategies that deflect attention from the real sources of pain and frustration among working-class voters of all backgrounds?

Ask yourself: What is the overall message now of the Democratic president, Democratic congressional leaders, and the Democratic Party leaders? If Republicans have defined minorities or immigrants or gay people as "the enemy," and "the problem," who are Democrats calling out as the real culprits? Who are Democrats holding responsible for the pain that so many Americans are experiencing?

It's not enough to simply say that the Republicans are engaging in ugly politics when they target immigrants, women, people of color, and the LGBTQ community. It's not enough simply to say that Trump and his followers are extremists who do not believe in democracy and the rule of law.

Democrats should be making it absolutely clear that the people the Republicans take their money from, and the people whom Republican policies serve—the very rich and the very powerful individuals who seek an America where uber-capitalism defines every aspect of our economy and of our society—are the problem. There is a reason why Republicans oppose treating health care as a right, oppose raising the minimum wage, oppose saving the planet, oppose taxing the rich, oppose regulating corporations. And oppose responding to inflation by addressing corporate price gouging and profiteering. They are delivering for their billionaire donors and their corporate sponsors. Pure and simple.

Democrats should be making it clear that they are prepared to challenge the rich and powerful on behalf of the working class. This will resonate with the American people in ways that the GOP lies never could.

Unfortunately, this economic justice message is rarely if ever delivered by the Democrats. And that has a lot to do with our broken campaign finance system and Democrats' dependency on campaign contributions from the wealthy and powerful.

There is no hiding from reality. Despite a lot of rhetoric, which fewer and fewer people believe, Democrats have not fought hard enough, or consistently enough, for working people. And this failure has cost Democrats at election time. The simple truth is that, as Democrats have turned their backs on working families, millions of working-class voters have turned their backs on a Democratic Party that their parents and grandparents strongly supported. This is a tragedy for our country, and has ominous ramifications for our future.

But that threat does not have to become our reality.

Democrats Must Show Up for the Working Class

If Democrats are going to effectively combat Republican right-wing extremism, they have to stop relying on inside-the-Beltway consultants, get out of the Capitol Hill bubble, cease their never-ending fundraising events with the rich, and start hitting the streets and engaging with Americans who feel left out and left behind.

They must prove to working-class people of every background and in every region that they are prepared to stand with them in their struggles for a better life. They must learn from the four terms of FDR. The world has changed a lot since the 1930s, but one political reality remains constant: You can't win elections and bring about real change without the overwhelming support of the working class.

How can Democrats win that support? They can start by showing up.

Today, when unions are more popular then they have been since 1965, Democrats need to align themselves closely with the growing grassroots trade union movement. They need to aggressively support workers who are attempting to organize, stand with workers who are out on strike, and demand that companies negotiate in good faith. In addition, Democrats must fight for labor-law reforms that strengthen the hand of the working class. And they must assure that those laws are enforced in every single state.

During the last several years I have been proud to join picket lines and to rally with Amazon and Starbucks workers as they have organized in communities across this country. I was at the side of Disney workers when they demanded higher wages. When workers have gone on strike, I've walked the picket lines with them. And, as chairman of the Budget Committee, I have held hearings to highlight the fact that the federal government can and must deny federal contracts to companies who violate labor law.

Have I been alone in Congress in these efforts? Absolutely not. But, if we're being honest with ourselves, the truth is that the prominent Democrats active in these working-class struggles have been few and far between. Yes, there is a lot of talk among Democrats about being pro-union, from the White House on down, but there's been way too little action.

What would it mean in this country if workers saw, with their own eyes, Democrats at their side, supporting unions and taking on corporate interests so that they earn decent wages, benefits, and working conditions? What would it mean if the president of the United States brought into the Oval Office the CEOs of major corporations that are trying to break unions, and made it clear that their illegal behavior will no longer be tolerated? What would it mean, when it became necessary for workers to strike, if the United States secretary of labor was there on Day One to walk the picket line with those workers?

Frankly, it would mean a lot. In fact, it would bring about a massive transformation of the American political system. It would change not just labor relations but the political culture of a country where too many working-class Americans have given up on democracy and elections because they do not believe that either party is on their side. If done honestly and aggressively, it would show that at least one political party was prepared to take on corporate greed and power and stand with the struggling working families of our country.

Transforming a Party of the Elite into a Party of the People

I am the longest-serving Independent in the history of the United States Congress. During my political career I have taken on and defeated Democrats and Republicans and, on occasion, candidates supported by both parties. In other words, I am not wedded to a two-party system.

We can argue about whether the multi-party parliamentary systems that exist in most countries around the world are more inclusive and democratic than our political system. I think they are. But here's the reality that we live with now: Today, we have a strongly entrenched and well-funded two-party system. Could that change in the foreseeable future? Maybe. But not tomorrow.

That means that, if we are going to bring about the kind of change this country desperately needs, if we are going to protect American democracy in this volatile moment, we need to completely transform the Democratic Party—from the bottom on up.

The Democratic Party must be more than just a well-funded, consultant-driven, ad-producing election machine. It needs to be a movement party that stands, unequivocally, with the working families of our country and addresses the most challenging issues facing our nation and the world. It needs to be a party that is rock solid in its commitment to economic and social and racial justice, to saving the planet, and to reordering policies to promote diplomacy and peace. Above all, it needs to be the party of a *united* working class. To do that, it needs to redefine what politics means in the twenty-first century by functioning 365 days a year, not just three months before an election.

The party must reach out and open its doors to working people, young people, and grassroots activists in a way that it has not done for decades. Instead of being an elite club that's difficult to join, and that tells newcomers they must wait their turn to be recognized, the Democrats have to become a party that empowers working people and delivers for them. Politics can be an integral part of people's lives, something they talk about every day. But that will only happen if the Democratic Party throws off its caution and gets into the fight.

Bringing fundamental reforms to the Democratic Party will not be easy. The corporate interests within the party, the consultant class, and establishment politicians will resist change every step of the way. But these changes can be brought about. Indeed, they must be brought about.

For a start, the Democrats must once again become a national party. Not only must they become a fifty-state party, they must become a 3,243-county party. They must be everywhere. Instead of spending many hundreds of millions in the few months before an election on political commercials, consultants, and pollsters, they must spend a small fraction of that by hiring thousands of full-time organizers to work in every state in the country. To the extent possible, these organizers should be local people of every age and background who know their communities and are part of them. The party should also be establishing neighborhood action centers that remain in operation year-round, linking up with grassroots groups and labor unions at the local level. At a time when many Americans want to rebuild a sense of community that has been lost in our modern, cell phone–driven, TV-streaming age, Democrats can be active in everything from youth athletics to senior dinners.

Democrats must also develop a national and local media strategy to counteract the extraordinary onslaught of Fox News and other right-wing media. This will not be an inexpensive or easy task, but it must be done. We cannot change political consciousness in this country when the only political information that tens of millions of people hear every single day comes from right-wing propagandists who peddle outright lies, conspiracy theories, and character assassination. The party must pour resources and creative energy into establishing a dynamic and compelling presence on television, radio, social media, and podcasts, and in new publications and books. In other words, the Democrats have to stop complaining about Fox News and right-wing talk radio and develop a compelling alternative to it.

Not only does the Democratic Party need major reforms in how it relates to the American people, it needs internal reforms as to how it functions organizationally. It must:

- **Transform the Democratic National Committee from a corporate-dominated fundraising apparatus into a source of support for grassroots activism and working-class struggles.** Right now, the DNC spends almost all of its time trying to keep on the right side of the millionaires and billionaires who write big checks to fund campaigns. It actually prefers candidates who represent corporate interests—or who are themselves wealthy. DNC members like candidates who defend the status quo, because they know those candidates will win the favor of the big donors. That has to change. The DNC needs to make a break from the current corrupt campaign-financing system.

- **Make certain that primaries are open, fair, and well run.** Needless to say, as I can well attest, it is beyond belief and a national disgrace that the Iowa Democratic Party in 2020 couldn't even count the votes cast in a timely manner in the vital Iowa caucuses, the first Democratic Party contest of the 2020 election season. And in California, the largest state in the country, which I won in 2020, it literally took weeks before the final results were announced.

- **Democratize the nominating processes.** In the 2016 Democratic primaries, because of the outrageous and undemocratic role that super-delegates played, Hillary Clinton started off with a roughly 500-delegate advantage before a single actual voter attended a caucus or cast a primary ballot. That year, I won every county in the West Virginia primary and secured a 16-point landslide statewide. Yet Clinton ended up with nineteen West Virginia delegates on the convention floor in Philadelphia that year to my eighteen. Why? She had a built-in advantage based on the votes of unelected super-delegates and party leaders.

  With a great deal of effort, progressives managed to curtail the role that super-delegates played in 2020. But we must go further. Party bosses, campaign donors, and officials should not be able to tip the balance of Democratic National Conventions against candidates that have won majority support in the states.

- **Restructure debates between contenders for the presidential nomination so that they are serious examinations of the issues.** They should stop relying on showbiz gimmickry, and on media personalities who parrot the talking points of advertisers. Moderators shouldn't go for "gotcha" moments. They should give candidates more than fifteen seconds to answer major policy questions. And they should seek thoughtful answers to questions that matter so that maybe, just maybe, debates will be enlightening.

- **Make conventions genuine convenings of the party membership, as opposed to choreographed media spectacles.** Delegates should be empowered to write platforms that address the needs of the country, and to engage in open and respectful debate on those issues. Then those delegates should head home with the resources and the support that will win elections and give meaning to the process.

Yes, Mass-Movement Politics *Can* Beat Uber-Capitalism

Good policy is good politics. Standing up to corporate greed and improving the lives of the majority of the American people is the right thing to do. It is also the smart thing to do politically. Democrats used to know this. That's why the party dominated congressional elections for the last half of the twentieth century.

Unfortunately, too many leaders of the current Democratic Party have rejected the vision that made their party strong in the past—just as they have lost sight of what could make it strong in the future.

The sad truth is that, if you boil it down, the essence of the Democratic message in recent years has been: "We're pretty bad, but Republicans are worse. So vote for us. We're the lesser of two evils!" Given the reality of the Republican Party today—their grow-ing attacks on democracy and women's rights, their abysmal record on climate change and the environment, their support for tax breaks for the rich and cuts in programs for working families and the poor—there's more than a grain of truth in that message. And it might be enough to win elections in the short term—as was the case in 2020, and to a lesser extent in 2022. But what it doesn't do is get to the root causes of the Democratic Party's problems, let alone the coun-try's problems. It doesn't generate grassroots excitement or coalition building. It doesn't strengthen our democracy. It doesn't create hope. It doesn't lay out a plan for the future that's based on the shared values that will bring Americans together to achieve great things.

It doesn't recognize that, when the oligarchs and the corporate world are waging class war against working Americans, the working class needs a party that will fight back. And win.

Our country faces unprecedented challenges today. They cannot be resolved with half-steps or compromises. There is not a middle ground between the insatiable greed of uber-capitalism and a fair deal for the working class. There is not a middle ground as to whether or not we save the planet. There is not a middle ground about whether or not we preserve our democracy and remain a society based on equal protection for all.

Democrats face the most fundamental of all choices. They must choose whether to be on the side of the working-class men and women who create the wealth of this country, or to be on the side of the billionaire class, the corporate elites, and the wealthy campaign donors who hoard wealth for their own self-interest.

By making an unequivocal decision as to which side they are on in the class war, Democrats can finally enact policies to overcome uber-capitalism and the greed, inequality, and bigotry that have de-nied this country the promise of "liberty and justice for all."

This is the stuff of a political revolution. A political revolution that every poll tells us the American people want. The danger for the Democratic Party is not being too bold. It's being too cautious.

It's time, finally, for the Democrats to recognize that good policy is good politics. It's good for the party. It's good for the country. It's good for the world.

Let's do it!

ACKNOWLEDGMENTS

Given my Senate schedule, this book could not have been completed on time without the very hard and excellent work of John Nichols. John, thanks very much. I also want to thank Warren Gunnels for his contribution to the book.

No elected official accomplishes much without a great staff, which is what I have. I want to thank all of my Senate staff in D.C. and in Vermont for their dedication and professionalism, as well as the men and women who are part of my political team. I especially want to acknowledge Misty Rebik, my Senate chief of staff in D.C.; Katie Van Haste, my Vermont state director; and Faiz Shakir, my political director.

Lastly, I want to express my appreciation to the millions of Americans who are part of the political revolution. Taking on oligarchy and fighting for transformational change is not easy. But it's a fight we must win, and will win. Thank you for all you do.

John would like to thank his daughter, Whitman Bottari, and his longtime editor, Katrina vanden Heuvel, for their unrestrained enthusiasm about this book project.